KEEPING THE WILD

KEEPING THE WILD

AGAINST THE DOMESTICATION OF EARTH

Edited by George Wuerthner, Eileen Crist, and Tom Butler

ISLANDPRESS

WASHINGTON | COVELO | LONDON

Published by the Foundation for Deep Ecology in collaboration with Island Press.
All rights reserved under International and Pan-American Copyright Conventions.
No part of this book may be reproduced in any form or by any electronic or mechanical
means, including information storage and retrieval systems, without written permission
from the Foundation for Deep Ecology.

Foundation for Deep Ecology
1606 Union Street, San Francisco, CA 94123
www.deepecology.org

Island Press
2000 M Street, NW, Suite 650, Washington, D.C. 20036
www. islandpress.org

ISBN 978-1-61091-558-8
Library of Congress Control Number: 2014935630

Grateful acknowledgment is made to the following authors and publishers: Tim Caro et
al.'s "Conservation in the Anthropocene" appeared originally, in a slightly different form,
in *Conservation Biology* and is reprinted with permission. Paul Kingsnorth's "Rise of the
Neo-greens" is adapted from a longer work that appeared originally in *Orion* and is used by
permission of the author. An earlier, shorter iteration of "The 'New Conservation'" by Michael
Soulé appeared in *Conservation Biology*; the version that appears herein is use by permission
of the author. Roderick Nash's "Wild World" appeared first in *New Scientist* and is reprinted by
permission of the author. "The Myth of the Humanized Pre-Columbian Landscape" is adapted
from Dave Foreman's book *True Wilderness* and is used by permission of the author. "An Open
Letter to Major John Wesley Powell" by Terry Tempest Williams appeared originally, in a
slightly different version, in *The Progressive*, and is reprinted by permission of the author.

Book design by Kevin Cross

Printed in Canada on recycled paper (100% post-consumer waste)
certified by the Forest Stewardship Council

For Michael Soulé—
scientist, conservationist, lover of the wild.

CONTENTS

PART THREE: THE VALUE OF THE WILD

EPILOGUE

Nature is gone. . . . You are living on a used planet. If this bothers you, get over it. We now live in the Anthropocene—a geological epoch in which Earth's atmosphere, lithosphere, and biosphere are shaped primarily by human forces.[1]

—ERLE ELLIS

"Wild" is process, as it happens outside of human agency. As far as science can reach, it will never get to the bottom of it, because mind, imagination, digestion, breathing, dreaming, loving, and both birth and death are all part of the wild. There will never be an Anthropocene.[2]

—GARY SNYDER

INTRODUCTION

Lives Not Our Own

TOM BUTLER

IN HIS "FAT MASTERPIECE," *The Fool's Progress*, Edward Abbey wrote of the protagonist's father: "Joe Lightcap was not a philosopher; he took ideas seriously. 'Ideas can hurt people,' he would say. 'Ideas are dangerous. I'd rather have a man come at me with an ax than a Big Idea.'"[3]

This is a book about ideas—ideas dangerous and ideas infused with restorative, healing properties. It's also about language and the way it shapes individual and collective views of the world, forging the deep "root metaphors,"[4] to borrow education reformer Chet Bower's term, which so fundamentally shape a culture's development that they become invisible to the people within that culture. Such is the idea of human hegemony, the way that our species, but one of millions on Earth and subject to the same forces and beneficiary of the same biological lineage, has (especially in its modern technological incarnation) come to believe that the community of life is merely a storehouse of "natural resources" subject to appropriation.

Keeping the Wild was conceived to confront the notion of human hegemony and also to join the growing conversation within the conservation movement about the so-called Anthropocene. That word describing the age of human dominion of Earth has been embraced by some academics, journalists, and environmentalists and is increasingly used to conceptualize, and often to justify, further domestication of the planet.

Cheerleaders for the Anthropocene have variously been called "neo-greens," "pragmatic environmentalists," "new conservationists," "Anthropocene boosters," and "postmodern greens." As there is not one dominant moniker for their camp, the editors have not enforced consistency among this volume's contributing authors.

The essays to come explore in detail the arguments made by the neo-greens, whose writings include the following claims:

- ▶ The Anthropocene has arrived and humans are now de facto planetary managers;
- ▶ If "pristine wilderness" ever existed, it is all gone now; moreover, focusing on wilderness preservation has poorly served the conservation movement;
- ▶ Nature is highly resilient, not fragile;
- ▶ To succeed, conservation must serve human aspirations, primarily regarding economic growth and development;
- ▶ Maintaining "ecosystem services," not preventing human-caused extinction, should be conservation's primary goal;
- ▶ Conservation should emphasize better management of the domesticated, "working landscape" rather than efforts to establish new, strictly protected natural areas.
- ▶ Conservationists should not critique capitalism but rather should partner with corporations to achieve better results.

These ideas, individually and collectively, are worthy of close inspection; respectful debate; and, in the view of the editors, vigorous rebuttal. While some contributors to this volume offer spirited rejoinders to the neo-greens, their criticism is nowhere intended to denigrate specific persons or organizations. Indeed, the editors have assumed that all of the players in these debates are acting in good faith, with genuine desire to see conservation succeed. Clearly, however, we have stark differences in worldview and thus disagree about strategies to protect the Earth.

Even a cursory look at the burgeoning Anthopocene literature will reveal celebratory, techno-triumphalist voices that seem not discomfited by but almost to revel in the belief that humans have become overseers of the planetary plantation. Other voices are more muted in tone, regretfully embracing a kind of environmental realpolitik—that, for better or worse, humanity is now in the global driver's seat and thus should manage Earth well. Whether celebratory or reluctant, the neo-greens' language creates a linguistic platform that reinforces and shapes anew humanity's resourcist agenda. The growing chorus of Anthropocene boosterism strikes us as an updated form of *noblesse oblige* inflated to a planetary scale—a call to humanity to rise to its globe-managing responsibilities—but actually embodying the type of hubris that David Ehrenfeld dissected so well in *The Arrogance of Humanism*.[5] This is all the more ironic because it is anthropocentrism—the worldview at the heart of this arrogance—that is leading Earth, and humanity, to ruin.

Before citing Stewart Brand's famous quote that opened the *Whole Earth Catalog*—"We are as gods and might as well get good at it"—contemporary Anthopocene proponent Erle Ellis gushes about the "amazing opportunity" that "humanity has now made the leap to an entirely new level of planetary importance."[6] But whereas one could read Brand's full passage as a whimsical entreaty to personal empowerment at the apex of 1960s countercultural zeitgeist, it is hard to interpret Ellis as anything but a straight-ahead celebrant for a cyborg generation alienated from the natural world, steeped in simulacra, and inclined to believe that any environmental problem can be solved through a techno-fix.

Are we truly "as gods"? Certainly humans now have the ability to destroy life on a scale formerly reserved for geological and astrophysical phenomena. But our godlike powers of destruction, rooted not in malevolence but in our sheer bulk and thoughtless ways of living, are not balanced by equivalently divine creative powers. Notwithstanding the efforts of synthetic biology engineers (whose goals are utilitarian—building new life-forms to serve humans), we do not have the ability to create diverse and beautiful life as nature has done on this globe for some 3.5 billion years. We are born of that epic evolutionary flourishing, and yet now are busy disrupting the primal force that gave us life. We are second-tier deities, conceited demigods, at best.

If the only choice before us were either to become good at being godlike or to remain inept and toxic to the diversity of life, then surely it would be right to choose the former—to make ourselves better "stewards" (a word that originally meant the ward of the sty, the keeper of domestic animals). This seems to be what the Anthropocene boosters in conservation are hoping for when they propose, "nature could be a garden." That is, a world thoughtfully manipulated, perhaps even "sustainably," for human ends.

But these prospects for the future of humanity are a false dichotomy. Surely there are other possibilities, including our potential choice to become plain members and citizens in the community of life and relinquish the delusion that we are "Lord Man."

Writing some twenty-six centuries ago, likely from a simple cabin in the woods, a Chinese sage considered what results when hubris prompts people's desire to possess the world:

> As for those who would take the whole world
> To tinker as they see fit,
> I observe that they never succeed:
> For the world is a sacred vessel
> Not made to be altered by man.
> The tinker will spoil it;
> Usurpers will lose it.[7]
> (Lao-Tzu, 6th century B.C.)

The proposed "Anthropocene" term for a new geological epoch and the Anthropocene-framed agenda for conservation based on domesticating Earth represent an unmistakable and, we contend, *illegitimate* claim on power. These developments not only make humans usurpers but advance this way of life as right. The present global extinction crisis tallies the ways we are indeed losing the sacred vessel of the world.

While perhaps little considered by those who are economically and politically power-hungry, a usurper always retains the option of renouncing and stepping away from a claim on power. In modern, techno-industrial society where the civil religion of progress means ever-more commodification of nature to serve economic growth, promoting a reasoned discussion about retrenchment puts one on the margins of polite society. In the world of ever *more*, the idea of *less*—of reducing human numbers and economic pressure on the biosphere—is almost unthinkable. But it is not impossible, and the act of forgoing technology-enhanced power has occasional cultural precedents. Such precedents include the nonuse of firearms, a technology already long known in Japan, during that nation's self-imposed, roughly two-centuries-long isolation from global trading networks prior to 1854, and the present-day Amish culture's decision to avoid technologies that undermine family and community life. Individuals, too, have the opportunity to step back from assumed godhood by embracing a personal philosophy based on deep ecology principles, which affirm the intrinsic value of all life-forms and the desirability of living on a planet of flourishing biological diversity. We can consciously choose to live in ways that minimize impact on the Earth by managing *ourselves*— lowering our numbers, scaling down our global economy, and making thoughtful decisions about the technologies we use.

Are such questions about worldview, power, and technology relevant to a book devoted to debating the future of conservation? Yes, for they help illuminate the foundations of the schism to be examined. Within every social change movement there are tensions between reformers and those who seek structural change. Our point is that if the conservation movement simply assumes that the current trajectory of population growth, economic development, and technological innovation *should* persist—or is just too entrenched to question—then it may be reasonable, as the neo-greens attempt, to craft human-centered conservation strategies that aim to reform that status quo by "greening" it. Within the context of the status quo it is sure to be deemed politically realistic and will bolster opportunities for conservation groups to partner with corporate interests.

But seeking to tinker with the whole world is, as Lao-Tzu warned, destined to spoil it. We believe that merely greening up a flawed system cannot stem the global eco-social crisis—the great unraveling of wild nature and indigenous human communities—and a different range of strategies will be needed. Those strategies will be oriented toward sustaining wildness and restoring degraded ecosystems. They will steer us toward domesticating less and doing so more skillfully, with our managed landscapes emulating to the extent possible the inherent vibrancy of natural ecosystems. Nature will be our measure, and the ultimate yardstick for cultural health will be the degree to which our species does not cause the extinction of others, allowing the rest of life to flourish. These aims cannot be accomplished without fundamentally changing our presence on the planet.

In short, the debate over the future of conservation hinges on our vision for the future of Earth: Do we continue down the path toward a gardened, managed planet with less beauty and wildness? Or take a wilder path toward beauty and ecological health, with a smaller human footprint, and cultures imbedded in a matrix of wildness, where we are "part of a seamless membrane of life"?[8]

CONTRIBUTORS TO THIS VOLUME are a luminary collection of writers, thinkers, academics, and conservation activists from North and South America, Europe, and Australia. We have grouped their writings into three sections:

"Clashing Worldviews," "Against Domestication," and "The Value of the Wild," with a personal essay by Kathleen Dean Moore as Epilogue. Unlike many anthologies, the contributions herein reflect considerable variety in tone, from academic to popular. Perusing some of the writings in section one will help orient the reader to the debate at hand, but each essay stands alone and can be understood by persons without extensive familiarity in the scholarly literature about wilderness, including earlier critiques of the wilderness idea by so-called wilderness deconstructionists.

Indeed, wilderness deconstruction—the literal kind, not the abstruse theorizing of academics influenced by postmodern literary criticism—concerns us most. Of primary importance is how "Anthropocene" thinking is influencing the communications and strategies of on-the-ground conservation practitioners, from the largest international NGOs to state agencies and local land trusts. If conservation is to be framed primarily within the context—and acceptance of—human domination of the planet, there will continue to be profound consequences for life: for the diversity of species and subspecies, populations of wild plants and animals, variety of ecosystems, ecological and behavioral processes, and evolutionary unfolding. The contributors to this volume submit that such a conceptual framing will almost surely lead to ultimate failure to protect the natural world. As never before, the Earth now needs a radical questioning of human domination coupled with creative, successful conservation strategies to restore and preserve the diversity of life.

It is this grim reality that wild and beautiful places continue to be destroyed by human action, that our numbers and behavior have precipitated a sixth great extinction event in Earth history, which challenges us to examine deeply our societal trajectory. Moreover, we cannot take on faith, nor encourage such faith in the mass of humanity, that the current dominant economic and political structures will persist indefinitely. The prospect of rapid and potentially catastrophic climate change is poised to accelerate the extinction crisis and, in worst-case scenarios, could make the planet unfriendly to much of life, including ourselves. Thorough, systemic criticism is crucial if conservationists are to become more effective. We hope that this and a subsequent, companion volume focused on protected areas—and the need to expand them and connect them—can help build the intellectual infrastructure of the global conservation movement and keep us from going down strategic dead ends. This is no mere academic exercise for all of us who are working to conserve wild places and creatures around the globe.

Conservation and environmentalism are big tents, and the history of these separate but related movements is rich with tension between people who saw their objective primarily as about preserving wild nature and those who sought "sustainable" use of "natural resources" for people. Many scholarly works cover that ground, which will not be repeated here, but it does seem to us that the current debate about the future of conservation is, as Curt Meine explains in his essay, not particularly new. Apparently each generation will have its "great new wilderness debate."

Why is it that domestication-versus-wildness is such a fascinating subject? Not just, perhaps, because of the dynamic historical and ongoing tensions within the conservation movement, nor because a new term, *Anthropocene*, has entered the popular lexicon. Perhaps it is because these competing inclinations and tendencies exist also within the human heart and psyche; we come from wildness, and those of us in the wild tribe embrace the power of wildness in every way that we can, even while immersed in a technocratic milieu. In order to live, most human societies, at least since the Neolithic Revolution, have domesticated their surroundings. And so we inhabit a world deeply affected by the activities of our own kind, and sometimes we have domesticated with skill and beauty. The accelerating domestication of the world, however, can make us lose sight of the love of wildness within us. As Barbara Kingsolver put it so well:

People need *wild places. . . . To be surrounded by a singing, mating, howling commotion of other species, all of which love their lives as much as we do ours. . . . It reminds us that our plans are small and somewhat absurd. It reminds us why, in those cases in which our plans might influence many future generations, we ought to choose carefully. Looking out on a clean plank of planet Earth, we can get shaken right down to the bone by the bronze-eyed possibility of lives that are not our own.*[9]

Just as the competing urges of the wild and the domestic live within us, they are likely to persist within the conservation movement until humanity embraces a land ethic that both places the well-being of the entire biotic community first and renounces the idea that Earth is a resource colony for humanity. Do we have the wisdom to exercise humility and restraint, to choose membership over Lordship? The lives that are not our own hang in the balance.

[ONE]

CLASHING WORLDVIEWS

Rise of the Neo-greens

PAUL KINGSNORTH

I HAVE BEEN (AND STILL AM) someone rather often quaintly known as a "green activist" for around twenty years now: for a lot longer than some people, and for a lot less time than many others. I sometimes like to say that the green movement was born in the same year as me—1972, the year in which the fabled *Limits to Growth* report was published by the Club of Rome—and this is near enough to the truth to be a jumping-off point for a narrative.

If the green movement was born in the early 1970s, then the 1980s, when there were whales to be saved and rainforests to campaign for, were its adolescence. Its coming-of-age party was in 1992, in the Brazilian city of Rio de Janeiro. The 1992 Earth Summit was a jamboree of promises and commitments: to tackle climate change, to protect forests, to protect biodiversity, and to promote something called "sustainable development," a new concept which would become, over the next two decades, the most fashionable in global politics and business. The future looked bright for the greens back then. It often does when you're twenty.

Two decades on, things look rather different. In 2012, the bureaucrats, the activists, and the ministers gathered again in Rio for a stock-taking exercise called "Rio +20." It was accompanied by the usual shrill demands for optimism and hope, but there was no disguising the hollowness of the exercise. Every environmental problem identified at the original Earth Summit has got worse in the intervening twenty years, often very much worse, and there is no sign of this changing.

The green movement, which seemed to be carrying all before it in the early 1990s, has plunged into a full-on midlife crisis. Unable to significantly change either the system or the behavior of the public, assailed by a rising movement of "skeptics" and by public boredom with being hectored about carbon and consumption, colonized by a new breed of corporate spivs for whom "sustainability" is just another opportunity for selling things, the greens are seeing a nasty realization dawn: Despite all their work, their passion, their commitment, and the fact that most of what they have been saying has been broadly right—they are losing. There is no likelihood of the world going their way. In most green circles now, sooner or later, the conversation comes round to the same question: What the hell do we do next?

There are plenty of people who think they know the answer to that question. One of them is Peter Kareiva, who would like to think that he and his kind represent the future of environmentalism, and who may turn out to be right. Kareiva is chief scientist of the Nature Conservancy, an American nongovernmental organization (NGO) which claims to be the world's largest environmental organization. He is a scientist, a revisionist, and one among a growing number of former greens who might best be called "neo-environmentalists."

The resemblance between this coalescing group and the Friedmanite neoliberals of the early 1970s is intriguing. Like the neoliberals, the neo-environmentalists are attempting to break through the lines of an old orthodoxy which is visibly exhausted and confused. Like the neoliberals, they are mostly American and mostly male, and they emphasize scientific measurement and economic analysis over other ways of seeing and measuring. Like the neoliberals, their tendency is to cluster around a few key think tanks: *back then*, the Institute of Economic Affairs, the Cato Institute, and the Adam Smith Institute; *now*, the Breakthrough Institute, the Long Now Foundation, and the Copenhagen Consensus. Like the neoliberals, they are beginning to grow in numbers at a time of global collapse and uncertainty. And like the neoliberals, they think they have radical solutions.

Kareiva's ideas are a good place to start in understanding them. He is a prominent conservation scientist who believes that most of what the greens think they know is wrong. Nature, he says, is more resilient than fragile; science proves it. "Humans degrade and destroy and crucify the natural environment," he writes, "and 80 percent of the time it recovers pretty well."[1] Wilderness does not exist; all of it has been influenced by humans at some time. Trying to protect large functioning ecosystems from human development is mostly futile; humans like development, and you can't stop them having it. Nature is tough and will adapt to this: "Today, coyotes roam downtown Chicago and peregrines astonish San Franciscans as they sweep down skyscraper canyons. . . . [A]s we destroy habitats, we create new ones."[2]

Now that "science" has shown us that nothing is "pristine" and nature "adapts," there's no reason to worry about many traditional green goals such as protecting rainforest habitats. "Is halting deforestation in the Amazon . . . feasible?" Kareiva and colleagues ask, "Is it even necessary?"[3] Somehow, you know what the answer is going to be before the authors give it to you.

If this sounds like the kind of thing that a U.S. Republican presidential candidate might come out with, that's because it is. But Kareiva and colleagues are not alone. Variations on this line have recently been pushed by the U.S. thinker Stewart Brand; the British writer Mark Lynas; the Danish anti-green poster boy Bjørn Lomborg; and the American writers Emma Marris, Ted Nordhaus, and Michael Shellenberger. They in turn are building on work done in the past by other self-declared green "heretics" like Richard D. North, Brian Clegg, and Wilfred Beckerman.

Beyond the field of conservation, the neo-environmentalists are distinguished by their attitude toward new technologies, which they almost uniformly see as positive. Civilization, nature, and people can be "saved" only by enthusiastically embracing biotechnology, synthetic biology, nuclear power, geoengineering, and anything else with the prefix "new" that annoys Greenpeace. The traditional green focus on limits is dismissed as naive. We are now, in Brand's words, "as Gods," and we have to step up and accept our responsibility to manage the planet rationally through the use of new technology guided by enlightened science.

Neo-environmentalists also tend to exhibit an excitable enthusiasm for markets. They like to put a price on things like trees, lakes, mist, crocodiles, rainforests, and watersheds, all of which can deliver "ecosystem services" which can be bought and sold, measured and totted up. Tied in with this is an almost religious attitude toward the scientific method. Everything that matters can be measured by science and priced by markets, and any claims without numbers attached can be easily dismissed. This is presented as "pragmatism" but is actually something rather different: an attempt to exclude from the green debate any interventions based on morality, emotion, intuition, spiritual connection, or simple human feeling.

Some of this might be shocking to some old-guard greens—which is the point, but it is hardly a new message. In fact, it is a very old one; it is simply a variant on the old Wellsian techno-optimism which has been promising us cornucopia for over a century. It's an old-fashioned Big Science, Big Tech, and Big Money narrative, filtered through the lens of the Internet and garlanded with holier-than-thou talk about saving the poor and feeding the world.

But though they burn with the shouty fervor of the born-again, the neo-environmentalists are not exactly wrong. In fact, they are at least half right. They are right to say that the human-scale, convivial approaches of many of the original green thinkers are never going to work if the world continues to formulate itself according to the demands of late capitalist industrialism. They are right to say that a world of 9 billion people all seeking the status of middle-class consumers cannot be sustained by vernacular approaches. They are right to say that the human impact on the planet is enormous and irreversible. They are right to say that traditional conservation efforts sometimes idealize a preindustrial nature. They are right to say that the campaigns of green NGOs often exaggerate and dissemble. And they are right to say that the greens have hit a wall, and that continuing to ram their heads against it is not going to knock it down.

What's interesting, though, is what they go on to build on this foundation. The first sign that this is not, as declared, a simple "eco-pragmatism," but is something rather different, comes when you read statements like this:

For decades people have unquestioningly accepted the idea that our goal is to preserve nature in its pristine, pre-human state. But many scientists have come to see this as an outdated dream that thwarts bold new plans to save the environment and prevents us from having a fuller relationship with nature.[4]

This passage appears on author Emma Marris's website, in connection with her book *Rambunctious Garden: Saving Nature in a Post-Wild World*,[5] though it could just as easily be from anywhere else in the neo-environmentalist canon. But who are the many "people" who have "unquestioningly accepted" this line? I've met a lot of conservationists and environmentalists in my time, and I don't think I've ever met one who believed there was any such thing as "pristine, pre-human" nature. What they did believe was that there were still large-scale, functioning ecosystems which were worth getting out of bed for to help protect them from destruction.

To understand why, consider the case of the Amazon. What do we value about the Amazon forest? Do people seek to protect it because they believe it is "pristine" and "pre-human"? Clearly not, since it's inhabited and harvested by large numbers of tribal people, some of whom have been there for millennia. The Amazon is not important because it is untouched; it's important because it is wild, in the sense that it is self-willed. Humans live in and from it, but it is not created or controlled by them. It teems with a great, shifting, complex diversity of both human and nonhuman life, and no species dominates the mix. It is a complex, working ecosystem which is also a human-culture system, because in any kind of worthwhile world, the two are linked.

This is what intelligent green thinking has always called for: human and nonhuman nature working in some degree of harmony, in a modern world of compromise and change in which some principles, nevertheless, are worth cleaving to. Nature is a resource for people, and always has been; we all have to eat, make shelter, hunt, and live from its bounty like any other creature. But that doesn't preclude our understanding that it has a practical, cultural, emotional, and even spiritual value beyond that too, which is equally necessary for our well-being.

The neo-environmentalists, needless to say, have no time for this kind of fluff. They have a great big straw man to build up and knock down, and once they've got that out of the way, they can move on to the really important part of their message. Here's Kareiva, with fellow authors Robert Lalasz and Michelle Marvier, giving us the money shot in their *Breakthrough Journal* article:

Instead of pursuing the protection of biodiversity for biodiversity's sake, a new conservation should seek to enhance those natural systems that benefit the widest number of people. . . . Conservation will measure its achievement in large part by its relevance to people.[6]

There it is, in black and white: The wild is dead, and what remains of nature is for people. We can effectively do what we like, and we should. Science says so! A full circle has been drawn, the greens have been buried by their own children, and under the soil with them has gone their naive, romantic, and antiscientific belief that nonhuman life has any value beyond what we very modern humans can make use of.

During my twenty years in the green movement, I've got a good feel for the many fault lines, divisions, debates, and arguments with which that movement, like any other, is riven. But to me, this feels like something different. The rise of the neo-greens feels like not simply another internal argument but an entirely new sloughing-off of some key green principles. It seems like a bunch of people keen to continue to define themselves as radicals, and as environmentalists, while acting and talking in a way that makes it clear that they are precisely the opposite.

The neo-greens do not come to rejuvenate environmentalism; they come to bury it. They come to tell us that nature doesn't matter; that there is no such thing as nature anyway; that the interests of human beings should always be paramount; that the rational mind must always win out over the intuitive mind; and that the political and economic settlement we have come to know in the last twenty years as "globalization" is the only game in town, now and probably forever. All of the questions the greens have been raising for decades about the meaning of progress, about how we should live in relationship to other species, and about technology and political organization and human-scale development are to be thrown in the bin like children's toys.

Over the next few years, the old green movement that I grew up with is likely to fall to pieces. Many of those pieces will be picked up and hoarded by the growing ranks of the neo-environmentalists. The mainstream of the green movement has laid itself open to their advances in recent years with its obsessive focus on carbon and energy technologies and its refusal to speak up for a subjective, vernacular, nontechnical engagement with nature. The neo-environmentalists have a great advantage over the old greens, with their threatening talk about limits to growth, behavior change, and other such against-the-grain stuff: They are telling this civilization what it wants to hear.

In the short term, the future belongs to the neo-environmentalists, and it is going to be painful to watch. In the long term, though, I suspect they will fail, for two reasons. Firstly, bubbles always burst. Our civilization is beginning to break down. We are at the start of an unfolding economic and social collapse which may take decades or longer to play out—and which is playing out against the background of a planetary ecocide that nobody seems able to prevent. We are not gods, and our machines will not get us off this hook, however clever they are and however much we would like to believe it.

But there is another reason that the new breed are unlikely to be able to build the world they want to see: We are not—even they are not—primarily rational, logical, or "scientific" beings. Our human relationship to the rest of nature is not akin to the analysis of bacteria in a petri dish; it is more like the complex, love–hate relationship we might have with lovers or parents or siblings. It is who we are, unspoken and felt and frustrating and inspiring and vital, and impossible to peer review. You can reach part of it with the analytical mind, but the rest will remain buried in the ancient woodland floor of human evolution and in the depths of our old ape brains, which see in pictures and think in stories.

Civilization has always been a project of control, but you can't win a war against the wild within yourself. We may have to wait many years, though, before the neo-greens discover this for themselves.

The Conceptual
Assassination of Wilderness

DAVID W. KIDNER

THE TIDES OF CHANGE are always harder to recognize when we ourselves are swept along in the same direction as everything around us. Specifically, as the tide of industrialism lays waste to the natural order, a complementary process occurs among those of us who inhabit the more affluent areas of the world, molding us toward an anxious individualism and generating an "empty self" that yearns to compensate for the loss of wildness and cultural meaning through consumerism and immersion in the distractions provided by the media.[1] Wildlife documentaries, TV travelogues, and colorful calendar images of nature reinforce the comforting illusion that the wild world continues to flourish; and the entire ideological system of industrialism suspends us within a sort of manufactured alternative reality, so that children can now grow up with almost no experience of wild nature. Thus the wider context of wilderness loss is a parallel ebbing of those human qualities that value, express, and resonate with wildness. In this essay I focus on the ways industrialized modes of thought have undermined our ability to recognize the degradation of wilderness and wildness throughout the world.

In the educational sphere, for example, Gene Myers has shown how children's felt connections to nature are replaced by less emotionally involving abstractions such as "food chains";[2] and David Sobel has argued that rather than being allowed freely to explore the natural world, children are instead steered toward PowerPoint presentations, videos, and closely manicured guided trails that deliver predigested experiences.[3] Given these powerful forms of socialization, it is hardly surprising that young people are persuaded to accept that "nature" consists of scattered islands of wildness in an ocean of domestication, so repressing their tacit, embodied expectations of a truly wild world.

Environmental thought is as susceptible to this tide of domestication as any other aspect of life in the industrialized world; and just as physical nature is being replaced by domesticated landscapes, so our understanding of nature as the outcome of evolutionary processes and ecological interaction is being replaced by a new origin myth that is more consistent with industrial beliefs. In recent academic writings, there has been a concerted effort to convince us that nature is "socially constructed" and that even wilderness is a product of industrial society. I will not review this debate here but will simply note that in the constructionist view, nature has more of a *symbolic* presence than a physical one. Even outside academia, nature is increasingly an *idea* rather than a physical reality, associated with images on a TV screen rather than embodied experiences of hiking in the wilderness; and it possesses much the same experiential status as Narnia, Middle Earth, or Hogwarts. If a person "loves nature," this doesn't necessarily mean that they enjoy experiencing it firsthand. More likely, they will have a Sierra Club calendar on the wall, will take their children to SeaWorld, and will donate to Greenpeace. It is as if we are no longer sure what is real—what our senses communicate to us, or what our minds, programmed through education and amplified by digital technologies, lead us to believe.

From this perspective, we are encouraged to accept that everything, including wilderness, is an artifact of the human world, because we define it, represent it, and communicate about it. Adrian Franklin, for example, defines nature as "whatever happens to result from the interaction between species including the actions and designs of man."[4] Furthermore, he continues, even "a caged wild animal in a zoo or the water in a fountain can be appreciated as nature."[5] Such definitions are both extremely broad and extremely vague; and "nature" is correspondingly malleable, being reduced to—in Steven Vogel's terms—"a kind of substrate that exists prior to our actions."[6] This is very close to the industrialist view that nature consists of "raw materials" without intrinsic structure, values, or tendencies, ready to be formed into useful products; and so social scientific understandings of nature, as well as everyday conceptions of it, are drawn into the industrialist web.

This sweeping aside of the properties of nature by industrialist ways of thinking has left its mark on the environmental literature to the extent that an attempted rewriting of history is well under way. Various theorists have argued not only that nature is conceptually constructed but that even wilderness areas have been *physically* constructed by humans. As Vogel puts it, "even the material landscapes we like to call natural always turn out to be more the product of human action . . . than we wanted to believe."[7] Likewise, Charles Mann argues that "the Amazon jungle, as a matter of brute fact, was not just construed but actually created by humans," and he writes that the shards of pots found there indicate that it is "fashioned as purposefully as Disneyland."[8] But as I have said elsewhere, this example "is somewhat more convincing as an example of the recalcitrance of nature in the face of human attempts to transform it, since the pottery—and the pottery-makers—have long since been re-assimilated by the jungle."[9]

In a similar vein, William Balée suggests that natural history is essentially a *human* history, as if humans are the only species of any significance in the evolution of wilderness. "Historical ecology," as Balée terms his disciplinary stance, "answers the call for an anthropocentric as opposed to an ecocentric or geocentric ecology";[10] and he argues that humans have had a uniquely significant role compared to all other creatures in shaping the landscape. By this logic, wilderness that is not shaped by humans is vanishingly rare; and the defender of "pristine" wilderness is portrayed as suffering from a romantic delusion. Given that people have at some time roamed almost every landscape on the face of the planet, virtually the entirety of nature, by this logic, becomes "fashioned as purposefully as Disneyland." There are immediate physical implications for such a view; for if nature is already "a product of . . . civilization,"[11] as William Cronon infamously argued, then further domesticating it does not violate nature's own structures but simply continues a natural process of change that began when *Homo sapiens* first chipped pieces of granite to make axe heads. And if, as Vogel argues, "all our artifacts are natural,"[12] then clearly any exploitation, development, or destruction of wilderness becomes acceptable as part of this process.

Not only do these authors claim that the history of the natural world is a largely human one, but so also, they allege, is its future. In Daniel

Botkin's terms, "nature in the twenty-first century will be a nature that we make,"[13] thus closing off any nonanthropocentric possibilities and ensuring an industrialist future that is necessarily an extrapolation of the present—bigger, better, and faster than before, with less "wasted" on things such as wilderness that are not efficient, profitable, or in some way useful to (industrial) humans. Similarly, we are invited by Peter Kareiva and his colleagues to accept that the battle to save wilderness is already lost, since "virtually all of nature is now domesticated";[14] and the key questions that remain simply "concern future options for the type of domesticated nature humans impose upon the world,"[15] any concern with other species being swept aside.

The belief that human influence necessarily makes nature a "human artifact" starts from the questionable assumption that humans are necessarily qualitatively different from any other creature. If bear scat, for example, is discovered in an area of wilderness, we don't say that this makes the landscape an artifact of bears—nor does the presence of salmon imply that the fish have constructed the river. Even a rudimentary ecological awareness makes it clear that nature emerges through the interaction between *many* forms of life; and absolute control by any single species does not signal a unique form of construction, but rather the death of the ecosystem. Thus the notion that humans have "constructed" the wilderness stems from a delusory anthropocentric arrogance that greatly overestimates human contributions while downplaying those of other life-forms almost to the point of nonexistence. This is the same sort of arrogance that is implied when we claim to "produce" oil, "have" babies, or "grow" apples; in other words, these descriptions grossly overestimate human control while taking for granted the natural processes involved.

Equally problematic is the inaccurate use of the term "human" in these arguments, implying that all humans are just variants of industrial humanity, and conflating industrialist and tribal ways of living in a sweeping and inaccurate generalization. As Arturo Gomez-Pompa and Andrea Kaus argue, we need to differentiate between those scenarios where humans are part of the ecosystem, and those that involve "modern production systems [that] have advanced technologies, from chemical fertilizers to hydroelectric dams, that are external to the local environment."[16] Industrial humanity does not so much "construct" nature as sweep it aside, replacing it with a quite different system that is hostile to and destructive of nature. In contrast, many tribal peoples have lived nondestructively for centuries as *members of* an ecosystem rather than as its conquerors;[17] and such groups often *enhance* ecosystemic diversity rather than destroy it.[18] Consequently they themselves are as threatened by industrialism as is any other part of the ecosystem.[19]

Indigenous peoples would (without exception, to my knowledge) regard the view that "humans construct nature" as bizarre and unrealistic, since their lives, both culturally and practically, are embedded within a *preexisting* natural realm. Thus meaning and structure, rather than being *imposed on* the world, are *derived from* the world; and as Tim Ingold suggests, knowledge of the world, for a tribal person,

is gained by moving about in it, exploring it, attending to it, ever alert to the signs by which it is revealed. Learning to see, then, is not a matter of acquiring schemata for mentally constructing the environment but of acquiring the skills for direct perceptual engagement with its constituents, human and nonhuman, animate and inanimate.[20]

This close engagement between people and nature may be why tribal groups often enhance ecosystems. This does not mean, however, that a "pristine" ecosystem *without* humans is necessarily unhealthy or unnatural, any more than an ecosystem without, say, anteaters is necessarily unhealthy or unnatural. What *is* clear is that where wilderness *has* been degraded by humans, this is generally the result of invasion by outsiders equipped with modern technologies and an anthropocentric worldview. It is essential, then, to distinguish between the potentially positive ecological influence of tribal groups and the invariably destructive actions of nonindigenous settlers armed with chain saws and tractors. For Kareiva, "human" equals the self-centered industrialist individual who has no concern for or empathy with anything or anyone else:

Most of the world's nearly 7 billion people don't care about biodiversity, and most don't think of nature conservation as essential to their ambitions and goals. People want to be safe and secure, have food and shelter, and have an opportunity to better their lives. And they will use natural resources in any way possible to further those objectives.[21]

According to Kareiva, we need "a vision of the future . . . [that is] based on the hard facts of growing population, huge climate impacts, and expanding agriculture and energy exploration."[22] His vision, therefore, is not only one in which pathological demographic and ecological scenarios are accepted as "hard facts" and *faits accomplis*; it also implies that the person is degraded from an empathic, moral, relational member of a culture and an ecosystem to a self-interested individual whose interests are "imposed" on the rest of the world, thus extending the dubious morality of the colonialist war to the natural world. Equally unfortunately, this sort of ecological zero-sum game, as Garrett Hardin's parable of the "tragedy of the commons" lucidly illustrates,[23] leads directly to ecological and social catastrophe. Kareiva's vision thus manages to combine ecological, moral, and social pathologies into a single disastrous whole. It is therefore not a vision that seeks to preserve nature at all. Rather, it is the offspring of industrialist ideology and seeks to materialize this ideology in the form of a fully domesticated world from which all forms of wildness, whether human or nonhuman, have been extinguished.

Ptolemaic Environmentalism

EILEEN CRIST

THE ANCIENT GREEK WORD *oecumene* came into broad circulation in the Hellenistic era to refer to the inhabited world. It was a world that stretched from the Mediterranean basin to India, and from the Caucasus mountains to the Arabian Peninsula, encompassing diverse peoples and cultures connected via trade routes and empire building, alliances and conquests. By "the inhabited world," *oecumene* of course meant the world inhabited by people. What the concept implied by exclusion, by what it passed over in silence, is that nonhumans do not inhabit. Only people are inhabitants, while animals, plants, and the natural communities they create merely exist in certain places—until they are forced to make way for, or be converted to serve, the oecumene.

Oecumene stands out as one of the first human imperialistic concepts. It is an idea constituted through omitting the actions that realize it—the appropriation of the natural world—presenting its meaning instead in a positive register: "the world inhabited by people." It suggested a kind of protoglobalization, since oecumene included a cosmopolitan terrain.[1] Indeed, through its later linguistic transformation into "ecumenical" (meaning universal), oecumene foreshadowed globalization—humanity's planet-wide occupation and the obliteration of the wild that the concept implied and through which it was realized.

Oecumene can be characterized as a "crystallization of culture,"[2] a significant sign of the lodging of anthropocentrism into language and thereby into broadly shared patterns of thought. It indicates that human beings, since civilization's beginnings, have proclaimed the separate and special prerogative of the human. For generations untold, people have been inheriting this belief system and living by its compass, through cultural constellations of concepts, philosophies, theologies, and theories, until ultimately—by such serial, ideological sedimentations over the course of many centuries—the anthropocentric belief system has acquired the foundational status of "commonsense." This belief system certainly has a different valence for different individuals and cultures. But broadly speaking, it professes that human beings, by virtue of the ostensible special nature of their consciousness and skills, are essentially distinct from other species, superior in their form of being (which includes, among other things, the ability to reason, foresee their own death, and terraform via technology), and entitled primacy with respect to having their interests met prior to all else. Anthropocentrism thus constructs an existential apartheid between, on the one hand, humans as a distinctive species-being with special privileges and, on the other, all other life forms regarded, more or less, as the usable or displaceable "merely living."[3]

Anthropocentrism's entrenchment accounts for its pervasiveness and apparent naturalness, yet it is not beyond the reach of critical inquiry, dissection, and refutation. To inquire into anthropocentrism is to ask what kind of belief system it is. The unquestioned conviction with which people uphold the anthropocentric credo belies its characterization as mere belief, because it is in the nature of belief to be open to questioning and relinquishment in the face of a better alternative. At the same time, to call anthropocentrism a kind of folk knowledge—that we *just know* humans are different and have special entitlements, by the sundry evidence all around us—is to normalize an understanding of the human which the evidence all around us surely reflects only because humans have *made* that evidence, through actions that their sense of specialness has inspired and informed, to do so. We find ourselves then in the awkward conceptual space of a "belief system"—that of anthropocentrism as I sketched it above—which cannot be convincingly characterized as either mere belief or certain knowledge.

To be open to discerning the historically constructed and reconstructed character of anthropocentrism—its achieved legitimacy as a matter of conquest and often violence, and not a result of the rightful prerogative, or nature, of the human; its commonsensical entrenchment as a corollary of the erasure of the nonhuman (physical obliteration, discursive belittle-ment, or the simple invisibility of the vanquished at all levels of percep-tion); its victory as a perhaps once-evitable, but increasingly inescapable, historical course which has been entraining a time of reckoning (the time when oecumene would be all there is to see)—to be open to discerning these qualities of anthropocentrism that inquiry makes available, thereby seeing it in a novel, non-commonsensical light, is to understand that it may compellingly be described as "false knowledge."

False knowledge is a most obstinate species of belief, for it tends to strongly resist dislodging. There exist notable examples of false knowledge systems, akin to the credo of anthropocentrism in the unswerving con-viction with which they were held and the enticements of grandeur that underpinned them: namely, the knowledge that the Earth is the center of the universe around which planets, Moon, and Sun revolve; and also the knowledge that humans were specially created in the image of God. Of the same epistemic status and kin content is simply knowing—deeply and almost irrefutably—that humans are different, special, and always come first. Indeed, it is this conviction that partially grounded the long-standing knowledge systems of Earth-centered astronomy and creationism, for what all three false ways of knowing have in common is self-glorification. When Nicolaus Copernicus wrote the tract that would refute Ptolemaic astronomy, he let the manuscript sit, virtually unread, on his desk for (at least) nine years.[4] Charles Darwin kept his knowledge of the fact of evolu-tion secret for twenty-one—and when he shared it with his botanist friend Joseph Dalton Hooker, he described the moment of confidence as akin to "confessing murder." These stories convey the following: Standard belief systems, even if highly respected and securely ensconced, can be inter-rogated; but false knowledge is confronted only at one's peril.

To characterize anthropocentrism as a (false) way of knowing is an-other way of saying that it describes *reality* for most people. And herein lies all the power that anthropocentrism claims. It possesses the moral power of always prioritizing human needs and desires. It provides the economic and political power of appropriating whatever humans can use from the natural world—from oceans, forests, rivers, grasslands, coasts, wildlife, domestic animals, genomes, or the crust of the Earth—by mak-ing the sources themselves invisible except in relation to our use of them. Anthropocentrism creates the ontological power to elide the acts of taking *as* acts of taking, through their ceaseless (small-to-mega) enactments as unremarkably ordinary. And, finally, through the power of its common-sensical standing, anthropocentrism keeps people under the spell of all of the above. For the dominant mindset, with nary a conscious thought, such is the real world: We came, we saw, we conquered. And to question this reality—the reality of human empire—places one outside, or at the margins, of every human club: academic, political, religious, or cultural. So while in the modern secular era questioning political regimes, religious dogmas, power structures, and even scientific theories or facts is kosher and often praiseworthy, questioning human empire is not. Questioning that particular reality will earn one certain unsavory labels. (And challenging that reality through activism can nowadays land one in prison or dead.)

Labels: for example, that you are being *unrealistic*. Or romantic. Juvenile. Probably misanthropic.[5] Environmental thinkers and activists with deep-ecological leanings, who have countered the human regime on Earth with the ideals of biotic membership and biospherical egalitarianism, have been called all these names. Recently their perspective has been proclaimed dead, dysfunctional, or passé. But while such labels impress with their dismissive power, we need not be led astray by that power—for it does not reflect on the sobriety of questioning human domination, but rather evidences the tremendous sway of that domination backed doubly by the authority of history and by certain almighty material interests that be. The establishment of human domination—with the penetration of anthropocentrism's myriad tendrils into the lifeworld, not to say into economic, political, and institutional power structures—means that those who question its legitimacy cannot be given audience but will invariably, for the time being, be written off. For it comes down to this: The ideational and institutional schemata of human privilege have long been championed by a dominant civilization, which has carved planetary reality to reflect the cult of human specialness, such that between the Scylla of anthropocentric ideas and the Charybdis of global terraforming, the human mind has virtually zero degrees of freedom to think outside the box of Earth takeover and self-arbitrated rule.

Be that as it may, after millennia of the empire's march are the consequences. The consequences are called the Sixth Extinction. They are called climate change, ocean acidification, and the Great Pacific Garbage Patch. They are called large-scale deforestation and desertification. The consequences are called 400 marine dead zones worldwide. They are called 90 percent of the big fish in the oceans are gone, and "empty forest syndrome." The consequences are called the stifling of animal migrations and the constriction of wild species' home ranges. They are also called the closing of the human heart to the suffering of farm animals. The consequences are called ecological amnesia, on the one hand, and a widening wave of grieving for lost beings and places, on the other. Today the whole planet is the oecumene and what the latter concept started out by implicitly erasing—the reality that nonhumans *do* inhabit and have equal prerogative to flourish here as we do—has become manifest by time, the revelator, as a nonhuman holocaust that is not even permitted to be called one. If at the heart of this juggernaut lies human self-appointed rule, then are we not called to take aim?

Neo-greens choose sustaining human dominion

Far from taking aim, a twenty-first-century vocal contingent of environmentalism—referred to variously as post-environmentalism, new environmentalism, eco-pragmatism, and eco-optimism, and often allied with the recent pitch to rename our geological epoch the *Anthropocene*—is disinclined from disputing human domination. Instead, it opts for the realistic work of *damage control* and of reforming the ways humans exercise planetary charge. Neo-greens, as I will refer to the exponents of this platform, seek to redress the adverse consequences of our impact while refraining from challenging the historical impulse toward Earth's occupation; and they often endeavor to recast the human presence in a more sanguine light.

The neo-green platform admits that there are serious environmental problems to grapple with, but the humanization of the planet is not one of them—let alone their root cause.[6] The problems are certain harmful side effects (most especially) of industrial civilization, with climate change usually considered the gravest. But the disposition of civilization to use the Earth as though it were deeded as human private property is left unchallenged and treated in the quotidian modality of "normal." Some neo-greens, recognizing the possibility that biophysical limits may have been (or might soon be) breached by human excesses, seek to identify and circumscribe planetary boundaries for key parameters in order to sustain a global environment that provides "a safe operating space for humanity" to continue its onward, if reformed, march.[7]

A critical mission of the neo-green agenda is to contain, mitigate, adapt to, or technically solve any consequences of civilization that might backfire, while essentially preserving the impetus of civilization's expansionism, and even celebrating its future extraterrestrial ventures.[8] The Earth's colonization is not portrayed as the exercise of power over the biosphere to serve human interests (and especially the interests of elites), but as a sign of the human race's godlike stature. Turning virtually the entire globe into "the inhabited world" showcases a superlative quality of the human, rather than manifesting the cumulative outcome of long centuries of dominating nature by the lights of a human supremacist worldview. Famously, in the words of Stewart Brand, we are as gods,[9] and—in the interests of keeping our planet a workable stage for our unfolding destiny—we have to get good at it.[10]

Getting good at being god involves making the takeover of the planet sustainable.[11] To that effect one requirement is sound global management of natural resources. While the idea of "wilderness"—a conceptual and pragmatic roadblock to such management, as well as to the legitimacy of constituting nature qua resources—is tirelessly assailed by the neo-green platform, the concept of "natural resources" (and kin cultural crystallizations of the anthropocentric credo) is left unpacked, as though its patently sensible import puts it beyond deconstructive exegesis.

Besides sound resource management, also imperative for addressing risks—such as resource depletion (for example, freshwater) or sink overload (for example, dangerous levels of greenhouse gases)—is the deployment of technological inventions and solutions, with special emphasis on cutting-edge technologies. (Genetic engineering and geoengineering are prominent examples). The appeal to cutting-edge technologies accomplishes the double task of offering promissory notes (which, if empty, no one will be accountable for) and of seizing ownership of the future by extending the exercise of technical power to address problems while simultaneously avoiding reflection on humanity's power-driven mode of operation and on the available choice of a more humble path. A predilection for the technological not only shuns wrestling with human planetary politics—in which everything from mountaintops to underground shale and from genomes to climate are treated as our rightful turf—but, at least tacitly, fortifies that planetary politics which tends to enforce its regime via technological means.

Alongside sound management and technological approaches, the neo-green agenda also embraces the surveillance of natural systems so as to scientifically monitor chemical, physical, and biological phenomena with the aim of maintaining or enhancing humanity's prospects. These interconnected strategies (management, technology, and surveillance) involve upgrading and fine-tuning the rationalization of technical means to serve human ends, such that current challenges, especially those which are civilization-threatening, can be grasped as an opportunity to veer ourselves out of danger and toward a more secure and greener human empire. "We can only hope," according to geographer and Anthropocene proponent Erle Ellis, "that human systems will continue to evolve in their capacity to create and sustain the biosphere we want and need."[12]

The strategy of creating and sustaining a human-ruled biosphere reaffirms the legitimacy of anthropocentrism, avoids interrogating our relationship with the biosphere and its whole ensemble of life as an ethical matter, and resolutely eschews confronting global civilization as a totalitarian system on Earth.

As alluded to above, neo-greens recast a dominant human presence as not-so-dire-a-prospect after all. According to this view, mourning the loss and depredation of the wild keeps us from appreciating the beauty that is part of all kinds of landscapes, including human-shaped ones; and obsessing over the exploitation and conversion of the natural world leaves us unable to recognize that nature is resilient and constantly changing anyway. Such environmental revisionism redefines humanity's impact as just another biogeological moment of Earth's history—and even a remarkable one; and it endeavors to banish the environmental blues by extending a more optimistic welcome to humanity's decisive presence. The metaphor of "garden" (or of "gardened planet") is invoked to envision the present and future world—tidy in some places, overgrown in others, but still beautiful, fecund, rambunctious, and ever in flux. This global garden in the making will not be, to borrow the words of ecologist Peter Kareiva (and his colleagues), "a carefully manicured and rigid one" but instead will be a tangle of natural ecosystems along with lands for food production, mineral extraction, urban centers, and so on.[13] The human-dominated era opening indefinitely before us can be an epoch, in Ellis's words, "ripe with human-directed opportunity."[14] It is a world that, if we cannot bring ourselves to embrace it, we can at least resign ourselves to. For "while there is nothing particularly good about a planet hotter than our ancestors ever experienced—not to mention one free of wild forests or wild fish—it seems all too evident that human systems are prepared to adapt to and prosper in the hotter, less biodiverse planet that we are busily creating."[15]

The state of the world captured via the garden metaphor sounds innocuous enough. But to invoke a different metaphor from popular culture, opting for the gardened-planet image is like taking the blue pill, instead of the red one, from Morpheus's extended hand—choosing "the blissful ignorance of illusion over the painful truth of reality."[16] The painful reality of Matrix-planet is that it will be chock-full of industrial agricultural checkerboards and grazing lands; factory farms; industrial fish-farm operations; industrial energy landscapes; theme parks and resorts; highway systems, roads, and parking lots; billions of cars and other vehicles; and sprawling cities, as well as suburban, exurban, and rural settlements; malls; landfills; airports; and beachfront development. Global trade and travel, with their 24/7 traffic of already huge quantities of stuff, will escalate enormously—as will the entropy of nature conversion, biodiversity loss, and pollution that accompany them.[17] The presence of humans will be palpable everywhere in this world devoid of any blank spots on the map—a world used, managed, monitored, gridded, and reduced to being knowable, with the map itself eventually turned into the territory. Thus, opting for Morpheus's red pill, the planet's ecological and existential predicament is plain, if painful, to see: "Gardened planet" is a euphemism for colonized Earth. And humanity is not penning another interesting chapter of natural history, but heralding the end of a sublime one—so long as we stay the course toward a coming world of 9, 10, or more billion people, running a global capitalist economy, and governing by the conceit that this planet is human real estate. To paraphrase author John Gray, the horror we should flee is making such a humanized world in which humans encounter only reflections of themselves.[18]

The view that humanity is an integral part of Earth's natural history, and that through our unique powers we are creating new expressions of nature, is a standard thread in the neo-green literature. This perspective on our shaping of the biosphere *naturalizes* the human impact—and usually in an offhanded manner: Because what is the human presence, after all, if not a manifestation of nature? According to environmental author Emma Marris, for example, since we know that ecosystems are never static, "this means that novel [anthropogenic or human-influenced] ecosystems, far from being a new phenomenon, simply represent the latest changes on a dynamic Earth."[19] Similarly, environmental journalist Fred Pearce asserts that constant change is a natural aspect of the world; "humans may have dramatically speeded that up, but novelty is the norm."[20]

And yet, the tack of naturalizing humanity's impact is profoundly contestable, because people (at both an individual and a cultural level) are capable of engaging in very different kinds of relationship with nonhuman nature and the Earth. I submit that far from humanity's impact being "natural," its character supervenes from a species-supremacist, actionable belief system that only recently has a minority of human beings awakened to and recoiled from. With respect to Western civilization—now dominating human affairs—from classical antiquity, through Judeo-Christian theology, to dominant strands of modern scientific and political thought, its intellectual canon and legacy have been *overwhelmingly* anthropocentric.[21] Anthropocentrism (or human supremacy) has shaped the dominant culture and has both orchestrated and legitimated a plundering human behavior toward the natural world.[22] Such human behavior can be regarded as "natural" only by espousing a hard-core neo-Darwinian view of life as ruthless, competitive, and fundamentally self-centered. But this Western, pseudo-scientific view is narrow and suspiciously self-serving, and thus cogent only as an ideology and not a comprehensive empirical representation of the nature of life.

More than fallacious, naturalizing our planetary takeover is an unwitting form of myth-making, fully intertwined with the neo-green elevation of the human to godlike status and with its ardent desire to christen a slice of geological time after *anthropos*. Mythmaking is integral to the human imagination, yet this currently propounded mythology is but the latest spin on humanistic narcissism; it is a mythology we would be wise to exorcise. Naturalizing the disfigurement and impoverishment of the biosphere—and simultaneously elevating this particular effect as stemming from humanity's power to create new expressions of nature—is a move accomplished by de-historicizing the human: "The history of the concept of man is never examined. Everything occurs as if the sign 'man' has no origin, no historical, cultural, or linguistic limit."[23] To inquire into humanity's anthropocentric mode of operation as socio- and psycho-historically constituted is to disclose that it is merely *one* constructed meaning of the human; such disclosure opens a horizon within which we become *free* to shift into the work of recreating ourselves and our way of life on Earth. This is a horizon of human freedom that cannot be forfeited without severely contracting the very scope of what it means to be human.

We are in danger of losing the freedom to remake ourselves as a compassionate and integral planetary member, if we embrace the pitch that humanity's identity as planetary overlord is natural.

Concerning the neo-green appeal to the priority of social justice

It is neither facile analogy nor rhetorical ploy to urge questioning anthropocentrism in the same spirit of inquiry and conscience that Caucasian-centeredness has been challenged. Human species supremacy and white racial supremacy are profoundly similar and, in fact, overlapping systems of thought. White supremacy drew its power from claims of racial superiority that were perceived as entirely commonsensical; moreover, to secure its hegemony, it leaned into the even more "obvious" reality of human supremacy over all other species by portraying non-Caucasian races as akin to "lower forms of life" (especially animals such as apes and insects). Inequalities between human groups, on the one hand, and the grand hierarchy of the human–nonhuman, on the other, have always been enmeshed, mutually supportive frameworks.[24]

The neo-green perspective alleges concern about inequities between people and about the lot of the world's poor. At the same time, it leaves standing the received hierarchy between humans and nonhuman nature—refusing to examine the troubled relationship between people and the natural world through the lens of justice. Issues of justice are reserved (in the time-honored Western intellectual tradition) for the human domain, and matters of social justice (the gap between the consumer classes and the poor) are judged as most immediately pressing. Environmental author Paul Hawken recently voiced the perspective of the primacy of social justice with the following appeal: "There is no question that the environmental movement is critical to our survival. Our house is literally burning, and it is only logical that environmentalists expect the social justice movement to get on the environmental bus. But it is the other way around; the only way we are going to put out the fire is to get on the social justice bus and heal our wounds."[25] Kareiva and his colleagues pursue a similar thread of reasoning: "Most people worldwide (regardless of culture) welcome the opportunities that development provides to improve lives of grinding poverty. . . . Conservation should seek to support and inform the right kind of development—development by design, done with the importance of nature to thriving economies foremost in mind."[26] Environmental analysts Michael Shellenberger and Ted Nordhaus are optimistic about the prospects: "By 2100, nearly all of us will be prosperous enough to live healthy, free, and creative lives. Despite the claims of Malthusian pessimists, that world is both economically and ecologically possible. But to realize it, and to save what remains of the Earth's ecological heritage, we must once and for all embrace human power, technology, and the larger process of modernization."[27]

What such analyses choose to ignore is that poverty has long been a social reality arising from civilization's peculiar relationship with the natural world: namely, of viewing nature as a container of coveted resources that can be appropriated (through the exercise of some form of power or other) for the creation of what we have come to call wealth. From time immemorial, just as today, the underclass and the powerless have been forcibly limited from accessing resources for their own material advantage. It is thus injustice toward the more-than-human world—stripping it of its intrinsic being and value, and turning it into being-for and value-for people ("resources")—that constitutes the foundation of social injustice and inequality.

Yet that foundation remains largely invisible, because a critical dimension of humanity's self-awarded entitlement to use nature as we will has *also* been to make it taboo to regard our relationship with the natural world as *having anything to do* with matters of justice or injustice. Thus the anthropocentric credo, today buoyed along through such ideas as "resources," "natural capital," "ecological services," "working landscapes," and the like—ideas specifically indebted to the erasure of any *intrinsic* modality (ontological or evaluative) of the nonhuman realm—is left untouched, as is its plainly colonialist vocabulary. At the same time, the solution to social injustice is portrayed as the "democratic" (ever the buzzword) sharing of planetary loot, loot described more politely through such commonplace concepts as those listed above. The poor will be lifted from their dire plight, so goes the promise, as the natural world becomes sustainably degraded for the benefit of all people. But as I now turn to argue, the problem with this solution to social injustice is that it will not work; and if it were to work, it could hardly be called justice.

Social relations between people do not transpire in a vacuum, despite the cult of humanity's long-cultivated fancy that the natural world is a stage for the grand show of human affairs. It is within the context of the dominant relationship between humanity and Earth that social relations have become constituted as material, normative, and historical realities.

As long as the living world is construed as a suite of resources to be seized or converted, human relations will tend to manifest the corollaries of this materialized belief: There will be competition, exploitation, corruption, struggle for access and control, posturing, and conflict over all manner of resources. Systematic distortions of human relations are inextricably coupled with the resourcist mindset—they are supported and inflamed by the relentlessly enacted regard of the natural world as a domain-to-be-used for human profit or advancement. The source of the disparity between the haves and the have-nots thus lies in the conception-*cum*-treatment of Earth's living beings and nonliving things as *resources*—a corrupt concept which continues to masquerade as merely a descriptive word.

While its pervasiveness normalizes it, it is worth investigating what kind of relationship to the biosphere this word signals. "Resources" is an abstraction for referring to a multitude of things in the living and nonliving world, while referring, as such, to nothing in particular: Simply put, it is a placeholder for designating the natural world in terms of its disposability for human needs, wants, desires, and whims. Thus, while seemingly an objective referent to things (oil, fish, soil, freshwater, and so on), the concept of resources reconfigures the natural world in terms of how it is usable, thereby entirely bypassing, and via its ceaseless use erasing, nature's intrinsic standing—both as being and as value. Indeed, "natural resources" blocks human thought from *seeing* the natural world in its intrinsic light. "Resources" is thus a linguistic accompaniment of the assault on and excessive exploitation of the natural world. The transfiguration of the natural world into resources has come to shape human thought and action at such an encompassing level that people largely perceive the natural world through this single framework: of how it is usable and/or profitable.

In a world thus diminished, enslaved, or otherwise turned into means for human ends, social justice is pragmatically all but unachievable, because people (as well as entities such as corporations and states which are run, and embraced, by people) will inexorably be incited to do what it takes to possess the useful or money-spinning means: land, freshwater, territory, fisheries, fur, genes, oil, coal, natural gas, uranium, timber, wildlife (dead or alive), livestock, metals, and minerals. As long as these means remain the perceived conduit toward wealth, privilege, and the good life, the goal of social justice is likely to remain elusive.

But assume for the sake of argument that social justice is achievable on a planet of resources—a planet used, managed, and engineered to be productive for human beings. Let's posit, along these lines, that humanity recognizes the folly of the unequal distribution of resources and decides to share the so-called commonwealth (the modern equivalent of the oecumene) fairly among all people. This thought experiment discloses the second reason that social justice is untenable without a radically new relationship between humanity and the more-than-human-world. Consider the following analogy: that Adolf Hitler had won the war and the Third Reich achieved global rule. People of Nordic descent established their dominion, while "inferior human stock" was exterminated, assimilated, or put to work; the Aryan race succeeded in founding its Golden Age, with its members enjoying, more or less equitably, all the amenities of the good life. Now map this thought experiment onto the achievement of a just world for all *humans* (regardless of race, ethnicity, class, caste, religion, gender, etc.), within a civilization built upon the subordination of the Earth's nonhumans and the appropriation of *their* oecumene (a.k.a. the wild)—a human world that, in order "to raise all ships," required the unavoidable side effects of (mass?) extinction, global ecological depredation, and techno-managerial planetary oversight; required, in a word, an occupied planet. Does this scenario not describe a victorious Human Reich—with all its members partaking equitably of the world's resources? Regarding such an advent of social justice, one might justifiably ask: What could the idea of justice possibly even mean at that point?

Social justice is not achievable as long as the natural world continues to be stripped of its intrinsic standing and reconfigured as a collection of resources. By virtue of the sorts of entities they are, resources not only encourage but also largely create the acquisitive mindset that undergirds human conflict, corruption, and injustice.[28] On the other hand, should people achieve greater material equity—while sustaining the anthropocentric representation of nature as made-for-humans—then social justice will come to pass at the price of planetary colonization, thereby evacuating the *very concept* of justice of any meaningful sense.

Earth is the origin and irreplaceable field of all human experience, the all-encompassing context of social life. Humanity's rupture from the Earth community along with humanity's takeover of the planet as an instrumental totality of objects-and-services-for-human-use have pathologized the human psyche in a way that will likely continue to prevent the healing of intra-human conflict. The ground for social justice and world peace is *literally* missing without Earth respected and restored as a living world and the rejection of the received hierarchy between humans and the rest of nature. Let us be clear about the magnitude of what is called for: the relinquishment of our fabricated, special and privileged identity.

It is a matter of becoming receptive to an idea whose time has come: that the Earth is not made for people, any more than it was made for the universe to frame itself around and for planetary bodies to circumambulate.

Saving the phenomena or revolutionary transformation?

The development of Ptolemaic astronomy originated around the time that the idea of oecumene had become pervasive; it offered a powerful model of the workings of the heavens that ruled people's understanding of the universe, and of Earth's place within it, for fourteen hundred years. A geocentric image was the unquestionable core of Ptolemaic astronomy—supported by the apparent nature of the phenomena, namely, the seeming motion of planets, Moon, and Sun and the seeming stillness of the Earth. But since the Ptolemaic picture corresponded poorly with actual astronomical reality (as opposed to a perceived and promulgated geocentric reality) problems with the model's predictions emerged and accumulated. These problems had to be solved—and so they were, but not by abandoning the geocentric picture and inquiring into alternatives. Instead, corrective mechanisms were affixed to the Ptolemaic model, such as "epicycles" which posited additional circular movements to a planet's standard Earth orbit (thus explaining that planet's "retrograde movement"). A number of corrective mechanisms (epicycles being but one) were able to explain—for a while—discrepancies between the dearly-held-onto geocentric model and actual observations.[29] As a consequence, over time, Ptolemaic astronomy became complicated and cumbersome, a proverbial Byzantine edifice, continuously reconstructed to sustain the Earth-centered gestalt and save the phenomena. But after a millennium and a half of laboring to make it hold, the central location of the Planet of the Humans had to be abandoned.

Neo-green environmentalism is holding onto its own version of Ptolemaic astronomy, namely, the core belief in the rightfulness or inevitability of a human-governed planet. Even as faith in human rule has soured, with oceans, forests, rivers, grasslands, species, and climate sacrificed to its bogus altar, the neo-green perspective seeks to add epicycle after epicycle to the model of human governance to keep it in place: nuclear power, biofuels, carbon capture and storage, and so forth to help stabilize levels of greenhouse gases; genetic engineering of crops and animals to solve the food crisis, the nitrogen and phosphorus overload, freshwater shortfalls, or what-have-you; geoengineering to cope with possible climate disruption, and eventually repurposed to adjust Earth's thermostat to favorable settings; desalinization projects and massive wind, hydropower, and photovoltaic industrial operations to continue funneling water and sustainable energy to many billions of people; placing monetary values on biodiversity and ecosystem services, so the market might safeguard some remaining natural areas; "de-extinction" projects and synthetic biology for the supposed instatement of human-made biological diversity sometime in the future; and efficient management and recycling to keep the flow of raw materials feeding a globalized industrialism. In other words, whatever it takes, so that the planetary authority of the human need not be confronted. The neo-green perspective would have us (enthusiastically or reluctantly) embrace a world that is massively complicated, mega-technological, engineered, risk-tending, used, biologically impoverished, overpopulated, and filled with (equitably shared) consumer stuff. The sole virtue of such a world is that it saves the historically bequeathed phenomenon of human rule.

There exists another path into the future, one which is more elegant, more beautiful, more ethical, and more becoming of the human spirit: on this path, wild nature—terrestrial and marine—is reinstated as the unbroken, rich-in-life tapestry within which human communities thrive in integration with their inhabited bioregions. Humanity must move *out of the center* and let the Earth and its whole community of life flourish there. Moving out of the center means scaling back humanity's presence enormously: humanely reducing global population to a far lower level than it presently is; ending overproduction and the excesses of global trade; ending industrial food production, along with its ecological, ethical, environmental, and public health horrors; and ceasing to stifle the freedom and creative powers of nature by playing Lord Man. Perhaps most fundamentally, moving out of the center means disowning the human supremacy complex—its blindness to the stupendous intrinsic power of the natural world and to the madness of its own heart.

With Friends Like These, Wilderness and Biodiversity Do Not Need Enemies

DAVID JOHNS

THE HUMAN FOOTPRINT is growing at the expense of other species and the integrity of ecosystems.[1] What poet-of-the-wild Gary Snyder called the "Growth-Monster"[2] remains not just unchecked but embraced, in theory and practice, by virtually all human societies.[3] There is nothing new in this situation—it has been accelerating for several millennia and especially for the last few hundred years; nor is there anything new in the arguments made by those who justify it.[4] Although the expression of self-righteous greed is rarer and sounds extreme amidst the claims of business and political leaders that biodiversity is important, human behavior—judged by its consequences—has not changed much: We take more and more, and we continue to squander a heritage that we can never replace. Each loss of species brought about by humans diminishes not only the Earth community but all who remain.

Those orchestrating and profiting from the ever-growing transformation of the natural world into commodities have always had apologists. In the mid-1990s conservationists responded to a wave of ideological attacks directed at wilderness and biodiversity.[5] In the last few years concerted attacks have again emerged, and, although they are shopworn, riddled with factual errors, and marbled with hierarchical values, they also appear well-funded, receive lots of media attention, and are advanced with great energy, as if careers depended on them.

In this essay I address five criticisms of wilderness and biodiversity conservation: that wilderness and biodiversity protection goals must be curtailed and tied to human interests in order to be achievable; that humans have always been everywhere and there is no real wilderness left; that our effects on other species, and our efforts to dominate or turn the world into a garden, are natural and therefore acceptable (if not good); that protected semi-wild and wild areas separate humans from the world; and that human wants should take precedence over the survival of all other species and entire ecological communities.

As a practical matter, factual assertions in arguments are entwined with the values, purposes, and meanings their proponents wish to further, but the distinction is important in analyzing arguments. Factual assertions about how the world works are generally subject to testing against reality. Individuals, groups, and even whole cultures may make factual assertions based not on testing for cause and effect but on compatibility with the purposes and meanings they hold. The distinction between knowledge and mere belief is important, and it led Senator Daniel Patrick Moynihan to say that people are entitled to their own opinion but not their own facts.[6] Critics of conservation often have their facts wrong. But even values, meanings, and purposes—plainly human creations—may be subject to a kind of testing over the longer term: Cultural orientations are more or less adaptive, serving the actual and long-term needs of groups or undermining them. Roy A. Rappaport observed that economic and political institutions which undercut "biological well-being . . . may be considered maladaptive."[7] From this perspective, many of the values and purposes advocated by critics of conservation are problematic. Let us turn now to the five criticisms:

*1) **Wilderness and biodiversity protection goals must be curtailed and clearly tied to human interests in order to be achievable.*** Justly unhappy that the world's governments are not meeting the biodiversity protection goals for 2010 established by the Convention on Biological Diversity, a group of pre-eminent scientists write that it is "critical" that goals for protecting biodiversity "be grounded in the real interests that people have in benefits provided by biodiversity."[8] In response to criticism that their view, if adopted, would leave much biodiversity vulnerable because many species or ecosystem functions might not clearly serve human interests, they state that because arguments on behalf of biodiversity's intrinsic value have failed to sway policy makers a new argument is needed based on human self-interest.[9] Peter Kareiva and Michelle Marvier make similar points.[10]

Scientists are not street fighters, although at least one editorial in *Nature* encouraged them to learn the trade.[11] Nonetheless, it is disappointing that some scientists seem prepared to backtrack on goals identified by scientific findings simply because such findings and the values that make such findings relevant fail to persuade. Scientific research is critical—it describes how the world works. This knowledge is essential to maintaining and recovering healthy species' populations and ecological integrity. But another kind of "argument" is needed to persuade societal decision makers—the type of argument that hinges on the capacity of groups seeking a policy to reward and punish decision makers more effectively than opponents. Carrots and sticks include campaign contributions or the equivalent;[12] bringing media resources to bear to define issues and acceptable solutions;[13] economic leverage—such as that possessed by banks "too big to fail" or by mass popular unrest;[14] control of information;[15] and personal relationships often based on long-shared interests.[16] These "arguments" help or hinder decision makers in gaining or keeping the power they desire, and therein resides their persuasiveness.

The intrinsic value argument has not failed conservation; it is conservationists' failure to organize enough people willing to act on behalf of biodiversity that has limited realization of conservation goals . The material consequences of biodiversity loss for various human groups inspire organizing groups to act, but so do moral arguments,[17] emotionally compelling stories,[18] the creation of a strong community around biodiversity,[19] and other factors, including transcending narrow notions of self-interest.[20]

Justifying biodiversity protection based on narrowly conceived human well-being (essentially cost-benefit analysis) ignores the fact that benefits are often difficult to quantify and that invoking future generations is not the same as applying political pressure in the here and now: The future does not organize and bring political pressure.

There is no escape for conservation from the need to organize a strong political force.

2) Humans have always been everywhere, have fundamentally changed virtually every place on Earth, and so there are no pristine lands (wilderness) to protect. There is no question that the collective human impact on other species and ecosystems is significant and has been accelerating rapidly since the availability of huge quantities of energy that magnify our actions.[21] We have been causing extinctions since we left Africa sixty thousand years ago,[22] although once the initial and significant large-animal extinctions accompanying human arrival had occurred, the impacts were much more limited.[23] Low population, low population density, stone technology, and a largely egalitarian social order that kept aggrandizing schemes of conquest, accumulation, and other sorts of domination[24] in check probably contributed to this. With the transition to agriculture, humans began a more systematic conversion of ecosystems to human use, reducing species' populations and range, causing extinctions, and generally simplifying ecological interactions. The fossil-fueled industrial revolution further ratcheted up the reach, intensity, and pace of human colonization and exploitation of ecosystems and other species.[25] If large mammals have been particularly hard hit because of either their range needs or perceived threat to humans, then forests have been the hardest hit ecosystems over the longer term.[26] But the world oceans' biota have also been seriously depleted from overfishing and other destructive fishing practices, and many areas have been damaged by the marine equivalent of clear-cutting (i.e., bottom trawling).[27] A review article about whether the human impact on the Earth merits the designation of a new age—the Anthropocene—notes that humans have significantly altered just over half of the ice-free land mass.[28] About 25 percent remain wildlands, another 20 percent or so are "semi-natural," and the rest consist of crops, grazing range, or heavily settled areas. And even wildlands and the oceans are affected by global forces such as climate change, airborne pollution, human noise, and the like.

More than significant, the human impact is negative: Humans have diminished biological diversity and disrupted, degraded, and in many cases simply destroyed ecological function. Yet those who claim wild lands and waters no longer exist are mistaken on two major points: that human influence so dominates every part of the Earth that nothing is wild ("self-willed"); and that this state of affairs is long-standing and universally pervasive and restoration to wildness is not possible .

Critics of the existence of wildlands usually posit a red herring: that *wilderness* by definition means "pristine" or "completely without human imprint." The U.S. Wilderness Act of 1964 (PL 88-577 §2(c))—the product of more than a decade of work by conservationists—does not use the term *pristine* but instead deliberately uses the term *untrammeled*,[29] a term very close to the original meaning of wildlands as undomesticated or self-willed land but not necessarily pristine.[30] Many conservation groups around the globe do focus on protecting largely intact lands and waters—often high in biodiversity—from further damage, including loss of native species, but they are not concerned with purity,[31] any more than civil libertarians cease defending the U.S. Bill of Rights just because they are routinely ignored by governments. Such places are wild and biologically critical. They offer the clear opportunity for halting further degradation, for healing, and for expansion and connection to other areas as part of a conservation strategy to hold the line against continued population growth and growing consumption—growth that has already overshot Earth's carrying capacity.[32] These areas, moreover, are not the exclusive focus of conservation.[33] But claims that humans are not simply destroying habitat but creating new habitat[34] are disingenuous and obfuscating—they ignore the comparative biological poverty of tree farms compared to intact forests and monoculture croplands compared to wild grasslands.

Largely intact places won't solve every conservation problem, but they are essential to preserving wildness, biodiversity, and ecological communities.[35] For intact areas to remain intact and evolve they need to be big and in the right location; to have good boundaries, buffers, and appropriate connections; and to have effective enforcement of their protected status.[36] Two *Nature* editorials call for addressing outside effects on wildlands and protected areas,[37] as have earlier scientific and strategic assessments.[38] Conservation is not served by counseling surrender to further encroachment.

The notion that wilderness no longer exists and that substantial biodiversity losses must be accepted as inevitable is often accompanied by claims that people have always been everywhere and therefore nothing can be done, because it might involve inconveniencing human colonizers, and that would be morally suspect. It is also often linked to the idea that significant human presence and impact means that humans are in charge—"already running the whole Earth."[39] Such literary imagination is coupled with massive denial about the overwhelming "evidence of" biological damage resulting from human presence.

This view of perennial and ubiquitous human presence fails to discern the difference between a few million humans and 7 billion, between dense and sparse settlement, and between differing levels of energy use, resource extraction, and technology; it also ignores humanity's short career as compared to the length of time other species have been present in places. Up until fairly recently, many areas on Earth either remained relatively free of human presence or were occupied only seasonally or transiently; and many areas were used only in a limited way (for example, for sacred purposes).[40] Claims, for example, that the Amazon is a human-constructed garden are dubious; settlement there has been sparse,[41] as it has been for many other regions, such as the boreal forests.

Although the cycle of intensification (population growth leads to more "resource" extraction to support more people leads to more population growth leads to more intense extraction) has its roots in the Neolithic,[42] in the last few hundred years—with greater populations and densities; more intrusive technologies; more energy at human command; self-aggrandizing elites making ever greater demands; the increasingly vast reach of population centers into distant areas; and the growing density of trade networks—that effect on wildlands and biodiversity has been globally devastating.[43] Globalization is not new, but its reach and intensity are.[44] To argue that this extreme and relatively recent state of affairs must be accepted despite its biological destructiveness is like arguing that colonial domination and exploitation must be accepted despite their obliteration of other peoples and cultures.

The view that we will never "return a substantial part of the Earth to a preindustrial state"[45] is an example of either Occidental (Enlightenment) fatalism or an effort to rationalize the current grim biological trend in the interests of those who benefit disproportionately from degrading the natural world. The inertia behind the current human trajectory is tremendous. But apartheid was overthrown, slavery in most of the world has been abolished, and women in much of the world enjoy improved conditions: Major change *is* possible. In some parts of the world the restoration of species and ecosystems has increased the store of wildness.

Species can be repatriated. Biologically degrading influences such as industrial incursions, roads, pollution, and exotic species can be halted. Injuries can be healed. Processes that have been suppressed or disrupted (such as fire, migrations, and succession) can be reestablished, enhancing ecosystem resilience. Humans can try to cast their interventions to mimic natural healing, while recognizing the limits of knowledge and wisdom, and work toward minimizing future need for intervention or intensive management, allowing for eventual self-regulation. Self-regulation requires very large areas and their linkage to other areas that are mainly intact.

Such restorative intervention contrasts with the violence done to spe-

cies and ecosystems by large-scale industrial or agricultural resource extraction—extraction based on the exercise of power and the object of control. Large-scale resource extraction refuses to acknowledge either that
other species are ends-in-themselves and are not merely means for human
purposes or that human well-being is antithetical to power and control
over others. Humans have a place and it is not as lords of creation.

For all of the ink (soy-based included) spilled over the idea of wilderness, the problem is plain: Humans are inadequate to the task of managing
Nature; humans lack the knowledge, intelligence, and wisdom. Although
management has achieved goods such as repatriating wolves, removing
roads, or restoring fire, to rely on it to ensure the future of biodiversity
would be akin to resting our fate on the failed Biosphere Project. John
Holdren, senior scientific advisor to President Obama, noted that he's "a
great believer in science and technology, but the notion that science and
technology will ride to the rescue is a pernicious one. Believing in technological miracles is usually a mistake."[46] A vibrant Earth requires large,
intact, and connected places (including restored places), off limits to exploitation by industrial and agricultural peoples whose inability to control
their numbers and wants has been more than amply demonstrated in the
last twelve thousand years.

**3) Humans are part of Nature and so our effects on other species, our ef-
forts to dominate, and our attempts to turn the world into a garden are
all natural.** How can human behavior be anything but part of Nature?
We are the products of evolution; we breathe air, eat, and are otherwise
dependent upon the Earth. Unless one invokes the supernatural then, by
definition, everything we do is natural, and that doesn't get us very far. But
if we reflect on the use of *natural* and *unnatural* we see that they designate
something as good or not good (a cultural judgment) and also seek to
transform the designation into a property of the world rather than a human creation. Much human behavior is not genetically determined and
is instead regulated mostly by culture (shared emotions, attitudes, and
worldviews shaped by experience and transmitted from one generation or
group to another). Where does this leave us? We must address the consequences for the living world of culturally shaped behavior.

For conservationists, behavior that converts, diminishes, or destroys
the Earth's biodiversity and ecological systems is morally wrong—we have
no right to cause extinctions or take so much for one species any more

than we have a right to enslave others (once considered natural). As a practical matter it is stupid ("maladaptive," according to Rappaport) to destroy systems we depend on and which we may not be able to fix once broken. As Leopold suggested, it's unintelligent to throw parts away when tinkering with something important.[47]

Acknowledging humans as part of Nature does not and cannot justify our ever-growing footprint. The human domination of other species and ecosystems is basically the same as the colonial domination of some people by others, visiting brutally stupid exploitation, displacement, and death on its victims. We might better ask whether the societal machinery that converts so much of the world into commodities for one species—and disproportionately benefiting a few million at the very top of our species' social hierarchies—is adaptive, healthy, or just. For James Lovelock the answer is clear: "[A]ll attempts to rationalize a subjugated biosphere with man in charge are as doomed to failure as the similar concept of benevolent colonialism. They all assume that man is possessor of this planet, if not the owner, then the tenant."

Lovelock is certainly not alone.[48] Brand's appropriation from another of the notion that we are "as gods" and should get good at it,[49] and Marris's view that we can be competent gardeners,[50] are just more examples of the same hubris that generates extinction, ocean dead zones, dust bowls, desertification and depleted soils, superfund sites, climate change, and nuclear power plants built in tsunami zones. We are about as godlike as a bull in a china shop.[51]

The conceit that humans are godlike rests on assumptions that gained dominance among European elites in the Enlightenment and have since spread to most elites and many others. These assumptions include notions that all problems are solvable by human reason, technology, or changes in social organization; that faced with great difficulties humans will rise to the occasion; and that resources are infinite or there will always be substitutes.[52] David Ehrenfeld, John Peet, Rob Deitz and Dan O'Neill, and Global Footprint Network have documented the mounting evidence undermining these assumptions.[53] Our capacity to problem-solve is limited by the world's complexity. Our pretensions to divinity are belied by our limited ability to grasp how the world works well enough to manage it, even if we actually had the requisite wisdom, judgment, and political will. As a result our "solutions" are inadequate and generate new and more complex problems that take more resources to address, in part because there is more inertia to be overcome.[54]

Bad "choices" are the result of structural constraints, not just limited wisdom and intelligence. The few thousands of decision makers at the head of government and business institutions are heavily invested in the current order and generally resist changes that could undermine their positions of power. Their awareness is also constrained by the insulation that technology and hierarchy provides from the consequences of their actions.[55] When united, decision-makers effectively constrain societal choices by controlling problem identification, formulation, and the range of acceptable solutions.[56] Even when divided they share much in common, such as preserving the system they benefit from. These decision-makers also influence or control the machinery of repression: laws, police, armies, prisons.[57]

Societal structure constrains choices in other ways. Dorothy Dinnerstein argued that it is not just our psychopathology that leaves us unable to confront what we are doing to Earth and ourselves; the societal process is now too mindlessly complex, unwieldy and overcentralized that even if we saw how bad things are it is questionable we could do much with the existing decision making apparatus. It is part of the problem; only relatively small groups can express healthy emotion and reason.[58] Harold Searles and Paul Shepard argue that a sense of self and a healthy identity depend on close contact with nonhumans and the broader ecology during development.[59] Only with such contact can we connect with and be grounded in reality, recognizing, among other things, that we are kin with the rest of the world. Absent such connection, people are left with the experience of human hierarchy as the only model of order.

4) Humans are part of Nature, and reserves of various sorts separate us from the natural world. It is not the advocates of placing some lands and waterways off limits to human exploitation who have separated humans from the rest of the world. Agriculture and civilization did that.[60] Agricultural and industrial societies depend on the systematic effort to control and reshape ecosystems for the benefit of humans at the expense of other species. They enhance human carrying capacity by subjugating other species—"the others," just as imperial Britain reshaped the Indian economy to serve British rather than Indian interests.[61]

Colonization and concomitant exploitation divides humans from the rest of the world just as surely as it divides peoples and nations despite the effort to mask it under Orwellian terms such as "interdependence." Colonization markedly ratchets up the intensification of extraction from and conversion of the natural world, generating ever-larger and more hierarchical human societies. Devaluing and distancing from what is conquered is a psychological necessity.[62] The ability to love and the drive to control are opposites.

Modern conservationists are not the first to lament the changes from forager to conqueror. The first-century-B.C.E. Roman poet Ovid (Publius Ovidius Naso) wrote that once the Earth gave "crops from fields unfurrowed / And fruits, and honey from a hollow tree, / And no one scored the soil with sturdy ploughshares."[63] Human cleverness changed all that, bringing tragedy. A few hundred years earlier Lao Tsu asked: "Do you think you can take over the universe and improve it? / I do not believe it can be done. / The universe is sacred. / You cannot improve it. / If you try to change it, you will ruin it."[64]

The idea of wilderness (self-willed land) emerged from the dualism that characterizes agricultural societies and their successors in order to describe those places not yet conquered.[65] Humans—not bears or birds or rivers—initiated the divorce. In seeking to conquer the natural world, humans set themselves at odds with the Earth—just as the slave master with the slave and the colonizer with the colonized.[66] Other creatures' homes and necessities merely constitute space or food the colonizer covets. To merely stop thinking—as the wilderness debunkers ask us to do—in terms of the wilderness/civilization dichotomy cannot, itself, resolve the actual material separation resulting from the quest to dominate.

Calls to make wilderness and comprehensive biodiversity protection subservient to growth—as if inequality could be solved by increased growth in the future any more than it has been solved by past growth—depends on the language of conquest and colonization using different words. It rationalizes the death warrants of large, intact areas and of the species dependent on them such as large predators and wide-ranging species. Marginalizing wilderness and biodiversity protection negates the best insurance we have against human foolishness. Gardening can neither replace wilderness nor heal the self-inflicted wound of estrangement from the natural world. Trying to make ourselves feel good about our overreach is like taking nineteenth-century medicine for a life-threatening disease. To abandon wilderness and large-scale restoration in the name of transcending dualism is to leave the Earth vulnerable to further impoverishment.

Those groups (the Hopi, the Hadza, the Bushmen, the Gwich'n—for example) who seem to remain most connected with the Earth have small footprints and share some obvious attributes: They are few in numbers, they lack dense settlements, and they do not rely on industrial technologies and vast inputs of materials and energy.[67] Most have been pushed to the margins of habitable land by more powerful societies and states. Can 7 billion people adopt these attributes? Foraging peoples left their way of life and adopted agriculture not because it offered a better way of life—it meant a poorer diet, more disease, and decreased stature—but because of population pressure.[68]

What, then, is the path toward healing our separateness if there is no return to the pre-Neolithic? This essay is not the place to set out a detailed vision or strategy to contain the machinery of control that separates humans from the world that gave birth to them. But if wilderness is destroyed, healing will become impossible. We cannot expect the path to reconnection to be led by those heavily invested in the status quo, as some have suggested.[69] The path forward is not about sacrifice. It is about recovering what we have long ago sacrificed—our wholeness and our connection to other life and our deepest selves. We traded these away for hierarchy and distractions in a deal we did not understand.

5) Human wants must take priority over the needs of other species, even to the point of extinction. The belief that human wants should have priority over the survival needs of species and the integrity of ecological processes is variously expressed, but the end is always the same: Humans have the right to alter the world for their benefit at the expense of other species regardless of the consequences—suffering, death, extinction, or the destruction of entire ecological communities. The Great Chain of Being has fallen before the Rights of Man, but it remains alive and thriving in human relations with other species.

That the Earth belongs to us rests on notions that we uniquely possess some attributes which other species lack. Why these attributes are a suitable basis for elevating us to godhood is never explained because it would reveal the contest to be rigged. It is difficult to know whether the claim of specialness is based on a genuine if misplaced sense of achievement, or if it arises from a deeply compensatory impulse: Like Gilgamesh, we are frightened by our mortality, we feel insignificant in a very large universe, or—having divorced ourselves from our wild home—we feel lost and so create grand narratives in which we can be the hero.

Unlike the notion that lightning manifests the anger of Zeus, the delusion that Earth belongs to us is not harmless. It is more akin to the inaccurate claims made by some supporting the belief that tiger bone and rhino horn have medicinal properties. Such claims, even if they were true, rationalize violence, disrupt ecological relationships, and increase the risk of extinction of irreplaceable creatures.

Claims by powerful states in the last century that they had the right to control other states or nations have lost legitimacy even though exploitation continues in different forms and carrying capacity continues to be transferred from poor to rich.[70] Today we see plainly that past exploitation was based on power, not on the merit of the colonizer. Colonialism is always violent. We can also see how the human need to feel good about ourselves leads us to create fantastical justifications for the theft and murder of conquest. In 1870 the Big Horn Association of Cheyenne, Wyoming, published the following:

The rich and beautiful valleys of Wyoming are destined for the occupancy and sustenance of the Anglo-Saxon race. The wealth that for untold ages has lain hidden beneath the snow-capped summits of our mountains has been placed there by Providence to reward the brave spirits whose lot it is to compose the advance-guard of civilization. The Indians must stand aside or be overwhelmed by the ever advancing and ever increasing tide of emigration . . . The same inscrutable Arbiter that decreed the downfall of Rome has pronounced the doom of extinction on the red men of America.[71]

Colonialism is nowhere more apparent and thriving than in the relationship between humanity and the rest of the Earth.[72] As a whole, humans take what they want with limited restraint and dress it up like the Big Horn Association.[73] That there is any restraint at all is the result of conservation success: protected areas that are *actually* protected and laws that are mostly enforced—such as the Convention on International Trade in Endangered Species (CITES) or the U.S. Endangered Species Act (U.S. ESA). This restraint is the exception and it must be constantly defended.

Rationalizing Nature's colonization does not hide the ugly realities. Remaking the Earth in the human image is violent: Forests and grasslands are transformed into tree farms, pasture, subdivisions, and endless corn and soybean fields or rice paddies. Inconvenient species are persecuted. Ecosystems are altered for the benefit of one species, and the community as a whole is discounted. Colonization diminishes the capacity of lands and waters to support diversity, replacing many species with a few or even a diverse ecosystem with a monoculture. Colonization means human numbers grow and consumption increases at the expense of other species' numbers, range, diversity, and even existence. Self-regulation of the community by all its adult members is replaced with control by a part of the community for its own exclusive benefit; and spontaneity, liveliness, and biological integrity are diminished. The tiger is caged or dead, and the oxen bred to plod endlessly before the plow. We do it because we can.

The human colonization of Nature and consequent destruction are unnecessary. We have long had the means to control our numbers—though some have always had fears about who will fill the armies and workshops and support the old. Much collective human consumption is unnecessary as well—a vain effort to control our anxiety over mortality.[74] The world's poor do not simply aspire to have full bellies; they want what the middle classes have.

There was a time when humanity was grounded enough to see ourselves as part of the cycle of things. We were troubled by killing.[75] We could see ourselves in the other and sought reassurance in ritual that acknowledged the "sacrifice" of the other. That insight and the imperfect restraint it brought is gone. The factory farms are invisible, and death is not real.

No other animal is as behaviorally flexible as we are. We have choices. Other species do not. It may be that most humans will never be biocentric. But if we do not behave *as if* we *are*, if we continue on the current path, we will impoverish the Earth and at last become the "stewards" of a graveyard. We cannot degrade Nature without doing the same to ourselves. To call "ethical" rules which rationalize human lordship is to make the notion of ethics meaningless.

IN THE END, what matters is not endless blather over gardening, pristine wilderness, how long people have occupied a place, or how much damage they have done. What matters is this: Humans are behaving like an asteroid hitting the Earth in slow motion. We are destroying what we could never create. The Earth did recover (after 10 million years) from the Cretaceous extinction 65 million years ago; it was not the end of the Earth, but it was the end of many creatures. Is being an asteroid the great purpose of our species—to steal the lives and homes of millions of species and billions of creatures?

Almost two centuries ago an astute observer of human behavior said that a person is wealthy in proportion to what they can leave alone.[76] By that measure, societies which enshrine striving for wealth, power, and fame are desperately poor and needy. Our stomachs are full, but we are hollow in our souls. In separating ourselves from the world by trying to control it we have created a hunger that things can never fill, though we keep trying. We have wounded our souls and our capacity for empathy and love. "This is what is the matter with us," D. H. Lawrence wrote, "we are bleeding at the roots, because we are cut off from the earth and sun and stars, and love is a grinning mockery, because, poor blossom, we plucked it from its stem on the tree of life, and expected it to keep on blooming in our civilized vase on the table."[77] This is the great sacrifice we have made, and it need not be.

What's So New about the "New Conservation"?

CURT MEINE

WE ARE BEING OFFERED a new story about human beings and the rest of nature. It goes something like this . . .

Once there was an environmental movement. It was a good movement—or at least it had good intentions—but it had some wrong ideas. All it really cared about was protecting and preserving the remote, unpeopled wilderness. It didn't care much about (or for) people. It ignored the places where people lived, worked, grew food, raised families, made things, and did things. What's worse, the "wilderness" to which it was so devoted did not really even exist in the first place, except as something that elite European people invented after they left Europe, colonized the far reaches of the planet, and displaced and subjugated its native peoples through waves of disease, conquest, and economic exploitation.

Some of the colonizers' descendants—the ones who felt remorse instead of pride—imagined the now-mythical "wilderness" to be pristine, unpeopled, static, timeless, fragile, and fraught with religious meaning. Ultimately they became conservationists *and, later,* environmentalists. *But their romantic fixation on the false ideal of wilderness led the well-meaning movement to create an impregnable divide between humans and nature, to disdain people, to care nothing for the poor and dispossessed, and to exude undue pessimism over human prospects and the fate of the planet. And, perhaps worst of all, this obsession led the otherwise worthy movement astray. Environmentalism did not work. The movement grew larger,· wealthier, and more influential, but it failed. It was unable to achieve its aims, many of which were actually quite sensible and laudable.*

Fortunately, and just in the nick of time, some rebellious "new conservationists" came forward to fix the wayward movement. They understood the fatal flaws in the old environmentalists' vision. They coolly explained: There is no wilderness, and there never really was; the natural world, in fact, changes; nature, far from being fragile, is actually quite tough and resilient; and with all this in mind, we can and should now turn our environmental concerns to the places where they are most needed, the "working" landscapes and cities in our thoroughly human-shaped and human-dominated world. In so doing, we can change the movement into what it ought to have been in the first place: humane, just, optimistic, and forward-looking. We can do what we human beings do best, and what in any case we must do: create a new world and manage it in a way that, while still respecting many of the wild things in our midst, does so in service of the human good, and the ever-growing human economy that promotes that good. It is the only way forward.

It's a compelling story, and an alluring one. Nobody wants to be considered old-fashioned, naive, ineffective, uninformed, and unjust. And absolutely no one wants to be thought uncool or stodgy. The story does what a good story must: It explains a lot. It has an awesome plot and fascinating characters. And since we humans are the main characters, it flatters us. Finally, it has this going for it: Portions of it are true.

Of course, this is not the only version of the story, and I'm not certain that I have done it justice. It is always risky to tell someone else's story. However, assuming that I have been accurate with at least the main story lines, they are worth examining more closely.

The "old" conservation/environmental movement had an idealized and illusory view of wilderness as pristine, and its adherents believed therefore that such wilderness can and should be walled off, separated from, and unaffected by human beings and human impacts. Nothing new here. Correctives to the "classic" view of wilderness date back, just in the relatively recent literature, more than twenty years.[1] But let's go back further, beyond the horizon of environmentalism and into the older world of conservation. We might pause in our time-travel to attend the landmark 1955 international symposium, *Man's Role in Changing the Face of the Earth*. The symposium brought together 75 leading conservation scientists, thinkers, and advocates in Princeton, New Jersey, to consider the fact of "man, the ecological dominant on the planet," and "to understand what has happened and is happening to the earth under man's impress." William L. Thomas, the editor of the conference proceedings, wrote: "The dichotomy of man and nature is . . . an intellectual device and as such should not be confused with reality; no longer can man's physical-biological environment be treated, except in theory, as 'natural.'"[2] Lewis Mumford, the guiding intellectual force of the symposium, suggested that "as the dominant biological species, man now has a special responsibility to his fellow-creatures as well as to himself."[3]

We might stop in 1933, to consider Aldo Leopold's textbook *Game Management*. Perhaps the readers of his day found it shocking to read: "Every head of wild life still alive in this country is already artificialized, in that its existence is conditioned by economic forces. Game management merely proposes that their impact shall not remain wholly fortuitous. The hope of the future lies not in curbing the influence of human occupancy— *it is already too late for that*—but in creating a better understanding of *the extent of that influence* and *a new ethic* for its governance" [emphases added].[4] Leopold saw the reality of human environmental impacts and ecological connections more clearly than most, and as deeply as the ecological science and environmental history of the day allowed. That did not deter him from his lifelong efforts to protect, sustain, and restore wildness, at any and all scales, in any and all places.

We might pause again to visit with the Progressive Era conservationists of the early twentieth century. The movement included utilitarians devoted to "wise use" of natural resources and preservationists devoted to protecting special and scenic wild places (largely *for* human recreational use). We are captivated by the dramatic narrative of the tension between these two conservation camps (and many apparently assume that little has changed since). However, we risk overlooking their shared disdain for reckless economic exploitation of the land. We forget that the early movement included many who were sympathetic to and active in both causes and intent on keeping them connected. We fail to diagnose what *both* approaches to progressive conservation missed.

We might return all the way to George Perkins Marsh's classic 1864 volume *Man and Nature*, the book that Mumford described as "the fountainhead of the conservation movement." In the opening sentence of his weighty tome, Marsh described his first aim: "to indicate the character and, approximately, the extent of the changes produced by human action in the physical conditions of the globe we inhabit." Marsh regarded as "doctrine . . . that man is, in both kind and degree, a power of a higher order than any of the other forms of animated life, which, like him, are nourished at the table of bounteous nature."[5] Instead of congratulating ourselves on our own discovery of human agency, we might give Marsh a deep and careful reading, to see just what he got right and wrong in his telling of the story, and to gain greater insight into what we have learned since.

In brief, it has long been understood by leading conservation thinkers that the natural world has been thoroughly affected by the actions of people, and that wild places cannot simply be preserved behind the walls of "fortress conservation." That understanding has not been an impediment to action on behalf of the wild, wherever and to whatever extent it exists.

The "old" movement aimed to protect this idealized wilderness, while ignoring and making no allowance for human action to promote more sustainable rural landscapes and cities. This statement would come as a surprise to those early progressive conservationists, led by game protectors responding to the bane of market hunting, foresters responding to the devastation of the forestlands of the upper Great Lakes, and agrarians responding to the destruction and degradation of soil. It would surprise the all-too-forgotten Liberty Hyde Bailey and Hugh Hammond Bennett (among many others of course) who, in the first half of the 1900s, focused on rural landscapes, livelihoods, and communities; built the movement for soil, water, and watershed conservation; and provided the foundations for the more recent sustainable agriculture movement.[6] It would surprise those who, over the last century, began to use the insights of ecology to actively restore degraded landscapes, waterways, and ecosystems. It would surprise those who pushed for and enacted the Clean Air Act (1970) and the Clean Water Act (1972)—among other signature laws of the modern environmental movement—legislation that had much to do with urban pollution concerns, and little to do with wilderness. And it now surprises the many contemporary conservationists who over the last generation have focused their work not on "classic" wilderness but on ecosystem management, urban and landscape ecology, private lands conservation, community-based conservation, watershed-based programs, maintenance of agricultural biodiversity, organic and urban agriculture, the local food movement, and other approaches to integrating conservation across the landscape.[7]

Meanwhile, appreciation of the embeddedness of cities within ecosystems, and of wildness in the city, is hardly new. For more than a century, a venerable literature has addressed the need and potential for better integration of cities and landscapes in the industrial age and for more socially and ecologically sensitive urban design and planning. The new conservationists need only consult such standard sources as Frederick Law Olmsted, Patrick Geddes, Jane Addams, John Nolen, Lewis Mumford, Jane Jacobs, Benton MacKaye, Jens Jensen, and Ian McHarg (again, among many others). The rising wave of interest in new urbanism and sustainable cities over the last two decades builds on these and other sources.[8] Evidently the effort in conservation to integrate the wild and the human is at least as old as the movement itself.

The "old" movement, blindly adhering to the mythical "balance of nature," assumed that nature in its pristine and undisturbed state was and would remain static. The new story seems to hold that the dynamism of natural systems and phenomena was discovered sometime in the late 1980s and came as a sorry surprise to naive environmentalists beholden to a "balance of nature" mythology. But the realization that nature changes is hardly new. Sticking just to the modern Western scientific tradition, we might point out that this view has been outmoded since the days of Alexander von Humboldt, Charles Darwin, Alfred Russel Wallace, and George Perkins Marsh. Even ecological succession, however flawed in its early formulations, was an effort to understand and explain patterns of ecological variation and change in time and space. We find Leopold cautioning in the 1930s that "the 'balance of nature' is a mental image for land and life which grew up before and during the transition to ecological thought. It is commonly employed in describing the biota to laymen, but ecologists among themselves accept it only with reservations, and its acceptance by laymen seems to depend more on convenience than conviction."[9] Scientific and popular understanding of a vast range of both natural and human-influenced phenomena—plate tectonics, climate change, glaciation, erosion and sedimentation, ecosystem disturbance, population cycles, population genetics, speciation, range expansions and contractions, biological invasion, extinction, etc.—has been compounding for decades, if not centuries. The theme may have required extra emphasis; it did not require *invention*. But it requires now that we understand more critically some fundamentals: that not all change is created equal; that the causes, rates, spatial scales, types, and impacts of ecological disturbance and environmental change vary; that natural and anthropogenic change are interwoven in complex ways; and that our challenge is to calibrate more finely our understanding of historic change, and to explore more carefully our ethical response to the human role amid such change.[10]

The "old" movement regarded nature as precious and fragile, whereas we now know that it is tough and resilient. *Resilience* has become the watchword of contemporary ecosystem science, but it has deep roots in ecological thinking and conservation practice. Leopold captured the essence of the modern formulation of resilience in the 1940s, when he advised his fellow conservationists to pay attention not only to the continuous supply of "natural resources" but also to the fountain from which all ecosystem goods and services flow. His term for this was *land health*, which he defined as "the capacity for self-renewal in the soils, waters, plants, and animals that collectively comprise the land."[11] For a generation that had witnessed epic deforestation, the depletion (and, in some cases, extinction) of wildlife populations, the widespread degradation of watersheds, and the Dust Bowl, the vulnerability of land to the ravages of unchecked economic exploitation was plain. Resilience was not merely a compelling ecological idea; it was a dire conservation need.

The more recent emergence of resilience as an organizing concept does not obviate the observable fact that ecosystems—human-modified and human-simplified worldwide, to varying degrees—for all their toughness and resilience, will not recover, on their own, their full complement of native diversity and their fine-tuned functionality. Ecological restoration recognizes and employs the potential "capacity for self-renewal" in ecosystems as a pragmatic standard—and it has done so since at least the 1930s. Restoration is not new, and anyone who works in restoration knows that it does not see land, or fragility, through rose-colored glasses. We can throw up our hands and take comfort in nature's inherent "toughness"; or we can choose to put our hands—and heads and hearts—to work on behalf of the vulnerable, the ruined, the ignored, and the desecrated.

In both cases—defining the concept of resilience and engaging in the practice of restoration—conservation scientists and practitioners have for decades turned to the wilder portions of our landscapes for insight, knowledge, and actual biotic materials (genes, species, seeds, pollinators, etc.). Vulnerability and toughness, fragility and resilience, turn out to be not opposing but interwoven qualities of ecosystems. But one needs history and perspective to make sense of the terms.

The "old" movement is, and always has been, inhumane and oppressive in dealing with people, especially by removing them from their home places in the name of preserving "pristine" nature. The observation that wrong, bad, and even tragic things have been done—to people and to the natural world in the name of conservation and environmentalism—is undoubtedly true. Large movements are not homogeneous. Movements do not control the actions of all who participate in them. Movements also learn, change, and grow. To represent conservation and environmentalism as inherently and forever inimical to social justice is to erect a very frail straw man. History does indeed provide plenty of examples of short-sighted social ethics in American conservation in the first half of the twentieth century, as well as the later environmental movement. It also provides much evidence of a shared conviction: that there is an intimate connection between society's treatment of our fellow citizens (both the indigenous and the more recently arrived) and of our fellow creatures and landscapes.

It is entirely appropriate to behold the mote—and the beam—that we find in our movement's eye. We engage in selective history, however, if we do not at the same time hold up those who have helped us to see more clearly the connections between social justice and conservation. In our critiques of, for example, the myopic utilitarianism of Progressive Era conservation, we may overlook its foundational commitment to economic equity and fairness. Bob Marshall, founder of the Wilderness Society, championed the people and culture of *Arctic Village* as much as he did the wild inhabitants of the *Arctic Wilderness*.[12] The eminent wildlife biologist Olaus Murie called for conservationists to broaden their ethical horizons, to mark "our heavy-footed progress in toleration of 'other' races of men," and to seek "tolerance for the views and desires of many people."[13] We cannot ignore historic tensions between advocates of social justice and nature conservation, but we can also build upon the efforts of those, from all sides, who have long sought to address those tensions and act upon commonality of purpose and values.

Then there is the question of respect for wild places and sacred spaces among indigenous peoples themselves. Is regard for the wild and nonhuman confined to only those with a Western worldview? Or is it reflected in varied cultures around the world, throughout history (and prehistory)? What are we to make, for example, of the Cree Nation of Wemindji, working in close partnership with Parks Canada and others to create, in 2008, the Paakumshumwaau-Maatuuskaau Réserve de Biodiversité Projetée, a protected area on the Wemindji lands along the east coast of James Bay?[14] Or the Red Cliff Band of Lake Superior Chippewa, which established in 2012 the Frog Bay Tribal National Park along the south shore of Lake Superior in Wisconsin—the first such tribal wildland park in the nation?[15] We could cite many other such partnerships. Perhaps we can make more than examples of these places and communities. Perhaps they can serve as reminders and guideposts, showing that concepts of *home* and *wilderness* are not, and never have been, as antithetical as we sometimes presume. Perhaps they can inspire others to make the same connections.

The "old" movement failed. This story line simply presents an inherent paradox.

The statement is true. Alas, it is also true of every other movement for social, economic, political, and environmental betterment that the world has ever seen. The civil rights movement has failed to eradicate racism. The women's movement has failed to do away with sexism. The labor movement has failed to eliminate economic injustice. Thinking that movements work this way—that they emerge, do their work, triumph, and then disappear—reveals a superficial understanding of history and social change, and the complexity of the human condition. Every movement involves steps forward, steps backward, and steps to the side—and an occasional leap to a new level.

The statement is also false. This movement for healthier relations between people and nature—call it what we will—has succeeded wildly. Over the last century and a half (at minimum), it has effectively challenged the currently dominant assumptions of human social and economic development: that humans are the sole source of meaning and value in the universe, and that other people and nature exist to be exploited for maximum individual and corporate economic benefit. Paul Hawken has described it as "the largest movement in the world": "I began to count . . . . I now believe there are over one—and maybe even two—million organizations working towards ecological sustainability and social justice."[16]

Hawken might have added that the movement is also the most complex, difficult, and necessary movement in human history. Because ecological relationships cannot be divorced from human social and economic relationships, progress in improving the former cannot be made without addressing the tensions in the latter. But the converse is also true: Healthier, more just human social and economic relationships cannot be achieved in any lasting sense without appreciation of the context of the biophysical world within which they exist.

Leopold had it about right in 1947:

I have no illusions about the speed or accuracy with which an ecological conscience can become functional. It has required 19 centuries to define decent man-to-man conduct and the process is only half done; it may take as long to evolve a code of decency for man-to-land conduct. In such matters we should not worry too much about anything except the direction in which we travel. The direction is clear, and the first step is to throw your weight around on matters of right and wrong in land-use. Cease being intimidated by the argument that a right action is impossible because it does not yield maximum profits, or that a wrong action is to be condoned because it pays. That philosophy is dead in human relations, and its funeral in land-relations is overdue."[17]

The power of the proposed story is that there is some truth in all of these story lines. Yet all of the story lines are, as I have argued, oversimplified and/or unoriginal. Considered together, they provide reasonable criticisms of the modern environmental movement, but they do so by painting a caricature of that movement, poorly informed by the history of conservation science, philosophy, policy, or practice.

There is another story about human beings and the rest of nature that we might offer. It is not a complicated one, and it is actually not so different from the one being proposed, especially in its concern for justice. But the story broadens this concern to include championing justice for the land, for its nonhuman denizens, and for future generations. This story would thus include in its narrative a firm place for the wild with, within, and (yes) without, the human. That story line is so important that it reframes the entire narrative. We are engaged in a collective effort to understand and redirect the relationship between the human (and humanized) and the "natural, wild, and free." To do so, we need to understand, in ways we do not yet fully understand, the complicated history of humans and nature, and the evolution of what we now call conservation and environmentalism, over decades, centuries, and millennia, among varied cultures, in varied places, according to varied traditions. It is a vast task of intellectual and spiritual synthesis. It demands more than oversimplification and caricature. It requires, above all, humility. We have work to do.

Without knowing how that task will finally work out, I have the feeling that it will all come down to a pretty basic set of principles in practice. We need to think of conservation in terms of whole landscapes, from the wildest places to the most urban places. We need to safeguard the wildlands we still have, at all scales. Where we can, we need to restore such wildlands specifically, and *wildness* more generally. We need to do more and better conservation work outside protected areas and sacred spaces; on our "working" farms, ranches, and forests; and in the suburbs and cities where people increasingly live. We need to meet our needs for food, fiber, and fuel in ways that do not simplify and deplete but actively replenish, ecosystems close to home and around the world. We need to treat water as the essential ingredient of life that it is, and we need to respect its function in the landscape. We need to sustain and restore the two great global commons: the atmosphere above and the oceans below. No part of the landscape—however wild, however humanized—is sustainable if the whole is not. And so we need to know and respect the connections among all these parts of any landscape, while building resilience into all those relationships. We need to build a just and restorative economy that serves all these goals. We need to do all these things for people, for human communities, for future generations, for all the other members of the community of life, and for the health of whole landscapes and the entire Earth. We are all in this together.

Conservation in No-Man's-Land

CLAUDIO CAMPAGNA AND DANIEL GUEVARA

OUR MAIN PURPOSE in this essay is to invite the concerned community of conservationists, from a variety of disciplines, to address the questions of conservation and of environmental ethics in a new way, and as frankly as possible. In our view, the crisis of biodiversity, conservation, sustainability, and any number of iconic environmentalist concerns must be radically reconsidered. Our sense is that after all the struggles against the environmental crisis—well-meaning struggles, that have employed the best science, thinking, and activism available—we are in a kind of trench warfare that can produce at best temporary and unstable "victories," many of which seem even to have backfired.

In response, our image is one of putting an armchair right on the battlefield—in no-man's-land—and, for all the risks involved, simply sitting down and thinking. At the very least, we can mourn, as we all do when we have lost something of incomparable and incomprehensible value, and when no words or deeds can quite express or mend the value of what has been lost, and continues to be lost. All other alternatives seem to us, at this point in time, to serve as mere distractions with deep negative consequences that the conservation movement does not seem to sufficiently reflect upon. These alternatives are sometimes offered in the spirit of reevaluation or of reforming environmentalism—as, for example, those we consider in the section immediately below, represented by their most famous contemporary proponents.

"Inconvenient" environmentalism: exposing the alleged myths, prejudices, and confusions of the traditional conservation movement

Environmentalist (American) heroes and their movement have been ostensibly exposed and disgraced. Their beloved, driving force—pristine and wild Nature[1]—has been laid bare as fraudulent: There no longer are any places "untrammeled by Man." Worse, there never were (!), or at least not in the last one thousand years;[2] moreover, national parks, supposedly intended to preserve wild Nature, have forcibly displaced native people from their homes (and continue to do so) for the sake of tourist attractions. Henry Thoreau and Edward Abbey, the high-brow and low-brow prophets of self-sufficient solitude and wildness, are exposed as hypocrites: Abbey for pining for companionship in his private journals while writing *Desert Solitaire*, and (worse) Thoreau for having his mom do his laundry, while he labored sublimely at Walden (only three miles from town, by the way).[3] After all, and most sadly, John Muir—who often *did* live wildly and self-sufficiently—was racist.[4]

These men are heroes of the conservation movement generally. They were not scientists, but many scientists do what they do now because of them. And there has been disgrace even among these scientists of Nature: Things are supposedly not as bad as they had predicted, since Nature bounces back with remarkable resilience and new things thrive where old ones have been lost—the way of the world from time immemorial. If the environmental movement is not dead, as some have declared it is,[5] then it ought to be.

These are the declarations of reformers and iconoclasts who have made such claims the basis of a manifesto for a new perspective—"conservation in the Anthropocene." (In this essay we refer to it as "the Anthropocene perspective.") This new perspective is considered by some as involving "new models for thinking and acting," and their arguments are seen to "demolish mythologies built around the environment." Here is their new, human-friendly vision: "The conservation we will get by embracing development and advancing human well-being will almost certainly not be the conservation that was imagined in its early days. But it will be more effective and far more broadly supported, in boardrooms and political chambers, as well as at kitchen tables."[6]

First reactions

Some of our main objections to this "new" or "inconvenient"[7] movement can be broken down into three basic categories:

1) *Ad hominem* arguments based on the characters of pioneers of the movement;
2) Factual arguments which contest the claims of the traditional environmental movement (pointing, for example, to bad predictions based on a lack of appreciation for the resilience of nature); and
3) Value arguments which oppose the idea of a "pristine wild" Nature, untrammeled by humans, and which show how unrealistic it would be to protect Nature in the way traditional conservationists want to.

Providing counterarguments to the vision of conservation in the Anthropocene involves adding to a controversy that has already generated much heat and many responses from the conservation community.[8] We believe that adding to the controversy distracts from the things really worth thinking about, but some brief counterarguments are in line with our general purpose.

First, the *ad hominem* arguments are the easiest to counter. Thomas Jefferson held slaves; Jean-Jacques Rousseau was a lousy father; Gottlob Frege (the architect of modern logic) was a rabid anti-Semite—so much for the ideals of constitutional democracy, education under the social contract, and modern logic. We can add to the list some of the classics of music or literature or painting, if we poke around in the right closets there. What is missed by continuing in this vein is the key point worth making: that the value, meaning, and significance of Nature—unlike democracy, human dignity, and logic—is something that, in our view, no one has been able to articulate philosophically or politically yet, though everybody grasps it. All commonly used words and concepts are proxies at best, "similes" in the language of Ludwig Wittgenstein's "Lecture on Ethics"[9] (which we will return to in a moment). Proxies for what you feel when, for example, you see an ancient forest razed by corporate lumber barons, a feeling that does not go away when someone points out that you, or those you love, enjoy the modern conveniences made from those trees. Examples abound: the carcasses of albatrosses with stomachs full of plastic; the fins of sharks in the market and their bodies agonizing underwater; the head of the gorilla on a plate; the rotting elephant without a tusk.

What we do know is that Thoreau wrote masterpieces, and Muir and Abbey produced works that people love and which inspired and sustain a movement—all in the effort of drawing our attention to the intrinsic values of Nature. We are limiting the analysis to the American cadre of environmentalist icons, as those have been the focus of the attack. It is a good bet that people will continue to be driven by their works for a long, long time, and perhaps all the more likely if the ideals in them are lost to view. We need to understand why this is so; and we simply give up trying to understand it if we think it useful to resort to superficial *ad hominem* dismissals.

Second, factual arguments. Here the attack is on what might be described as the "failed metaphors" and hasty generalizations of the traditional movement. An example of a failed metaphor: *Nature is primeval, fragile, and at risk of collapse from too much human use and abuse.* In fact, states the counter-claim, Nature is so resilient that it can recover rapidly from even the most powerful human disturbances. But the crucial point in reply is that the claims, on either side, are *not* purely factual. For example, the human population has often bounced back after epidemics, genocide, and wars, but we do not take epidemics, genocide, and wars in stride because humanity has proven resilient to their onslaughts.

And third, regarding the value claims of the Anthropocene perspective, two central examples:

1) Traditional conservationists, in the Anthropocene view, are set for failure as they have an idealized notion of "pristine nature"—of untouched Nature as a source of solitary spiritual renewal, aesthetic appreciation, and support for diversity of life. The anathema of this unsupported nostalgia for wilderness is the "national park" or "wilderness park." In contrast, for the Anthropocene perspective the concept of pristine Nature has no basis in reality, and it is anachronistic, counterproductive, and unfriendly to people, especially in the poor regions where the protected lands have forced people from their traditional homes and livelihood.

2) Traditional conservationists see people as the original sinners who caused our banishment from Eden. From the Anthropocene platform's perspective, the traditional movement pits people against Nature, and it creates an atmosphere in which people see Nature

as the enemy. If people do not believe conservation is in their own best interests, then it will never be a societal priority.

In response to these claims, however, consider that the most numerous and brutal human displacements in the history of our species are unrelated to the creation of parks or any other conservation efforts. Wars and occupations have obviously played a more significant role than protecting land for wildlife; and, perhaps even more significantly, national development priorities have been, and continue to be, of utmost relevance in this context. Again, examples abound, a high-profile one being the Three Gorges dam on the Yangtze River, which displaced over a million people. Are these the salutary effects of self-interest? If not, then how much confidence can we put in self-interest? As for "pristine" Nature: In fact, nothing of comparable value and beauty that we try to preserve is "untouched." Think of the masterpieces of art, of how they are housed and preserved, and of the injustices and astronomical costs incurred in our effort to preserve them. What should our attitude be to this? What in fact is our attitude? Complicated and thorny, because even as the ethical and other violations may be crystal clear, so is the value to us (to humanity) of what we are trying to preserve.

Finally, the notion that Nature is "the enemy" is an even older perspective than the nostalgia for pristine wilderness. And, of course, at some level it is *true*. Nature is often *not* friendly. Nature can be terrifying and wild and dangerous. This is the only realistic perspective. And yet, as Thoreau and Muir and many others have felt, Nature's peculiar value lies in these untamed facts about it. Nature is about death as much as it is about life, about terrible sublimity as much as it is about soothing beauty. We all intuitively seek from Nature the opportunity to be intimate with both dark and light things, things we are normally busy running away from and that we often need solitude to experience properly, points made famous by Martin Heidegger as part of his philosophy[10]—if we dare cite another flawed genius.

The deepest issue

Analysis. In our view, the deepest issue—and real crisis— is that we do not have the concepts or language for expressing, or explicitly understanding, the intrinsic value of Nature; nor, therefore, for articulating its violation.

We cannot understand the full meaning of "extinction," for example. We cannot overemphasize this point about language and about the conceptual or intellectual lacuna of the many crises we face. The economic and biological aspects we may grasp, but these are just the outward aspects of a deep phenomenon that we cannot even name. Nature has a supreme value that (we believe) everyone recognizes in some way, but one for which, when it comes to expressing it explicitly, the common terms and concepts available are inadequate, or at best proxies—or worse, the language of the "enemy," inasmuch as what is commonly available to us is a language and philosophy of value that has been honed for centuries in an effort to clarify the value of *humanity*.

Herein lies the deepest issue for the conservation and environmental movements (old or new), because until this point is absorbed, all well-meaning efforts will have lost touch with the values supposedly driving them, and their accomplishments will tend to be pyrrhic. The critical concern here is not only our inability to articulate a shared understanding of the intrinsic value of Nature but also a confusion in language, reflected in how the conservation crisis is depicted, thought about, understood, and related to in our attempts to solve it.

This can be illustrated clearly, with the example of the language of "rights." The most thorough philosophical development of the concept of rights for Nature has been in the "animal rights" movement. Of course, this is because the concept is being extended to beings who are, relatively speaking, closest to the human, where the concept gets its rationale and paradigmatic application. But then, as many have objected: What of the rest of Nature? Was not the whole point to get away from man as the measure of all things? And even when we remain within the animal kingdom, we find (from one of the most distinguished philosophers working out a theory in this direction) the idea entertained that perhaps prey (deer, for example) ought to be protected from the predator (for example mountain lion), like victim from violent attacker.[11]

We should be grateful for any intelligent attempt to theorize the intrinsic value of Nature, but we believe that entertaining such conclusions likely signals that we lack the conceptual tools or the language adequate to the task of a theory, or properly articulated knowledge, in this area. We believe that, so far as the value of Nature goes—an "ethics of Nature" (if even this is not already a misapplication of language)—we are in a position closest to that described by Wittgenstein in his 1929 lecture on ethics more generally.

An unsolved issue of values. Without defending everything Wittgenstein says in this lecture about science and ethical value, we think that the thoughts he expresses are a sound starting point for environmental ethics. Wittgenstein says, for example, that "my whole tendency and, I believe, the tendency of all men who ever tried to write or talk Ethics or Religion was to run against the boundaries of language." Earlier, he states that "there are no propositions, which in any absolute sense, are sublime, important or trivial," and "ethics, if it is anything, is supernatural and our words will only express facts."[12]

We will comment on the other quoted remarks in a moment, but when Wittgenstein contrasts relative and absolute value he echoes a well-known distinction in ethical theory, one that is useful for understanding the fundamental distinction between so-called consequentialists and non-consequentialists—a distinction quite germane to our discussion. The vision of conservation in the Anthropocene movement is best understood as a *consequentialist* view of value, where the point is always to bring about the on-balance best state-of-affairs, after weighing costs and benefits—with nothing absolutely or intrinsically valuable other than that. Accordingly, essentially no effort is put into grappling with the question of the intrinsic value of Nature. If species are being lost and decimated in one place, we may need to make trade-offs to save more in another place, or to trade off with some urban human-centered concern, or etc. Consequentialists are famous for being impatient with the non-consequentialist's idea of a value that transcends and constrains the best state of affairs on balance. The only value that seems to make any sense for the consequentialist view is one relative to some given end. Wittgenstein illustrates the idea with the example of the right road. To speak of a right road makes sense only in relation to an end, like a desired destination. There are many ends in life. Get clear about the ones you want and do your best to satisfy them, with the necessary and available means. This is a schema for thinking about value in a way that fits comfortably when considering questions of conservation policy in light of an array of other issues: issues that could fall under the rubric of one science or another; values that are in effect just conditional facts.

This is how the vast majority of conservation questions and other environmental issues are approached today by governments and the biggest conservation societies in the world, where there is little or no discussion of the intrinsic value of Nature, or its absolute value or sacred value, as some put it. The attitude is that there is no time for such (semantic) things; trade-offs and compromises need to be made. And the issue is made all the more difficult by the fact that whatever we say about the relevant values must involve aesthetic values (as Wittgenstein also suggests more generally about ethics.). Aesthetic values always have had a troubled relationship to the ethical, being putatively only subjective ("in the eye of the beholder"). We ourselves do not endorse this purely subjective view of aesthetic value;[13] we mean only to draw attention, again, to common obstacles to our understanding in this area. In fact, one obstacle lurking here, in the distinction between aesthetic and ethical value, is that we overlook the relevance of the expressions of emotions in connection with the values we *do* understand and can articulate philosophically.

We have words and moral systems to articulate the worst that has been done to humanity. But it took a long time, indeed many centuries, even for the worst cases (such as slavery) to find and build them. Words and moral systems were found and built, to begin with, on a relatively inarticulate, emotionally *felt* reaction to the evil involved, and they were laid down amidst all manner of contradictions. As a consequence, we can be ethically articulate about what it is to enslave a human being, or to kill one unjustly. We even have a deep understanding of the mind-boggling evil of mass murder and genocide, beyond mere statistics. But who understands what is lost in the loss of a whole species? It is not satisfactory to say that species have been lost from time immemorial or that forests may grow back and that life goes on, probably no matter what we do. Think of how we would react to someone saying something like this in response to human genocide. It would be unspeakable. And we believe something like the same reaction is a clue to understanding our experience of the destruction of Nature, even though at the same time we also know that talk of equal "rights," or the like, for Nature does not really illuminate anything, and, on the contrary, can lead to absurdities. For example, there is a sense in which it seems obvious that if our values are not human-centered, then the preventable and regular loss of whole species from the face of the Earth is worse than genocide. But it is as yet impossible to express an understanding that makes such a point without involving oneself in seemingly callous and reprehensible implications from the point of view of our most humane values. Are we really forced to choose either the one or the other? Our point is that the dilemma is false, or better, meaningless, because the only way to assess or resolve it is with a language equal to the task—which is to say, a language for the value of Nature that is not shot through and through with language meant to express the value of humanity.[14]

The dilemma which *is* clear and real, especially in light of the practically minded conservationist is this: When all we can say of something valuable is that it is intrinsically valuable, or sacred and inviolable, we paradoxically seem to disqualify ourselves from the wide and complex questions of public policy. Issues of public policy, often mixed up with scientific claims (as they so intimately are in questions about conservation), tend to leave no place for intrinsic values. By invoking such values we therefore seem to remove ourselves from a language game that is suited to questions of the form "What do you want?" and to answers having to do with the most realistic means for obtaining one's end. Then, it appears we must choose between effectiveness and an obscure conception of value. But our contention is that we *must* remove ourselves from that language game if we are to have any hope of understanding why Nature is deeply valuable to us. In his lecture, Wittgenstein thinks we violate the boundaries of sense *whenever* we speak of intrinsic value. However that may be, the point is important for talk of the intrinsic value of Nature. The language and conceptual tools available for illuminating, theorizing, instituting such talk are forged from ethical theories and thinking that were developed with humanity in mind. And in the rare cases where the language is fresh and free of such human-centered constraints—as in talk of the wild, sublime, and beautiful in Nature—a profound clash between the two language games is everywhere evident. One is for civilized society, the other not. Either way, we find language of one kind being pushed into directions it was not made to go, into ways that lead to absurdities. Language may fabricate problems, but it may also hide them.

And yet as Wittgenstein says at the end of the lecture, the tendency to do this is not to be ridiculed or dismissed as ordinary useless nonsense. It points to something of the greatest importance. But how to begin to unravel it, if indeed it can be unraveled?

In summary

We conclude with this observation, all too briefly. Our deepest evaluations begin in the more inarticulate and intuitively felt values. This is true of our sense of the value of humanity. The environmental ethic likewise begins in deep reactions (hard to distinguish from our deepest aesthetic evaluations) like, say, those to slavery (and sexual slavery perhaps most poignantly). The evaluation lies in a place deeper than words or concepts, even if later we find some that seem up to the task of moral theory. But it can take a long time to theorize or judge properly about such things explicitly and discursively (as is clear in the case of slavery, accepted everywhere for centuries, for all that we take for granted now about the rights of all human beings). And for a long time one can be made to feel romantically unrealistic and counterproductive for clinging to the unspeakable nature of the evil involved.

In our view, it is not clear how if ever we will articulate properly the value of Nature, or the evil of its destruction. Wittgenstein famously says, in another place, that whereof we cannot speak thereof we must be silent. And however that is to be interpreted in the broader context of Wittgenstein's writings, we think it fitting and instructive here. The concepts and language of the conservation movement and environmental ethic more broadly need a proper burial, which of course is a form of respect. Who knows what will happen then, or what will happen from sitting in the middle of no-man's-land and simply contemplating what has happened so far (perhaps a renewal of certain terms). We are early in this thinking, even earlier than the equivalent of displaying a white flag to gain time before being swirled by the confrontation. Consequentialists may receive with horror this proposition of halting action until we understand the play better—after all, they are anxious to monopolize Nature through facts that rarely change the path of destruction. They are the first who need to recognize the failure of their propositions. Given that the original spiritual sources, at least in English, of the conservation and environmental movements today include Thoreau and Muir, and activists like David Brower, we submit that one constraint to place on future thinking about the value of Nature is for it to not proceed along consequentialist lines.

We proclaim the need for *intellectual* activism, a form of paradigmatic change that starts at the theoretical roots of the movement and refounds it on new conceptual ground. Intellectual activism is about reformulating the discourse by creating a new language game that is not played by those on either side of the trench. We may not yet have the rules or tools for this activism; it lies in no man's land and may not ever happen. But precedents exist, even for the environmentalists. The 1987 Brundtland Report, (*Our Common Future*, published by the World Commission on Environment and Development), catapulted the concept of "sustainable development" into the established discourse—an example of intellectual activism by consequentialists—and channeled the movement in a new direction (a wrong one in our perspective) by creating a new relative value: sustainability. While the discourse remains the same, we have no solutions to offer, no actions besides pointing at the demise of this concept,[15] and remain in hopeful silence for a radical new beginning.

The authors are thankful to Luigi Boitani, Janette Dinishak, and Douglas Tompkins for their comments and suggestions on an early version of this paper and to Victoria and Eugenia Zavattieri as well, for their earlier technical help.

The "New Conservation"

MICHAEL SOULÉ

> *Man has lost the capacity to foresee and to forestall.*
> *He will end by destroying the earth.*
>
> —ALBERT SCHWEITZER (1875–1965)

RECENTLY MY WIFE AND I spied on some female endangered leatherback sea turtles depositing their Ping-Pong-ball-sized eggs at Trinidad's Grande Riviére, on the famous "turtle beach" where the river enters the Atlantic.

During our first night at Grand Riviére the skies gushed for hours, previewing the rainy season. By morning, the swollen river had cut a new channel through the beach where many female leatherbacks had already nested. Hundreds of turtle eggs were being either washed into the ocean or consumed by dogs and black vultures. We felt compelled to collect the doomed eggs and rebury as many as possible in new "nests" at a safe distance from the river and the ocean's waves. So for an hour we gathered turtle eggs from the sand and reburied them in safety.

That incident was like a coda for a piece that had begun forty years earlier during a sabbatical in Australia. During a research break on Heron Island in the southern Great Barrier Reef, my family and I watched green turtle hatchlings poke through the sand and awkwardly scramble to the water through an obstacle course of ravenous gulls. Some didn't make it, but witnessing their indomitable will to live deepened my fascination with the universal struggle—*élan vital*—that drive to thrive and to leave behind some genetic or cultural flotsam, a legacy of genes or memes.

Granted, our "rescue" of a few hundred turtle eggs is evolutionarily meaningless. Nonetheless, emotions usually trump rationality, even in science where pride and status are the rewards. So I readily confess that rescuing the eggs of an endangered turtle was thrilling, even while knowing that for millions of years the jellyfish-eating leatherbacks had survived untold numbers of calamities, including major marine extinctions, without humanity's help. My rescue attempts stemmed from my faith in turtles, actions compelled by a loyalty akin to that described by poet Gary Snyder:

> *I pledge allegiance to the soil*
> *of Turtle Island,*
> *and to the beings who thereon dwell,*
> *one ecosystem*
> *in diversity,*
> *under the sun,*
> *With joyful interpenetration for all.*

The French used to ask, "What difference will it make in four hundred years?" Few human projects leave tracks. Nowadays, however, with everything speeding up, even "fifteen minutes of fame" is more than most people will get, unless you are Bill Clinton. The global speedup affects everything, from the pace of elections to how fast we walk, to happiness metrics, stock trades, and the rate of species extinction—which is expected to grow by a factor of 10,000 compared to its preagricultural baseline rate.

The shrinkage of time scales is partly due to population growth. In addition, earth-scalping technologies like mountaintop-removal mining, dam construction, and forest clearing for cattle grazing are exponentially expanding humanity's ecological footprint.[1] Cultural and environmental changes, which once took centuries, now take only decades. Time is contracting while ecological entropy expands, and wild places, like human languages and cultures, are blinking out much faster than they can be rescued.[2]

No wonder conservationists are accused of sending messages filled with "doom and gloom." Conservation biologists are certain that providing enough shelter, food, water, and smartphones for 3 or 4 billion more humans by the end of the century means wildness will survive only in highly secure parks, most of them in already industrialized nations. Assuming that commerce and growth carry on as usual, soon virtually all wild rivers will be dammed, tropical forests will be replaced by commercial plantations, marine fish stocks will continue to be depleted, oceans will be increasingly acidified, and deserts will be "improved" with desalinated seawater, wind farms, and solar collectors. The greatest blow of all, climate change, will likely extinguish most remnants of biodiversity and cripple civilization, but—owing to successful lobbying by powerful vested interests—the subject remains taboo.[3]

The so-called new conservation

Is there hope? Yes, if you believe the copious chatter coming from a group of environmentalists associated with the Breakthrough Institute, Santa Clara University, and The Nature Conservancy (TNC). Calling themselves the "new conservationists," they wish to divert monies donated for the protection of nature to projects that would benefit the economic well-being of workers. Their vision is described in detail at the end of this essay. In the meantime, most conservationists are depressed to the point of despair as the final curtain descends on the most majestic creatures to have survived the Pleistocene massacres of megafauna coincident with the arrival of the first humans; the latest of these majestic creatures are elephants, whose valuable ivory fetches goodly sums in China.

That said, I remain hopeful. My faith springs from an attitude I call *possibilism*. No condition or state in the cosmos is permanent, and change is inevitable. Surprises occur, and saving nature remains a possibility. Sure, possibilism is a delicate reed, but it is my only solace.

One problem with the emotion of hope, however, is its cunning companion, denial. Both hope and denial are evident in the "new conservation." The new conservationists, including the chief scientist at TNC, decry the doleful whining of conservationists and biologists about the loss of wildness and biological diversity while predicting, hopefully, a future of economic well-being for rural and poor communities that partner for economic development with large corporations like those affiliated with current or recent members of TNC's board. These corporations include Goldman Sachs & Co., Google Capital Group Companies, General Atlantic, Alibaba Group, Eagle River Inc., Meritage Capital, Blackstone Group, Applied Materials, Duke Energy, The Bridgespan Group, Inc., AP Capital Holdings Inc., Hewlett Packard, and others.

Perhaps not coincidentally, TNC is the financial behemoth in the constellation of conservation NGOs. Its annual budget approaches $1 billion in good economic times. In comparison, the budget of Conservation International in 2011 was about $123 million; the budget of the WWF–US (World Wildlife Fund–United States) in 2011 was about $182 million; and the budget of the Wildlife Conservation Society in 2010 was about $200 million.

The "denial" element of their sanguine strategy is the absence of evidence that this top-down, for-profit strategy will work when it is brought to scale.

Supporters of the so-called new conservation promise that an engineered, people-friendly "garden world" will thrive in the hypothetical new geological era—the *Anthropocene,* literally "the Age of Man." These new, corporate-sponsored environmentalists cheerfully predict that investors and companies will flock to create jobs for the poor in profitable enterprises such as mining, oil drilling, logging, water capture, and agriculture while creating "gardens" to save some beneficial elements of wild nature at the same time.

The new conservation is now being promoted by Wall Street and by some neoliberal think tanks. But before I elaborate on this emerging campaign, it would be helpful to place it in a broader moral and social context, one that recognizes the existence of a set of movements devoted to the affirmation of life more inclusively—not just human life.

Caring about life

How people define "saving life," "caring for life," or "saving the world" is all over the map. In 1989 I discovered, to my dismay, that 95 percent of my students in the Environmental Studies department at the University of California–Santa Cruz interpreted "saving the world" to mean kindness directed at under-privileged sections of humanity, whereas I meant saving all of nature with the emphasis on wild creatures. I was depressed for a week.

A similar compartmentalization is obvious among many of my friends in the North Fork Valley of western Colorado where my unscientific observations reveal that people here care about living beings roughly in this order of life-forms: friends and family, large dogs, horses, small dogs, cows, elk, hay, peaches, tomatoes, cherries, sweet corn, zucchini, honey bees, cats, on down to mushrooms and other useful creatures.

What about major, compassion-based movements dedicated to the protection of different life-forms? I classify such life-affirming movements into three groups. The biggest of these is *humanitarianism,* a great umbrella of diverse crusades that share the goal of boosting human well-being. The next largest movement, based on amounts of money donated, is *animal welfare*; its mission is the protection of domesticated animals and other kept creatures that people maintain for companionship, food, entertainment (such as in zoos), research, and doing work such as plowing, hunting, hauling, racing (dog and horse), and so on.[4]

I've already alluded to the third movement, *conservationism*; it emphasizes free, relatively wild ecological communities including their native animals and plants. Before I briefly describe humanitarianism and conservationism, I think you need to know about the relative popularity of these movements.

A metric of caring—donations

It surprises many to learn that about 98 percent of charitable donations in the United States target socially beneficial, humanitarian nonprofits and foundations that support religion (35 percent); education; human services; health, arts, and cultural institutions; international affairs; etc.[5] Many humanitarian charities work hard to fight diseases like malaria, cancer, addiction, obesity, and heart disease, and other humanitarian NGOs battle injustice and poverty, issues that may seem more tangible to the average citizen than Earth's unraveling ecological fabric.

The good news is that the vast majority of people and foundations are life-affirming in some sense. However, most donating households and foundations in the United States are strongly biased toward the pro-people movement, with more money directed toward programs related to environmentalism and the welfare of kept animals, for example. The bad news is that only a sliver is left for the wilder set of creatures and places.

A catchall category called "Environment" gets about 2 percent of charitable donations, including donations benefitting animal welfare, as well as humanitarian causes such as clean air and water. Conservation's share of the funding pie is puny. Less than 1 percent is given to a hodgepodge of charities supporting open space, outdoor recreation, hunting, fishing, national parks, endangered species, wilderness protection, ecological restoration, wildlife corridors, and habitat protection. I estimate that wild nature and biodiversity conservation, including protection of vulnerable species, gets about one-half of 1 percent of American charitable giving. Financially, conservationism is the runt of the pro-life family of movements.

Humanitarianism

Our species quickly achieved near-absolute global domination of the biosphere in the last ten or twelve thousand years. The catalyst for this unprecedented ascendency appears to be a linked series of cognitive breakthroughs that occurred between two hundred thousand and one hundred thousand years ago, beginning with language and artisanal innovation, the subsequent evolution of language, and cooperation within and between clans. These changes eventually led to the emergence of hyper-sociality, religion, planning, art, dance, language, and agriculture, leading in turn to city-states, capitalism, and institutionalized warfare.[6]

In the last few hundred years, humanitarianism—the promotion of human welfare—has propagated widely in many societies. Originally the province of the church, this movement has diffused into secular institutions, particularly in Europe and North America. It has benefited the arts and has sometimes, and in some places, reduced human violence, expanded the spheres of freedom and justice, raised standards of living, and greatly improved the human condition overall. Even cynics must admit that humans are without peer in many cognitive and behavioral realms. Compassion is one of these realms, and the moral impulse to care about the well-being of others—at least of some others—can ennoble individuals and institutions.

Today, humanitarianism comprises thousands of specialized causes and campaigns and is by far the biggest and wealthiest of the three pro-life movements. But humans are not angels, and the ideal of a universal, loving humanity is still beyond our reach. Inter-group aversion and hostility are ubiquitous. Chauvinism ("groupism") obviously constricts and distorts humanitarianism. Racism, fanaticism, and religious fundamentalism are major obstacles to a messianic reunion of humanity.

Generally, every group or "ism" assumes that its ways—its ideologies and policies—are the most beneficial and true. Thus liberals, fascists, capitalists, socialists, atheists, religious fundamentalists, pacifists, and terrorists descend into out-group aversion.

Take me for instance. As an educated, intellectual nature lover and a practitioner of Zen Buddhism, I am dead certain (but nonjudgmental) that deniers of both anthropogenic climate change and the extinction crisis are morbidly ignorant. I think that oil exploration will kill most life in the Arctic Ocean and that the planet will be virtually unlivable for people and the majority of large animals by the end of this century. My neighbor across the street is a coal miner and a Mormon. His bumper sticker states "Earth First! We'll Mine the Other Planets Later." My stickers say "Got Science?" and "Public Lands Protect America the Beautiful." When we meet in the street we smile and don't mention our bumper stickers.

We are all humanitarians to a degree, but so too do we all have preferences, biases, inconsistent beliefs, stuff we hate, ideologies we cling to, and those we despise. On a recent bike ride I saw a squashed, eight-inch turtle barely alive in the middle of the road—it had been run over. I stopped, got off my bike, and carried the dying turtle to the curb. Then I noticed the people in a parked car looking and laughing at me.

I happen to despise despoilers of nature (with compassion of course). If you live long enough, you will discover that most of the wild places you loved as a young person have been peopled to death. The woods, the streams, the shores, and even the national parks are being quickly defunded and degraded, even in California, the richest state in the richest nation. I grew up in San Diego County and witnessed its destruction. In 1936, the population was 270,000; in 2010, it was 3.1 million and growing. As a teenager I roamed its network of canyons, its Borrego desert, its Palomar and Cuyamaca mountains, and its pristine Pacific shores nearby. I harvested abalone and lobsters in tide pools, carrying my bounty home in a gunnysack. Now pollution, pathogens from sewage, and people have degraded the coasts; what still lives isn't safe to eat. It is hard for me not to judge real estate developers as a group.

My disgust at the actions of "rape-and-run" developers as a group is an example of a universal trait of highly social animals: groupishness—allegiance within groups and animus between them. The anthropological literature on "ethnocentrism" is enormous, and the social psychologist Jonathan Haidt declares that groupishness generates conflict more often than it nurtures peace and love.[7] People simply prefer to "hang" with those who look, think, and worship like they do. Naturalists and conservationists are just as groupish as those who detest their values.[8]

The groupish impulse is one of many great challenges to humanitarianism. Groupishness reflects our primate origins, but the relative youth of *Homo sapiens* may explain its virulence. Humanity is thought to be the most recent large mammal to evolve—having appeared only about one hundred fifty thousand years ago. This immaturity, I think, is why we seem unable to behave like grownups. It may be why we cannot stop the population explosion, arrest the extinction of most species, and prevent the termination of civilization by climate change.

Our clannish and clownish nature also contributes to an us-against-them aversion to life-forms—including creatures such as wolves, prairie dogs, and mosquitoes—that challenge our hegemony. A related bias is "resourcism," the notion that nature has little value except as a human resource and that nonresource creatures have no value or "purpose." (It always astounds me when people ask the pre-Darwinian question "What good are cobras, chiggers, cockroaches for example?" But what can one expect in a country in which nearly half the people believe that the Bible is literally true?) Our impulse to dominate and control nature reflects this resource/nonresource dualism—one of the darker hairs on the underbelly of humanitarianism.

E. O. Wilson believes that humanity is a biological outlier and the epitome of primate sociality, a "eusocial" species like ants, bees, wasps, and naked mole rats. It is true that the social organization of human beings is extraordinarily complex. On the other hand, human sociality is double-edged. The volatile mixture of evolutionary immaturity and super-sociality might also explain why our species is also "eu-competitive." Eu-competitiveness spawns scads of mutually antagonistic groups and movements. Today, for example, those urging timely responses to climate change are stalemated by business-funded climate change deniers who lobby for governmental procrastination and effectively abort initiatives that could save civilization. Naturally, both sides of the climate debate don the mantle of humanitarianism. Stalemate is as good as it gets. As Edward Abbey put it:

We are slaves in the sense that we depend for our daily survival upon an expand-or-expire agro-industrial empire—a crackpot machine—that the specialists cannot comprehend and the managers cannot manage. Which is, furthermore, devouring world resources at an exponential rate.[9]

Conservationism

The mission of conservationism is threefold: first, protecting Earth's extraordinary, autochthonous diversity of wild plants, animals, and ecosystems; second, ensuring the perpetuation of the 3.5-billion-year saga of biological evolution and speciation; and third, ensuring opportunities for people, now and in the future, to benefit spiritually and physically from wildness and the diversity of wild beings. The values associated with wildness were most clearly elucidated in the deep ecological writings of Arne Naess as popularized by Bill Devall and George Sessions.[10]

Most people, including the majority of environmental professionals, continue to conflate environmentalism with conservationism. This is understandable but unfortunate. Dave Foreman has clarified the distinction between these two movements.[11] Foreman notes that the goals of environmentalism are anthropocentric, aiming to improve the health and welfare of people, while conservationism—at its core—is biocentric or ecocentric but often humanitarian in its recreational and spiritual manifestations.

Many environmentalists simply assume that biological diversity is meant for human consumption, exploitation, and recreation. Theirs is a world of resources and hoped-for wealth.[12] In stark contrast, the goal of conservationism is other-centric. It stresses the intrinsic (for-itself) value of nonhuman beings and aims to protect Earth's 5 million or so different kinds of surviving creatures *for their own sake*.

But we can overparse things, including our attitudes. I venture into wild places—from the hillside behind my house to national parks—for personal enrichment and enjoyment. I rejoice when seeing a bear cub climbing an aspen tree for the fun of it, a lizard basking on rocks in a desert arroyo for the warmth of it, or hatchling turtles making a "beeline" to the sea for the safety of it. Incidentally, I have similar, positive feelings when watching our cat snooze in front of the woodstove. But you and I "contain multitudes" as poet Walt Whitman wrote—we are big enough to embrace all life-affirming impulses and emotions, including humanitarianism, animal welfare, and conservationism.

Recently while watching my grandchildren play at a lake in the Elk Mountains in Colorado, I became aware of the two conflicting emotions I experienced—the pride of my grandparenthood versus my considerable chagrin about how much more at ease the children are when playing indoors with their parents' iPads. I wondered if I would ever see them become confident and skilled sojourners of the wild. The supporters of both conservationism and humanitarian environmentalism agree on one thing: The inexorable growth in human numbers and the expansion of civilization is accelerating the conversion of wild nature into amenities, commodities, and derelict landscapes. And perhaps the "singularity," when human feelings are replaced by silicon-based algorithms, is not so many decades in the future, and no one will care.

Environmentalists are good at inventing miraculous fixes, such as payment for ecosystem services and sustainable development. Sadly, even the United States, with all its resources and public lands (40 percent of the land base in the West), lacks the will and heart to provide a safety net for vulnerable, threatened, and endangered species, including wolves, grizzlies, sage grouse, amphibians, native fishes, songbirds, and so on. I used to believe that federal-agency land managers could overcome political and bureaucratic interference and do what was right for nature. I used to believe that a new administration would not always cave in to vested interests and political exigencies, including today's drill-and-frack mania, at a time of huge gas surpluses.

Today, the conservationists who still assume that wild creatures and wilderness have intrinsic value doubt that they will ever be able to arrest, let alone slow, the extinction of species, globally.[13] The obstacles are widely understood:

- ▶ Fewer youngsters are exposed to nature during their formative years; even children who can spend time outside are seduced by the power of electronic, digital gadgets.
- ▶ Conservationism is just as fragmented as the other pro-life movements, and internecine squabbles between groups are common, particularly when donations dry up during times of economic stress.
- ▶ The diversity and surplus of conservation organizations is confusing to the public.
- ▶ Conservation "wins" are becoming rare, and bad news for nature is depressingly ubiquitous, exacerbated in the last twelve years in the United States by a coal train of anticonservation policies and legislation from both Republican and Democratic administrations and from Congress, virtually all of which favor extractive industries.
- ▶ Conservationism, like humanitarianism, has its darker attributes and suicidal impulses. One is the tendency to judge and attack other groups before sincerely seeking ways to cooperate. Another is that grassroots organizing has nearly vanished, which may account for dissipating citizen awareness of environmental and conservation campaigns. Exceptions, however, occur. My own small community (the North Fork Valley of the Gunnison River on the

western slope of the Colorado Rockies) has twice succeeded in blocking attempts by the Bureau of Land Management to lease adjacent public lands for gas drilling—the kind of development that has devastated so many communities in the western states.

The "new conservation"

A high-profile but chimeric movement is rapidly gaining recognition and supporters. Its goal is to replace the biodiversity-based model of traditional conservation with campaigns emphasizing human economic progress. Christened the "new conservation" (or the "new environmentalism"), this movement promotes economic development, poverty alleviation, and corporate partnerships. Its proponents justify its conservation payoffs on the grounds that helping disadvantaged people, blue-collar workers, and others to achieve a higher standard of living will kindle their public sympathy and affection for wild creatures. Because its goal is to supplant the biodiversity-based model of traditional conservation with something entirely different, namely a human-centered (economic growth–based) "green" or humanitarian movement, it is certainly not conservation.

Institutional allies and supporters of the new conservation include the Long Now Foundation, the Nature Conservancy, and the Breakthrough Institute. The founders of the latter write—in the style of the Enlightenment—that "we must open our eyes to the joy and excitement experienced by the newly prosperous and increasingly free [persons]. We must create a world where every human can not only realize her material needs, but also her higher needs."[14]

Leading spokespersons for this form of humanitarianism or social justice include University of Santa Clara faculty Peter Kareiva and Michelle Marvier, and the author Emma Marris. Kareiva is a theoretical biologist, ecological modeler, and Chief Scientist at TNC. The "new conservation" manifesto, coauthored by Kareiva, Marvier, and TNC marketer Robert Lalasz, asserts that the mission of conservation ought to be primarily a humanitarian one, not nature protection: "Instead of pursuing the protection of biodiversity for biodiversity's sake, *a new conservation should seek to enhance those natural systems that benefit the widest number of people, especially the poor*" [emphasis mine].[15] In light of its humanitarian agenda and in conformity with Dave Foreman's distinction between environmentalism (a movement that historically aims to improve human health, mostly by reducing air and water pollution and ensuring food safety) and conservation, it is obvious that the term *new conservation* is a misleading misnomer.[16]

Kareiva and his colleagues also declare that "nature could be a garden" and that their new conservation will measure its achievement in large part by its relevance to people, including city dwellers. Underlying this humanitarian vision is the belief that nature protection for its own sake is a dysfunctional, antihuman anachronism. In interviews and talks Kareiva defames the characters of past conservation champions such as Henry David Thoreau, John Muir, and Edward Abbey, whom he caricatures as hypocrites and misanthropes, but he never refers to contemporary conservation leaders or writers.

Another of their assumptions is that biodiversity conservation is out of touch with the economic realities of ordinary people, even though this is manifestly false. Since its inception, the Society for Conservation Biology has included scores of progressive social scientists among its editors and authors.[17] The "new conservationists" also assert that national parks and protected areas serve only the elite. The fact is that nearly nine out of ten U.S. voters say they agree that it is important to protect national parks.[18] Further, the new conservationists argue that it should be the mission of conservationists to spur economic growth in commercial sectors such as forestry, fossil fuel extraction, and agriculture, including support for patented, genetically modified crops.

A key claim of the "new conservation" platform is averring a correlation between standard of living and people's affection for (or, tolerance of) wildlife. As incomes grow, they posit, affection for wildlife and nature will also grow. The problem is that evidence for this trickle-down theory is completely lacking. But what a boon it would be for conservation if beneficence really did percolate from prospering human communities into imperiled biological communities. What a godsend for creation, if higher standards of living really did increase people's affection for wild creatures. To date, however, the proponents of this sanguine theory have failed to produce any credible evidence for the notion that economic development and affluence are ethically and behaviorally transformative. In fact, the evidence points in the opposite direction, in part because affluence is correlated with per capita ecological footprint.[19]

There are other nettlesome issues:

▶ Which life-forms will lose and which will win if the economic growth agenda replaces long-term protection in secure protected areas? Will there be a movement to start ranching in national parks? Will the creation of designated wilderness areas be terminated?

▶ Will funds be skimmed from the dwindling budgets of conservation NGOs and government wildlife agencies in order to acquire monies to support the TNC-birthed, development-based "new conservation"?

▶ Is conservation destined to become a zero-sum game, pitting the greed and prosperity of the dominant species against the millions of other life-forms? Many conservationists believe that this has already happened.

▶ Is it ethical to convert the shrinking remnants of wild nature into playgrounds and gardens beautified with nonnative species, following the prescription of writer Emma Marris?[20]

▶ Will an engineered, garden planet designed to benefit rural and urban communities admit inconvenient, bellicose beasts like lions, elephants, bears, jaguars, wolves, crocodiles, and sharks—the keystone species that maintain much of the wild's biodiversity?[21]

Among the least credible assumptions of the "gardeners" are, first, that the benefits of economic development will trickle down and protect biodiversity; second, that children growing up in a garden world will be as adventurous as their forebears; and third, that a leap in humanity's love for the more-than-human world will occur once per capita consumption passes the threshold of "enough stuff." Personally, I doubt that people will be impressed by a faith-based, trickle-down, data-free economic growth theory of "conservation." Nor will mainstream, working conservationists ever believe that the extinction crisis could be halted by an increase in per capita consumption.

Most shocking is the new environmentalists' dismissal of current ecological science. The best current research solidly supports the connection between species diversity and the stability of ecosystems. It has firmly established that species richness and genetic diversity enhance the plant growth, productivity, and stability of terrestrial and marine ecosystems, resistance to invasion by weedy species, and agricultural productivity. Furthermore, the research has shown that greater species and genetic diversity reduces transmission rates of disease between species.[22]

Sadly, implementation of the new environmentalism would inevitably exclude the very creatures whose behaviors stabilize and regulate ecological processes and enhance ecological resistance to disturbance, including climate change.[23] Conservationists and citizens alike, therefore, ought to be incensed by a preposterous scheme that replaces wild places and national parks with pretty gardens animated with well-behaved, convenient animals. Those who promote a Disney World should just move there.

Conclusions

Progress in all three compassion movements over the last century is undeniable. People today are heir to a world with less violence and injustice than in any past era.[24] Thanks to generations of animal-welfare promoters, kept creatures—at least in some parts of the globe—suffer less abuse than in the past. And thanks to generations of committed conservationists, hundreds of thousands of species have been saved from extinction in secure protected areas, notwithstanding that such projects subsist on about 0.5 percent of charitable giving.[25]

In the meantime, the global speedup has accelerated the frenzied rush for energy and raw materials and is devouring the last remnants of the wild, largely to serve the expanding, affluent, consumer classes in industrialized and developing nations alike. At current rates of deforestation, dam construction, extraction of fossil fuels, land clearing, and water withdrawals, many expect that the two major refugia for biological diversity on the globe—the wet, tropical forests of the Amazon and Congo Basin—will be gone by the end of this century.[26]

Thus, the situation for millions of species is worse than dire. So a pro-life person must ask if the sacrifice of so much natural productivity, beauty, and diversity is prudent, even if some human communities and stockholders might be enriched for a few years. I believe it is not. We know a few things. We know that evidence is lacking for the proposition that people are kinder to nature when they are more affluent, if only because they consume much more. We also know that the richer nations may protect local forests but at the expense of forests elsewhere where officials are more easily corrupted. Another thing we know is that climate change, probably the greatest threat to civilization, is still denied by the most powerful, wealthiest sectors in society, including some of the supporters of so-called new conservation.

Finally, we know that the notion of faith-based, trickle-down "conservation" lacks scientific rigor. The naive and unscientific new environmentalism, if implemented, would accelerate extinction and would be a disaster for civilization, hastening ecological collapse globally while pulling the trigger on thousands of beautiful kinds of plants and animals. The issue is not whether human beings care about life. They do. The central issue is whether the biggest conservation organizations should spend monies donated for nature protection in order to fund a morally suspect and scientifically naive theory of human economic development, and pursue a program of corporate partnerships that supposedly advance conservation.

Conservationists don't demand that humanitarians stop helping the poor and underprivileged, but the humanitarian, "new conservationists" suggest that nature conservation stop protecting nature for its own sake. What hope is there in the face of all this cumbrous discordance?

This essay began with a quote from Albert Schweitzer, "Man has lost the capacity to foresee and to forestall. He will end by destroying the earth." Schweitzer was one of the most compassionate thinker-activists of the twentieth century. His moral breadth and tenacity of benevolence[27] may point the way and give us solace. Schweitzer was a humanitarian, theologian, musician, philosopher, physician, medical missionary, and winner of the Nobel Peace Prize. He is still celebrated for his global compassion, including his humanitarian work in Africa, and for his dedication to animal rights. As his words testify, Schweitzer also bore witness to the devastation of nature.

There is no accounting for what makes a person become a humanitarian as opposed to becoming a naturalist or an animal welfare advocate. But I think it possible that all human beings, like Schweitzer, can learn to manifest a broad, all-of-life compassion encompassing wild things and places, kept creatures, and humanity. Schweitzer's breadth of compassion and generosity of spirit are a standard to which all life-affirming people might aspire. The obstacles are daunting, so we must be just as determined as turtle mothers who journey thousands of miles to remote beaches and just as driven as hatchling sea turtles to return to the sea.

[TWO]

AGAINST DOMESTICATION

The Fable of Managed Earth

DAVID EHRENFELD

We must judge with more reverence the infinite power of nature, and with more consciousness of our own ignorance and weakness. . . . Why do we not remember how much contradiction we sense even in our own judgment, how many things were articles of faith to us yesterday, which are fables to us today?
—MICHEL DE MONTAIGNE, *ESSAYS*, 1580

HUMAN CIVILIZATION can thrive only in a healthy natural world. For at least two centuries, environmentalists, conservationists, and ecologists—greens—have, to their everlasting credit, made this point, showing that technology, for all its genius, will not last if it stands alone, damaging the natural world and disregarding the essential place of nature in our lives. Techno-optimism is a deeply flawed worldview—not only morally and ethically but also technologically. Yet in the midst of planetary-scale destruction, technology remains seductive; even some greens now proclaim the coming of a gardened planet, in which all nature is tamed, preserved, and managed for its own good by enlightened, sophisticated humans.[1] But these "neo-greens," or "ecological modernists" as some call them, are doomed to disappointment: The gardened planet is only a virtual image; it will never happen in the real world.

We do not need to be prophets to know that we do not have the technological ability to produce and sustain a smoothly running, completely managed Earth. Of the existing technologies that are supposed to service a managed Earth, it is easy to show that many don't work well now, and they will be even more prone to failure in a future without extensive natural systems to serve as emergency backup.

From a human perspective, planetary gardening can be divided into a number of critical management areas. These include: food production; energy production; global climate control by geoengineering; accident prediction/control/repair; restoration of damaged ecosystems; assuring water supplies; regulation of human population size; and the maintenance of cooperative working relationships among nations. I will concentrate on the first four, but the others are also critically important. All of these processes must interact smoothly; positive adjustment of one set of variables should not negatively affect others.

Sustainable food production

Beginning in the 1940s, a technology that came to be known as "the Green Revolution" created enormous increases in crop production, primarily the grains—rice, wheat, corn, etc.—which comprise the bulk of our food supply. These increases were achieved by breeding dwarf plants that could respond to the application of synthetic nitrogen fertilizer by increasing their production of edible grain rather than growing longer stems and more leaves. The dramatic increase in food production brought about by the Green Revolution saved many millions of people from starvation. Yields of rice, the first crop to benefit from Green Revolution technology, increased as much as tenfold, and prices fell accordingly. Norman Borlaug, the geneticist who was the father of the Green Revolution, was awarded the Nobel Peace Prize for his achievement.

An essential feature of the new agricultural technology was the growing of grains in fertilized, irrigated monocultures—only one crop at a time in supersized fields. In these very large fields, the plants were more accessible to the machinery that applied not only the necessary chemical fertilizer but also the newly developed insecticides, herbicides, and fungicides needed to protect the vulnerable crops from the insect pests, weeds, and fungi that thrive in monocultures. The big fields also allowed more convenient use of the irrigation apparatus that provides water to wash the fertilizer into the soil, and to water the dwarf crops, whose small root systems are less able than roots of traditional varieties to extract water from dry soils.

The dramatic yield increases brought about by the Green Revolution peaked in the 1960s, 1970s, and 1980s. By the 1990s, it was becoming clear that yields, especially of wheat and rice, had started to plateau. Farmers around the world had achieved the maximum benefit that the technology had to offer. Lester R. Brown, then president of the Worldwatch Institute, wrote in 1997:

In every farming environment, where yields are increased substantially, there comes a time when the increase slows and either levels off or shows signs of doing so. . . . During the four decades from 1950 to 1990, the world's grain farmers raised the productivity of their land by an unprecedented 2.1 percent per year, but since 1990, there has been a dramatic loss of momentum in this rise.[2]

According to *Vital Signs 2006–2007*, world grain production per person peaked around 1985.[3] A growing world population (a growth propelled, ironically, by the Green Revolution) needs more food, but supply is no longer increasing proportionally.

Nevertheless, people had become accustomed to the idea that technology would solve their food problems, and technology appeared to be about to respond. Genetic engineering of food crops rose to the fore in the 1990s and in the early twenty-first century. People hoped that genetically modified (GM) crops would end world hunger.

But the great increases in crop yields that were supposed to be the result of genetic engineering have not materialized, and they seem unlikely to do so in the foreseeable future. In fact, compared with conventional crops, GM yields have often decreased, and sometimes the quality of the GM seeds is poor.[4] Yet despite this mixed performance, by the beginning of the second decade of this century, the acreage planted to GM crops in the United States, Brazil, China, and other countries had increased substantially. This increase happened for a variety of reasons, some related to transient agricultural advantages of the new crops but another significant factor being the link between economic subsidies and the political power of the multinational corporations that produce the GM seeds. By contrast, the nations of the European Union and India have largely rejected GM crops out of fear of their biological and socioeconomic side effects.

At the time of this writing, the proponents and opponents of genetic engineering are waging a fierce battle, with victories and defeats on both sides. Genetic engineering is not likely to disappear, but its claims of potentially ending world hunger have no basis in reality; GM crops are not another Green Revolution.

What went wrong after forty years of the Green Revolution, and then, more quickly, with genetic engineering?

The Green Revolution has fallen victim to a host of intractable problems. It entirely depends on cheap energy to produce the synthetic nitrogen fertilizer; to make and run the machinery that is needed on the monoculture farms; and to package and transport the crop surpluses to distant markets. By the 1970s well into the 1990s, cheap energy was starting to become a thing of the past.

The monoculture fields that were so much a part of the green revolution were also causing serious problems. The heavy equipment used on the fields was compacting and breaking down the soils, increasing erosion, and decreasing soil fertility. The chemicals used to combat the pests, weeds, and diseases that are a hallmark of monoculture were affecting the integrity of ecosystems as well as the health of humans and other species. Irrigation required large amounts of energy, and it was drawing down scarce groundwater reserves. And the shift from many small farms to a smaller number of large ones, combined with the displacement of farmworkers by machine labor, caused a mass migration of people from rural areas to cities all over the world, from Sao Paolo to Manila, creating huge urban slums.

Genetic engineering has had less time than the Green Revolution to reveal its problems, but so far they seem just as numerous and intractable. Some are specific to this technology; others are shared with the Green Revolution.

One problem specific to genetic engineering is that its exaggerated claims are based on a genetic fallacy. It is common knowledge that most genes have more than one function, often many more, and that expression of these functions can be influenced by the changing environment of the cell, of the entire organism, and of the external world. But the hype surrounding genetic engineering is grounded in the false belief that one gene does one thing—even when the gene is moved from one species to another—and that its expression remains constant over time. Sometimes this is true; frequently it is not. The public sees only the illusion of one gene, one function; the high failure rate of genetic engineering is proof that this hype cannot be trusted. For example, in March of 2012, Reuters reported that a group of plant scientists were warning that Monsanto's GM corn, which had been engineered to resist corn rootworm, was "losing its effectiveness," potentially leading to "significant production losses." Similarly, in November of 2011, the U.S. Department of Agriculture, in an extensive study of Monsanto's "drought-tolerant" corn (MON87460), concluded that "equally drought resistant varieties produced through conventional breeding techniques are readily available."[5]

Contrary to the claims of agribusiness, genetically engineered crops have caused an increase in the use of pesticides. This is hardly surprising, because the companies that develop and sell the genetically engineered seeds are the same companies that produce the agricultural chemicals. For example, seeds genetically engineered to contain a bacterial pesticide, Bt (*Bacillus thuringiensis*) toxin, a naturally occurring bacterial toxin, kill some pests, but its use results in enabling other pests, previously viewed as minor disturbances, to rush in and fill the ecological void, with unexpected consequences. In a May 2010 *Nature* article, Jane Qiu gives an example:

More than 4 million hectares of Bt [GM] cotton are now grown in China. Since the crop was approved, a team led by Kongming Wu, an entomologist at the Chinese Academy of Agricultural Sciences in Beijing, has monitored pest populations at 38 locations in northern China, covering 3 million hectares of cotton. . . . Numbers of mirid bugs, . . . previously only minor pests in northern China, have increased 12-fold since 1997, they found. . . . [and according to Kongming Wu] 'Mirids are not susceptible to the Bt toxin, so they started to thrive when the farmers used less pesticide [for the bollworms].' [The mirids also eat] green beans, cereals, vegetables and various fruits. . . . The rise of mirids has driven Chinese farmers back to pesticides.[6]

A perhaps more serious problem caused by agricultural technology—both Green Revolution and genetic engineering—is the erosion of the genetic base upon which all of agriculture depends. For more than ten thousand years, farmers have been cultivating and saving the seeds of the plants they have found most productive; most resistant to pests, diseases, droughts, and floods; and most delicious. Tens of thousands of local varieties of hardy crop plants that yield high-quality food even under adverse conditions are the heritage of these millennia of farming. The best seeds have always been saved and passed on to the next generation by the farmers who grew them, and, since the nineteenth century, they have also been produced and sold by many seed companies. However, starting with the Green Revolution, and accelerating with the rise of genetic engineering, restrictive patent laws and the growing power of the agricultural chemical companies (which now own the major seed companies) have caused the loss of thousands of preexisting crop varieties. Many corporate owners of these varieties have deliberately discontinued them in order to make way for their own, patented seeds. Restrictive laws in some countries now punish farmers who save their seeds. Loss of agricultural varieties is a worldwide phenomenon. For example, according to Dr. H. Sudarshan, in India, where in the first half of the twentieth century there were an estimated 30,000 indigenous varieties of rice, it is now predicted that soon just 50 varieties will remain, with the top ten accounting for more than three-fourths of the subcontinent's rice acreage.[7]

The spread of genetically engineered crops is causing a threat to traditional varieties and wild relatives of our crops. Corporate claims to the contrary, genetically engineered genes are escaping from the planted fields and contaminating the gene pools of traditional crops and their wild relatives. It is a paradox that the success of the Green Revolution, GM crops, and conventional agriculture largely depends on the preservation of the gene pools that are now being deliberately discarded by industrial agriculture, wiped out by herbicides, or accidentally contaminated with engineered genes. The genetic engineers are sawing off the very branch on which they sit.

Another effect of the genetic contamination is the transfer of the genes conferring the genetically engineered traits from the crops to the weeds. In another, more recent *Nature* news article, in August 2013, Jane Qiu reports that transgenes from rice crops genetically engineered to resist the herbicide glyphosate have crossed over into weedy relatives of the rice. Not only have the weeds become resistant to the weed killer, but they now have higher rates of photosynthesis, grow more shoots and flowers, and produce 48–125 percent more seeds per plant than their non-transgenic relatives. An ecologist at Shanghai's Fudan University stated that "making weedy rice more competitive could exacerbate the problems it causes for farmers around the world."[8]

Monocultures have been praised for their high yields, but even these appear to be an illusion. The physicist and agricultural scientist Vandana Shiva has exposed what she calls "the myth of productivity."[9] Traditional polyculture systems, where many different crops are grown close together on the same farms, actually produce more food per acre than do modern monocultures. A mixture of corn, cassava, and peanuts yields less corn per acre than a GM corn monoculture, but it produces two and a half times as much total *food* per acre. As Shiva points out, "The Mayan peasants in the Mexican state of Chiapas are characterized as unproductive because they produce only two tonnes of corn per acre. However, the overall food output is twenty tonnes." Shiva concludes that "industrial breeding has actually reduced food security by destroying small farms and the small farmers' capacity to produce diverse outputs of nutritious crops."

Sustainable energy production

It was cheap energy that powered the Green Revolution and the entire industrial revolution of the twentieth century. Chief among the sources of energy was oil, a concentrated energy source that was easy to extract from the ground. Coal and natural gas completed the trio of "fossil fuels," carbon-rich substances that were the end result of millions of years of decay of plants buried deep underground. Although vast, the underground reserves of fossil fuels are finite, and the easily extracted parts of these reserves have been largely depleted.

As the physicist Albert Bartlett pointed out,[10] with an increase in fuel consumption of 7 percent per year, a typical twentieth-century growth rate, the amount of a fuel consumed in ten years is equal to the grand total of oil consumed in the recorded history prior to that decade. In other words, simple arithmetic shows that if oil consumption grows at a rate of 7 percent per year between 2010 and 2020, we will have used during that same decade an amount of oil equal to all the oil consumed in all the years before 2010. Clearly, these extraction rates cannot continue, and they haven't. The economist Herbert Stein put it succinctly in what has become known as Stein's Law: "If something cannot go on forever, it will stop."

The cheap energy that helped produce industrial civilization is nearly gone, as anyone who buys gasoline knows. This author remembers once, in the midst of a "gas war" during the 1950s, buying gas at 11 cents a gallon to fill the tank of his gas guzzler; now gasoline is more than thirty times as expensive. Some of the difference is due to a drop in the value of the dollar; most is because of dwindling supplies of cheap oil. Modern technologies of prospecting for new oil reserves are very sophisticated, yet new oil discoveries peaked in the 1960s. And oil consumption continues to grow, propelled by consumer demand and industrial expansion in China and India. However, according to World Energy Outlook 2010, global oil production peaked in 2006, and it is expected to decline from 70 million barrels per day in 2006 to less than 16 million in 2035. The International Energy Agency, the U.S. Joint Forces Command, and the oil companies themselves all know that cheap oil is a thing of the past.

The loss of cheap oil (and cheap oil = cheap energy) is an incontrovertible fact, so the technophiles have turned to the idea that technology will invent oil substitutes to power our technological civilization, and they keep alive their hopes that cheap energy will continue to be available to run a managed planet. Coal-to-liquid conversion; nuclear fission or fusion; hydrogen; tar sands and oil shale; fracking for natural gas; offshore and deep-sea oil and gas drilling; and the "renewables," including solar power, wind power, and biofuels, are expected to rescue us.

But the cold facts tear this dream to pieces. True, nearly all of the celebrated energy substitutes are technically feasible and have been shown to work, but all suffer from one or more major problems. They require large-scale investment and have long lead-in periods. They frequently need expensive government subsidies. Some routinely cause serious environmental damage and have high greenhouse gas emissions. Some are subject to major accidents. Their processing may place great demands on scarce freshwater supplies and can require high energy inputs for production. They may not be capable of producing enough energy to replace what we now use. And all the new energy substitutes are guaranteed of being more expensive, often much more expensive, than conventional oil.

The University of Manitoba's Vaclav Smil, one of the world's leading energy experts, writing in the May–June 2011 issue of *American Scientist*, looked at the substitutes for conventional oil and dubbed them "the latest infatuations."[11] They reminded him of the scientist at the grand academy of Lagado, in *Gulliver's Travels*, who had spent eight years on a project for extracting sunbeams out of cucumbers. (Actually, as mentioned below, cucumbers probably could be used for biofuel, but nobody in their right mind would think that the world's energy needs could be met by cucumbers.)

Enthusiasm for the new energy sources waxes and wanes, as it does for any new fad. A few years ago the fad was hydrogen: Hydrogen-powered cars and distributed energy systems were the rage. But when people stopped to think, they realized that hydrogen is not a primary energy source (there are no hydrogen wells)—it takes money and energy to extract it from natural gas or water. Also, hydrogen is highly explosive (remember the Hindenburg disaster); is corrosive; and, in liquid form, even contains much less energy per gallon than does oil. Not surprisingly, we hear less about hydrogen cars now than we did in 2000.

Before hydrogen, nuclear fusion was going to save us. It was thought that ordinary seawater, believed to be in endless supply, could have acted as the fuel for a fusion reactor. The first patents for fusion reactors were registered in 1946. In 2012, sixty-six years and millions of research and development dollars later, I heard a lecture from a prominent fusion scientist who was equally enthusiastic about the limitless potential of fusion. When asked how long it would take to get a working reactor, she replied about thirty to forty more years.

Nuclear fission power plants have existed for decades in many countries. The oldest operating commercial nuclear power plant in the United States, New Jersey's Oyster Creek plant, has been producing power since 1969, and it is not scheduled to shut down until 2019. Until the Fukushima Daiichi disaster caused by the Tohoku earthquake and tsunami in March of 2011, many assumed (despite the earlier accidents at the Three Mile Island and Chernobyl plants) that nuclear power would ease the transition to a new, renewable energy world. Since Fukushima, fission has become an increasing cause for concern: Few new reactors are being built; Germany has announced that it will abandon nuclear power completely by 2022; and, after Fukushima, Japan closed or suspended its 50 nuclear reactors.

Moreover, as noted by Mark Bittman in *The New York Times*, on August 24, 2013:

The dangers of uranium mining, which uses vast amounts of water . . . [are] barely regulated or even studied. Thousands of uranium mines have been abandoned, and no one seems to know how many remain to be cleaned up. The cost of that cleanup . . . will be borne by taxpayers. . . . Then there's disposal of spent fuel. . . . Decades into the nuclear age there remains, incredibly, no real plan for this. . . . The economic viability of nuclear power is no more encouraging. Plants continue to close and generation rates continue to drop. . . . Subsidies for nuclear power have been more than double the expense of power generation itself.[12]

U.S. oil shales and the Canadian tar sands contain large reserves, but the environmental damage associated with the extraction of the oil is enormous; a great deal of freshwater is used in the process; the energy ratio, Energy Returned Over Energy Invested (EROEI), is terrible—only about three barrels of oil out for every two barrels put in; and the need to construct new pipelines to transport the heavy, toxic crude oil from remote production sites many miles to distant refineries generates grave political and environmental problems. Offshore oil, another heralded energy source, is extremely expensive, and it was dealt a serious blow by the *Deepwater Horizon* explosion. The *Deepwater Horizon* drilling rig cost a billion dollars to build and a half-million dollars a day to operate—while it lasted.[13]

Improvements in the efficiency of energy generation and use can save us a great deal of energy. These improvements are both desirable and possible. Again, however, they are unlikely to meet the energy needs of a highly managed planet. Modern agriculture has a much lower energy efficiency than that of traditional farming systems, which take advantage of the free energy subsidies offered by nature. And even when efficiencies materialize, there is the Jevons Paradox, first described by the English economist W. Stanley Jevons in 1866: Increased efficiency of energy production leads to increased consumption. Using the coal industry as his model, Jevons showed that improvements in efficiency led to lower cost of the product, which in turn caused a rebound increase in consumption of the coal. This paradox applies to other sources of energy besides coal.

Renewable energy. Let us take a closer look at renewable energy—solar, wind, and biofuels, the great hope of the neo-greens. According to Smil, the renaissance of renewable energy "has led to exaggerated expectations rather than to realistic appraisals." In 2011, he wrote:

Promoters of new renewable energy conversions that now appear to have the best prospects to make significant near-term contributions—modern biofuels (ethanol and biodiesel) and wind and solar electricity generation—do not give sufficient weight to important physical realities concerning the global shift away from fossil fuels: to the scale of the required transformation, to its likely duration, to the unit capacities of new converters, and to enormous infrastructural requirements resulting from the inherently low power densities with which we can harvest renewal energy flows and to their [irregularity].[14]

Solar power. In his well-researched book *Green Illusions*, environmentalist Ozzie Zehner states:

If actual installed costs for solar projects in California are any guide, a global solar program [to replace fossil fuels in powering the planet] would cost

roughly $1.4 quadrillion, about one hundred times the United States GDP.
Mining, smelting, processing, shipping, and fabricating the [solar] panels and
their associated hardware would yield about 149,000 megatons of CO_2. And
everyone would have to move to the desert, otherwise transmission losses
would make the plan unworkable.[15]

Future costs of solar panels may come down with technological in-
novations (costs may already have started to plateau), but as Zehner notes:

Cheaper photovoltaics won't offset escalating expenditures for insurance, war-
ranty expenses, materials, transportation, labor, and other requirements. Low-
tech costs are claiming a larger share of the high-tech solar system price tag.[16]

Passive solar power, which involves energy savings in heating and
cooling achieved by sophisticated architectural design and construction,
has been proving its worth for millennia, as the natives of New Mexico
demonstrated in the tenth century with their incredibly energy efficient
housing complex, which we call Pueblo Bonito. These energy efficiencies
were built into Pueblo Bonito from the start of construction. Modern passive solar houses constructed today can be equally energy efficient and
are a joy to live in. But many, perhaps most, existing homes have a limited
potential for passive solar improvement.

Solar power has an important role to play among the energy sources
of the future, but it does not seem to be about to replace cheap oil in maintaining our present industrial civilization.

Wind power. Wind power, like solar, is receiving a great deal of enthusiastic praise, some of it justified. I am among those who find the sight of a
row of giant, stately wind turbines with their slowly moving blades thrilling and beautiful, but, admittedly, I don't live near them. Denmark is the
pioneer in wind energy: In 2012, Denmark got 25–30 percent of its power
from the wind, and now the country hopes to raise this figure to 50 percent or more. Denmark also produces half of the world's wind turbines.
Like solar power, wind has a great deal to offer an energy-challenged future. Wind power is not, however, all smooth sailing.

In *The New York Times* on August 15, 2013, Diane Cardwell chronicled the problems experienced by Green Mountain Power, whose wind
turbines line the ridge of Lowell Mountain in Vermont.[17] These problems

are typical of those experienced by the wind power industry. Some of the difficulties include "curtailments," mandated cutbacks in energy production when the grid will not accept the wind power energy, either because the electric company can get energy cheaper elsewhere or for technical reasons involving the interface between fossil fuel generated electricity and wind power. Other difficulties involve the size of the lines carrying the power. When curtailments occur, the wind turbines must operate at a fraction of their potential output. In her article entitled "Intermittent Nature of Green Power Is Challenge for Utilities," Cardwell writes:

Because energy produced by wind . . . is intermittent, its generating capacity is harder to predict than conventional power's. And a lack of widely available, cost-effective ways to store electricity generated by wind only compounds the complex current marketplace. . . . [One wind power CEO noted that] at full operating capacity he can lose $1,000 an hour if the electricity is not sold. "We have a grid system that's not smart . . . it's a 100-year-old system—and they run it like fossils and nukes are the only things that matter and the rest of us, they can fiddle with," he said.[18]

Integrating wind power into an electrical system that receives inputs from fossil fuel and nuclear plants plus, increasingly, solar installations involves daunting economic and technical challenges. Some of these will be fairly straightforward to resolve over time; others, like the difficulty or impossibility of storing excess wind power when the grid cannot accept it, are much harder to fix.

Among the other problems that are an inseparable part of wind power are the fact that wind turbines kill bats and migrating birds, that wind power installations on the roofs of city buildings are noisy and hard to maintain, that turbine installations on ridgetops damage and fragment some of the last undisturbed wildlife habitats, and that many people complain that the huge turbines spoil their view of the countryside or of their neighboring coastal waters.

Bat and bird kills by turbines are easy to document. Numerous counts have been published of dead bats and birds collected under turbines; but there is as yet no evidence that any populations are threatened by wind power, and some radar studies have shown birds flying well above the turbines during migration. Urban wind power production on the tops of tall buildings has been promoted by neo-greens as a renewable source of energy in cities, but noise and maintenance issues are likely to limit the potential of urban wind energy for the foreseeable future. Even outside of cities, some people living in rural areas near wind turbines complain of health problems such as insomnia, anxiety, palpitations, and nausea, allegedly related to the low frequency noise. The existence of this "Wind Turbine Syndrome" is still debated.[19] As for the question of unsightliness of the windmills, there is no right answer; some love them, some don't.

Biofuels. Biofuels are another mixed blessing as a replacement for vanishing cheap fossil fuel energy. The idea of biofuels is straightforward: Use plants to capture the energy of sunlight (like the Lagado cucumbers), and get some of that energy back by extracting energy-rich substances from the plants (sugars and other hydrocarbons) that can be either turned into fuel, such as ethanol, by chemical processing or used directly as a diesel fuel substitute. Corn, sugarcane, soy, rapeseed, palm and other tree oils, grasses, algae, and the desert plant called *Jatropha* are some of the plants used for biofuel.

Like solar and wind power, biofuels have a dark side. Some of the plants grown for biofuel, especially the grasses, can escape from cultivation and become invasive species, particularly harmful in agricultural fields.

The EROEI of biofuels is troubling. Corn ethanol from the American Midwest has an EROEI ratio of about 1.0 or even lower, meaning that if we total the energy costs of growing the corn, harvesting it, and then processing it, we find that the amount of energy we get back is only equal to or less than the energy we put in, clearly a losing proposition. Meanwhile, we have wasted land that could have been used for growing food and have also driven up the price of corn. The EROEI of other biofuels can be better than that of corn ethanol, but not always enough to offset the other difficulties of the technology.

If the results for corn ethanol are so poor, why does the Midwest in the United States continue to produce so much of it? The answer is political: Midwestern states receive huge federal subsidies for growing corn and producing ethanol, and few politicians are willing to tell the truth about corn ethanol and risk the wrath of midwestern voters.

The land used to grow biofuel plants is unavailable for growing food in a hungry world. True, plants like *Jatropha* grow well in dry, nutrient-depleted soils that are not suited for crops. But the conceivable supply of *Jatropha*-derived biofuel could run only a tiny fraction of the world's vehicles.

Timothy Beardsley summed up the problems with biofuels in an editorial titled "Biofuels Reassessed," in the October 2012 issue of *BioScience*:

It takes a lot of land, a lot of water, and a lot of energy to produce biofuel crops and convert them into usable fuels. The displacement of food crops by biofuels has already increased food prices, and many have argued that such effects will put limits on the biofuel enterprise. . . . The enthusiasts are right that improvements [in biofuel technology] are possible . . . and the seriousness of the looming energy crisis—only partly ameliorated, at substantial environmental cost, by fracking—argues for the continuation of such efforts. Still . . . it is important to understand biofuel's limitations.[20]

Beardsley cites scientific studies showing that the amount of biofuel that globally could be produced is four times lower than previously published estimates:

All these numbers exclude losses due to manufacturing the fuel. . . . Actual current global primary productivity suggests strongly that biofuels have less promise than many had thought. . . . Some new biofuels may yet alleviate the human predicament, but nobody should be under any illusions about the constraints that nature—ultimately through the laws of thermodynamics—has put in the way.[21]

In concluding this section on renewable energy, we should heed the words of Vaclav Smil: "None of us can foresee the eventual contours of new energy arrangements—but could the world's richest countries go wrong by striving for moderation of their energy use?"[22] In other words, the best thing we can do to sustainably run the Earth and our own civilization is to depend less on technologies of control and more on regulation of our own self-destructive consumption.

Geoengineering to control climate change

To begin, climate change is a reality. In 1981, NASA physicist James Hansen calculated the extent of global warming he expected in the near future, based on man-made CO_2 emissions. Three decades later, these calculations have proven exceptionally accurate.[23] Temperatures have risen to meet or exceed Hansen's predicted levels; polar ice is melting; and drought-prone areas are receiving less rainfall. In recent years, other consequences of climate change—more frequent and more violent storms, and rising sea levels—have forced themselves on our attention. In a May 9, 2012, article in *The New York Times*, Hansen writes that if we were to continue to burn conventional fossil fuels and to exploit Canada's tar sands:

Concentrations of carbon dioxide in the atmosphere eventually would reach levels higher than in the Pliocene era, more than 2.5 million years ago, when sea level was at least 50 feet higher than it is now. . . . Disintegration of ice sheets would accelerate out of control. Sea levels would rise and destroy coastal cities. Global temperatures would become intolerable. Twenty to 50 percent of the planet's species would be driven to extinction. Civilization would be at risk. That is the long-term outlook. But near-term, things will be bad enough. Over the next several decades, the Western United States and the semi-arid region from North Dakota to Texas will develop semi-permanent drought, with rain, when it does come, occurring in extreme events with heavy flooding. Economic losses would be incalculable. More and more of the Midwest would be a dust bowl. California's Central Valley could no longer be irrigated. Food prices would rise to unprecedented levels.[24]

Other parts of the world, including its most populous nations, China and India, are already experiencing the effects of climate change. In China, the Gobi Desert is expanding, moving toward the Yellow River, and is within 100 miles of Beijing. Growth of the Gobi is the result of not only climate change but also careless use of groundwater and indiscriminate logging in the past. Groundwater use and logging can be and are being controlled to some extent by the government, and millions of trees are being planted at the edge of the desert to halt its advance, but global warming is a continuing presence. In India, now the world's sixth-largest emitter of greenhouse gases (carbon dioxide, methane, and nitrous oxide), disastrous floods have been attributed to climate change; melting of the Hindu Kush ice mass is accelerating; and sea-level rise is forcing saltwater into coastal aquifers, contaminating drinking water.

The solution to the problem of climate change is obvious: We must immediately halt the expansion of greenhouse-gas release and quickly start to reduce it below present levels. A number of well-publicized, high-level meetings of governments have confronted this issue, with some positive results. But international environmental agreements are subject to compromise and delay; meanwhile, greenhouse gas levels continue to rise.

Impatient with the political process, some scientists have decided that geoengineering offers the best hope of managing our planet. Geoengineering solutions fall into three categories: dimming the sunlight reaching Earth; using plant photosynthesis to take up and reduce the carbon dioxide already in the atmosphere; and capturing carbon dioxide, turning it into charcoal, and burying it in the Earth.

There are various proposed ways to reduce the sunlight reaching the Earth. One solution, inspired by the observed effects of volcanic eruptions, would be to spray solar-reflective sulfates into the stratosphere, perhaps from a giant balloon. Other schemes include using rockets to send tiny reflectors into space, growing lighter-colored crops genetically engineered to reflect sunlight, painting all roofs white, and covering the Earth's deserts with reflective Mylar.

Some of these ideas, like desert Mylar and lighter-colored crops, are too preposterous to deserve comment. After careful evaluation, most of the schemes, like painting roofs white, would not have enough effect to make a significant difference in global warming. Injecting 5 million tons of sulfates per year into the stratosphere (like other sunshade schemes) could make a difference, especially in the tropics, but could also disrupt monsoons, bringing famine to millions, and, according to Oxford's Tim Palmer,[25] "You might turn the Amazon to desert." Sending enough tiny reflectors into space could require an estimated 20 million rocket launches. And if there were bad side effects, how would we get our little reflectors back?

Using plants to pull carbon dioxide out of the atmosphere through photosynthesis has no obvious adverse side effects, and it does have the added benefit of putting oxygen back in place of the carbon dioxide removed. Planting forests of relatively fast-growing trees can tie up a good deal of carbon dioxide. Reforestation is generally a good idea, not just because of carbon sequestration but because of beneficial effects on local climate, water storage, and stream flow.

Reforestation, however, is slow, varies greatly from country to country, and can present ecological and social challenges. Reforestation can be a win-win procedure to slow climate change. But planet managers are an impatient lot—reforestation is too slow for many of them.

Algae in the world's oceans remove a great deal of carbon dioxide by photosynthesis, and some climate engineers might ask, Why not fertilize the oceans, increase the algal numbers, and pull out more carbon dioxide?

This would slow climate change, benefit marine food webs that are based on algae, and even, in closed systems, provide algal biomass to be used as animal food or for biofuels. That's the theory, and it works to some extent. Dumping iron fertilizer in the ocean does stimulate algal growth; the algae do remove carbon dioxide; and, when they die, some of them take the carbon out of harm's way by sinking to the bottom of the ocean.

Unfortunately, ocean fertilization with iron can also stimulate toxic algal blooms and cause production of the greenhouse gas nitrous oxide. And when the algae die, as they do in vast numbers during blooms, the decomposition of algal bodies that stay at the surface pulls oxygen from the water while putting carbon dioxide back in the atmosphere. In closed, artificial systems, unlike ocean fertilization, the main difficulties are the costs of building, maintaining, and aerating the containers for the algae and the problem of scale—these systems will have limited impact on global climate change and biofuel energy production.

Carbon capture and storage is a geoengineering method that can reduce climate-changing carbon dioxide. The carbon dioxide is captured and removed at point sources, usually the smokestacks of large fossil fuel power plants, and then moved to sites where it can be deposited underground. This is a good idea, but one whose impact is limited because there are so many non-point sources of greenhouse gases. The principal risk of carbon capture and storage is leakage of the gas back into the atmosphere from its underground burial sites (declining oil fields, saline aquifers, un-mineable coal seams, and other suitable geological formations). Deep-well injection of unwanted substances has caused earthquakes. Needless to say, carbon capture and storage is a great deal more expensive than simply letting the gas escape into the atmosphere, and it may require government-sponsored incentives and subsidies.

Geoengineering has a great appeal to those looking for quick and simple solutions to overwhelming, complex problems. Such searches tend to promote tunnel vision, in which the gaze is always on simple models and their associated technical solutions, not on the many, sometimes serious, unpredictable, and unmanageable side effects produced by geoengineering technologies. Vaclav Havel, author and first president of the Czech Republic, wrote in *The New York Times* on September 27, 2007:

I'm skeptical that a problem as complex as climate change can be solved by any single branch of science. Technological measures and regulations are important, but equally important is support for education, ecological training and ethics—

a consciousness of the commonality of all living beings and an emphasis on shared responsibility.[26]

Accident prediction, control, and repair

Our global management systems rest on a precarious edifice of predictions. These include predictions about the sustainability of industrial agriculture; the safety of nuclear power plants; the stability of the global political structure; the efficacy of our ecological restorations; the future of globalization—especially global trade; the continuation of economic growth; and, above all, the ability of our technology to solve any problems we face, now or in years to come.

These predictions are often unwarranted and very dangerous. One would think that the first priority of the planet managers would be to look at their past predictions and assumptions and see how well they have worked out. But this might involve admitting failure and, more important, shutting off sources of revenue for the failed projects. Consequently, risk assessments made at the start of projects are frequently "cooked," unwarranted justifications for enterprises scheduled to go ahead no matter what.

In their book *Useless Arithmetic: Why Environmental Scientists Can't Predict the Future,*[27] geologists Orrin Pilkey and Linda Pilkey-Jarvis show how a model of future beach erosion and coastal sand movements has been used to justify escape from reality and allow construction of questionable shoreline structures and buildings. The standard model used in beach engineering is the Bruun Rule, which describes how shorelines retreat in response to rising sea levels. This simple model to describe a complex process has some general validity, but, as the authors note:

The Bruun Rule resides in a world dominated by engineers rather than scientists. It is a world where it is not possible to admit defeat and walk away or to respond flexibly, one where an answer must be found . . . and where the answer, to be credible, is best found by the most sophisticated means possible. . . . Evidence continues to accumulate from all over the world that the basic assumptions behind the Bruun model are very wrong. Yet it continues to be widely applied by coastal scientists, who should know better, and blindly applied by social scientists, planners, and international agencies concerned with how future global trends will affect coastal cities.[28]

When the Bruun Rule is used to predict the rate of erosion of a particular shoreline, one has to know only the rate of sea-level rise and the slope of the shoreface on that particular beach. Two variables; it's easy. But as Pilkey and Pilkey-Jarvis show, there are at least 31 variables that matter, including beach subsurface geology, sand grain size, coastal sediment supply, beach nourishment projects, storm types and frequency, shoreline vegetation, upland bluffs and dunes, dam construction and removal in neighboring rivers, and history of dredging.

Even if you know how each of the factors works and interacts with other factors, including sea-level rise, in causing shorelines to retreat, you still can't predict the future because you don't know the order in which the factors will occur. . . . On different shorelines the various parameters will be of varying importance, over varying time frames. This is ordering complexity. This is why shoreline retreat related to sea-level rise cannot ever be accurately predicted.[29]

Ordering complexity can make some management predictions absurd. Pilkey and Pilkey-Jarvis give, as the ultimate preposterous example, the Department of Energy's Total System Performance Assessment (TSPA) for the proposed nuclear waste repository at Yucca Mountain, Nevada. The assessment of the chances of radioactive leaks from the underground repository, based on hundreds of models, is that it will be safe for more than a hundred thousand years. Yet, as the authors show, there are at least 15 important factors that will affect the seriousness of future leaks. None of these factors were known when the TSPA was formulated, and many will never be known.

In 2009, the Environmental Protection Agency issued a rule requiring that the Department of Energy (DOE) strictly limit the amount of radiation from the facility to no more than 15 millirems per year for the first ten thousand years after the facility's closure, and requiring the DOE to show that the nuclear waste repository will resist earthquakes, volcanic activity, climate change, and container leakage for 1 million years. The risk assessment charade came largely to a halt when work on Yucca Mountain was ended by Congress in 2011, for political reasons. It remains to be seen whether it will be started again.

Ordering complexity is only one kind of complexity that makes the long-term predictions and assumptions used in planet management unreliable. The other is structural complexity. The pioneer in studying the hazards of structural complexity is Charles Perrow, Professor Emeritus of Sociology at Yale. Using the well-studied 1979 accident at the Three Mile Island nuclear plant as his model, Perrow showed how the sheer complexity of the nuclear plant made accidents inevitable and unpredictable—"normal."

The operating system of a nuclear power plant has a large number of separate subsystems, many of which interact in ways that cannot be directly observed, and in ways that might not be understood even if they were observed. Moreover, the operating systems interact with safety systems, which are themselves complex and often cannot be directly observed.

In his book *Normal Accidents: Living With High-Risk Technologies*, Perrow describes how the accident at Three Mile Island was caused by failure of a pressure-relief valve, which resulted in radioactive water boiling out and onto the floor of the reactor building.[30] This could have been determined only indirectly by the control room operators from a variety of gauge readings; while three audible alarms were sounding and simultaneously many of the 1600 lights on the control panels were flashing. Only 13 seconds elapsed between the time of the valve's failure and the time when the accident became irrevocable. The scene in the control room was chaos.

Several hours after the start of the accident, control room personnel and supervisors were still arguing about what was happening. The valve stayed open for two hours and twenty minutes until a new shift came on and somebody thought to check it. But the accident was just getting started. Two reactor coolant pumps did not work (possibly because of steam bubbles in the lines), and levels of coolant began to drop alarmingly, the most feared happening in a nuclear plant. The two dials indicating reactor pressure gave diametrically opposite readings.

Then, thirty-three hours into the accident, an ominous bang was heard in the control room. It was a hydrogen explosion inside the reactor building. No one had expected this. Frantic discussions occurred between the plant operators and the commissioners of the Nuclear Regulatory Commission. The emergency pumps, like all electric motors, can produce sparks; when hydrogen accumulates, a spark can cause an explosion that could destroy the reactor building. Should the pumps be turned off or kept running? Opinions varied. That an explosion did not happen was in good measure a matter of luck.

Because of the vast complexities of nuclear plants, paradoxically including their safety systems, the operators did not actually know what was happening while the accident was going on. But they had to do something. In this sort of situation, Perrow notes, you form a mental model of events.

You imagine what is happening, based on the inadequate and partially erroneous information that you have. "You are actually creating a world that is congruent with your interpretations, even though it may be the wrong world. It may be too late before you find that out."[31]

In other words, the complex systems that we invent to manage and run our world cannot be made fail-safe. And if we add economic and ecological interactions, our constructed systems become still more complicated and accident-prone.

Here is an example: On April 20, 2010, the *Deepwater Horizon* oil drilling rig in the Gulf of Mexico suddenly exploded in flames. As chronicled by Joseph Tainter and Tadeusz Patzek, in their book *Drilling Down: The Gulf Oil Debacle and Our Energy Dilemma*:

Everything seemed to be under control, with the computers in charge and their sensors humming. The people assigned to watch these computers, and act on their advice, were content and getting ready to go to sleep. . . . Suddenly all hell broke loose, and it became clear that the people watching the computer screens did not understand what the computers were telling them. It took just a few seconds for their false sense of security to go up in the same flames that consumed the Deepwater Horizon *in two days.*[32]

When the flames were extinguished, the accident was far from over. Several months later, the well was finally capped. By then, an estimated 210 million gallons of oil had leaked into the gulf. Various attempts were made to contain the oil or mitigate its effects. State of the art technologies were used. But several years later, we still do not know the long-term effects of this accident on the thousands of species living in the immensely complicated gulf ecosystem, or on the human communities of the adjacent land areas.

Tainter, a professor in the Department of Environment and Society at Utah State University, and Patzek, Chairman of the Department of Petroleum and Geosystems Engineering at the University of Texas, analyze in detail the causes of the accident. At the end of their book, they conclude:

The Deepwater Horizon *was a normal accident, a system accident. Complex technologies have . . . ways of failing that humans cannot foresee. The probability of similar accidents may now be reduced, but it can be reduced to zero only when declining [energy returns] makes deep-sea production energetically unprofitable. It is fashionable to think that we will be able to produce renewable energies with gentler technologies, with simpler machines that produce less damage to the earth, the atmosphere, and people. We all hope so, but we must approach such technologies with a dose of realism and a long-term perspective.*[33]

Three Mile Island and *Deepwater Horizon* teach us a simple lesson: We cannot predict all the accidents that will occur in our managed world; and even if we could predict them, we could not prevent many of them from happening. Disasters in our complex systems are bound to take place, and the techno-utopians' models offer no credible ways of fixing them.

Other global management concerns

Successful global management requires addressing issues of necessity besides the concerns listed above. To describe them briefly, they include:

Ecological restoration and preservation: In some cases, restoration of damaged ecosystems is possible if done with care and ecological knowledge; in others, it can be difficult or impossible. Restorations are often confounded by ignorance of the component species and complexity of the specific ecosystem; by prior species extinctions; by major soil or water changes; and by lack of sufficient funds to do the restoration properly or to monitor it after the restoration is complete.

Preservation can be as hard as restoration. Moving species endangered by climate change to more favorable climate zones ("assisted colonization"), and attempts to reintroduce recovering populations of endangered species to their original habitat are challenged by the limitations of our ecological knowledge. This is not a reason to abandon restoration and preservation efforts, but it should make us think twice before we boast about how green the coming garden planet will be.

Maintenance of adequate supplies of clean freshwater will be essential for sustainable global management; it is not happening now, and there are no affordable technologies on the horizon that will assure water for everyone, especially in the face of climate change. Already, international fights over water management complicate tense politics in the Middle East, South Asia, and parts of Africa. Water will undoubtedly be one of the greatest obstacles to a managed planet.

Growing populations require more space, more food, more water, more mineral resources, and more energy than stable ones; and they produce more waste. The Earth's population is growing: Estimates published by the United Nations (UN) in June of 2013 suggest an increase from today's 7.2 billion to 9.6 billion by 2050.[34] Population growth models are no more reliable than any long-term predictions involving thousands of variables (climate and sea level, disease, ethnic conflicts and warfare, economic changes, etc.), and this sort of unreliability will greatly increase the difficulty of managing a gardened Earth. A point to consider is that per capita consumption is increasing more than twice as fast as population in many places around the world.

A managed world assumes *good working coordination between nations.* The Convention on International Trade in Endangered Species of Wild Fauna and Flora (CITES) shows that this is occasionally possible.[35] By 2013, 178 nations had ratified the convention, which protects—at least on paper— thousands of endangered animal and plant species from over-exploitation. With exceptions, this protection has been moderately successful. A great weakness of the treaty, however, is that reservations (exceptions) can be taken by member countries for specific species. Iceland, Japan, and Norway have taken reservations that allow them to hunt some baleen whale species, and Saudi Arabia has taken falcons as an exception. CITES is an encouraging model; nevertheless, the proliferation of regional military conflicts, terrorism, religious and ethnic strife, exhaustion of resources, and political instability do not bode well for cooperative management of the planet.

I have considered the various threats to the neo-green vision individually, but of course they interact, usually making the situation worse. For example, scarcity of cheap energy affects modern food production and water availability, while causing us to rely on increasingly dangerous energy technologies, which are prone to accidents that we are unable to predict. Similarly, climate change has a major impact on food, water, international relations, and energy use.

IN CONCLUSION, the paragraphs above give only an incomplete sampling of the reasons why many of the dreams of the planet-managing neo-greens and ecological modernists are likely to turn into nightmares. In his chilling short story "The Machine Stops," written more than a century ago, E. M. Forster described the chaos and total collapse that descended on a managed world when the "Mending Apparatus," which had always repaired everything that was broken, itself began to fail: "Man, the flower of all flesh, the noblest of all creatures visible, man who had once made god in his image . . . was dying, strangled in the garments that he had woven."[36]

The dream-to-nightmare scenarios outlined here do not have to become reality. We *can* keep trying to make the world a better place, using any safe technology that is proven or seems promising. For instance, we already know that traditional polycultures can reliably produce far larger amounts of food than can industrial monocultures year after year, with less input of chemical fertilizers and pesticides. The field is wide open to apply careful, modern scientific research to improve this performance still further. And in the case of our energy deficit, reduction of consumption is safer, easier, faster, and more effective than deep-sea oil drilling or nuclear power.

Wendell Berry wrote in *The Unsettling of America* that "what has drawn the Modern World into being is a strange, almost occult yearning for the future. The modern mind longs for the future as the medieval mind longed for Heaven."[37] This yearning, embodied in the blind worship of technology, has led us astray—if we open our eyes and look at who and where we are, we have our best chance of finding out where to go next. I end with a quote from my book *The Arrogance of Humanism*, published in 1981, with words that I believe are as applicable now as the day they were written:

Not all problems have acceptable solutions. . . . There is . . . no need to feel defeated by the knowledge that there are limits to human power and control. . . . [We should start] with the honest admission of human fallibility and limitations, and from this realistic base [rise to the] challenge to construct a good life for oneself, one's family, and one's community. . . . We simply start with realism and then free the human spirit for high adventure, struggle, and an unknown fate.[38]

Conservation in the Anthropocene

TIM CARO, JACK DARWIN, TAVIS FORRESTER,
CYNTHIA LEDOUX-BLOOM, AND CAITLIN WELLS

IT HAS BECOME COMMONPLACE to remark that humans are now the dominant environmental force on the Earth. The indications are strong and diverse. They range from paleontologists reaching a consensus that humans contributed to megafaunal extinctions on at least two continents, North America and Australia;[1] recognition that formerly intact marine ecosystems have changed enormously;[2] suggestions that climate has changed sufficiently that no ecosystem is immune from alterations in species composition;[3] remarks that pollution is widespread even in Antarctica;[4] and arguments that human predation on mammals is pernicious and the principal driver of changes in phenotypic traits of exploited species in many areas.[5] Some scientists use geographic data to show that human activities affect almost every terrestrial system (e.g., the human footprint[6]). Indeed, the current epoch is now being referred to as "the Anthropocene,"[7] which has led geologists to formally debate stratigraphic evidence for this new phenomenon and to argue over not if but when it began.[8] With the catchword *Anthropocene* in ascendancy, one might easily come away with the impression that nowhere on Earth is natural, in one of the word's specific meanings of ecosystems being untouched by humans,[9] and indeed it is common to hear the phrase "humans have altered everything."

Although we agree that humans are a dominant species and have affected natural systems at a global scale, we suggest that humans may have less influence at smaller extents of specific regions and even ecosystems. We fear that the concept of pervasive human-caused change may cultivate hopelessness in those dedicated to conservation and may even be an impetus for accelerated changes in land use motivated by profit.

Airborne and waterborne chemicals, lowered water pH, rising temperatures, increasing rates of extinctions, habitat fragmentation and loss, nonnative invasive species, and new diseases have not yet altered key aspects of every ecosystem. There are still ecosystems that are sufficiently intact to retain key ecological functions and species (see Table), and it is vital to identify and protect them now. We define intact ecosystems as those in which the majority of native species are still present in abundances at which they play the same functional roles as they did before extensive human settlement or use, where pollution has not affected nutrient flows to any great degree, and where human density is low. This definition is similar to Russell Mittermeier et al.'s definition of wilderness areas,[10] but it does not specify the size of the area. Ecosystems where human influence is relatively mild in terms of exploitation, pollution, and climate change include newly discovered ecosystems;[11] large, relatively intact areas with low human densities;[12] newly discovered areas of high species diversity or places with no recent history of human activity;[13] areas with very low human population densities at both large and small extents;[14] and places of still extraordinarily high species diversity.[15]

We recognize that humans have had at least marginal influence on most if not all of the world's biomes, but there are several reasons to doubt that "humans have altered everything" (a phrase that is generously interpreted as including nutrient flows and species composition and interactions). First, the human footprint—a compilation of human population density; land-cover and land-use change; human accessibility via roads, rivers, or coastlines; and electrical power infrastructure[16]—shows large gaps at equatorial (central Africa), subtropical (central Australia, Sahara), temperate (Himalayas), and Palearctic (Russia and Canada) latitudes. Second, increases in global temperature, touted as now affecting everything from patterns of migration, plant phenology, and laying dates of birds to species' range expansions,[17] have occurred principally in northern and southern latitudes and at high elevations. It is acknowledged that temperature increases, at least, will be smallest in the lowland tropics, where most of the world's species occur. Third, species diversity, apex predators, intact food webs, functioning ecosystems, and nutrient cycles may be little af-

EXAMPLES OF RELATIVELY INTACT ECOSYSTEMS

Type of ecosystem	Location
Unexploited by humans	Lake Vostok and other lakes under Antarctic ice sheets Southern Ocean deep sea

Wilderness areas	*North America*
	  Rocky Mountains
	  Alaskan Pacific northwest temperate rainforest
	  Southwestern deserts
	South America
	  Amazonia
	  Chaco
	  Patagonia
	  Pantanal
	Africa
	  Congo Forest
	  Miombo-Mopane woodland
	Asia
	  central Asian deserts
	  boreal forest

Ecoregions with virtually no human presence	Central Greenland Antarctica high-elevation Himalayas central Sahara
Smaller sites little influenced by human activity	waters around the Line Islands in western Pacific Foja Mountains, Papua Ndoki-Likouala, central Africa
Sites of extraordinary species richness	Rupununi, Guyana Province Nord, New Caledonia Monte Alen region, Equatorial Guinea Cameroon Mountains Congo, edaphic grasslands

fected by humans in areas inhabited by people living at low densities.[18]

We believe that there are four reasons to acknowledge that some areas of the globe are still intact. First, if nothing is believed to be intact, it allows humans to think that species invasions are inevitable and not problematic and may open the floodgates to human manipulation of species assemblages. For example, if species composition in northern temperate ecosystems now is a mélange of species formerly found at lower latitudes, then it may be fair to argue that it is better to construct new ecosystems through assisted migration in order to conserve species as climate changes,[19] or to initiate Pleistocene rewilding programs to reconstruct former functioning ecosystems or reinstate past evolutionary drivers.[20] Although the ideas of assisted migration and Pleistocene rewilding are debated,[21] they seem more acceptable if one believes that everything has already been anthropogenically altered.

Second, planning and setting goals for conservation action usually require relatively intact areas that serve as baselines for comparisons and to set targets.[22] Without spatial comparisons it is difficult to understand how ecosystems have changed or to frame management goals. If there are no contemporary intact benchmarks for comparative purposes, one must rely on incomplete data and memories of past ecosystems, which are known to change over time (i.e., shifting baseline syndrome[23]). Although restoring poorly functioning ecosystems is a conservation goal, protecting nearly intact ecosystems also is a fundamental conservation priority.

Third, if no ecosystem is intact, governments can more easily argue, and societies concur, that land use ranging from subsistence farming to extensive resource extraction is acceptable because the environment has already been degraded. Dam building in major rivers, oil exploration in western Amazonia or the Arctic National Wildlife Refuge, and construction of housing developments become more tolerable in an irrevocably modified world. Especially worrying to us is the ongoing change in conservation agenda from identifying and protecting sites of high conservation priority to conserving "working landscapes" with extensive human influence.

Fourth, if the idea that Earth is already spoiled further permeates the general mindset, monetary contributions to and efforts for conservation may seem futile to the general public, whose support is vital to conservation. Already a doom-and-gloom discipline, conservation science may want to obviate this pessimism by focusing on the reality that not every place in the world has been severely affected by anthropogenic activities and that these places can serve as models for the structure of and interactions within natural communities.

While accepting humans' enormous effect on the planet, we see a crucial need to identify remaining intact ecosystems at local extents, to protect them, and to remind the public of them. We need to do this for scientific reasons so that baselines for determining, for example, extent of pollution and declines in ecosystem function are preserved.[24] We need to do this for practical reasons so that goals for restoration projects have a basis in reality. We need to do this for public relations reasons, to reiterate that natural ecosystems exist and to engage society in conservation. And, we need to do this for ethical reasons; we have a duty to future generations to enhance their quality of life by providing them with the opportunity to observe the wonders of nature. We acknowledge that this is the goal of many conservation organizations, but we are concerned that the increasing adoption of the concept of the Anthropocene will undermine both conservation and restoration objectives.

The authors are grateful to E. Fleishman, P. Sherman, and three reviewers for helpful comments. This essay was published previously in slightly different form in Conservation Biology; *T. Caro, J. Darwin, T. Forrester, C. Ledoux-Bloom, and C. Wells, "Conservation in the Anthropocene,"* Conservation Biology *26 (2012): 185–88. doi:10.1111/j.1523-1739.2011.01752.x. At the time of publication, Tim Caro, Jack Darwin, Tavis Forrester, and Caitlin Wells were associated with the Department of Wildlife, Fish and Conservation Biology at the University of California, Davis. Cynthia Ledoux-Bloom was associated with the Department of Animal Science at the University of California, Davis.*

The Myth of the Humanized Pre-Columbian Landscape

DAVE FOREMAN

GEOGRAPHER WILLIAM M. DENEVAN of the University of Wisconsin is a leading researcher of what he calls "The Pristine Myth." He claims that "the Native American landscape of the early sixteenth century was a humanized landscape almost everywhere. Populations were large."[1] Arturo Gomez-Pompa and Andrea Kaus echo this assessment: "Scientific findings indicate that virtually every part of the globe, from the boreal forests to the humid tropics, has been inhabited, modified, or managed throughout our human past."[2] J. Baird Callicott similarly claims that "the wilderness idea is woefully ethnocentric. It ignores the historic presence and effects on practically all the world's ecosystems of aboriginal peoples."[3]

How true are these theoretical assertions? What do research and facts tell us? Questions we must ask about the Pristine Myth are:

- ▶ How many native people were there?
- ▶ How widespread were native people?
- ▶ How widespread were the impacts of native peoples?
- ▶ Do ecosystems recover from human impact?
- ▶ And, finally, is the Pristine Myth necessary to the *Wilderness Area Idea*?

After exploring these questions, I will second University of Oregon geographers Cathy Whitlock and Margaret Knox, who write: "It's not surprising that assigning a large role to prehistoric peoples is a popular concept among those who advocate active management of wilderness and commodity lands today."[4] Indeed, ranching apologist Dan Dagget calls for livestock grazing in the arid lands of the West, and for the final domestication of wilderness, because he believes American Indians had already domesticated the land before North America was colonized by white settlers.[5] Michael Soulé writes that right-wing anti-conservationists in the United States contend that, "because the West is no longer pristine, there should be no regulatory constraint on the pursuit of maximal short-term profits from public lands," and that the left-wing social ecologists' claim that the Amazon rainforest was created by Indians therefore justifies "further material refashioning."[6] The political and ecological implications of the humans-have-always-been-everywhere perspective are chillingly clear.

How many native people were there?

Denevan has suggested a total population for the New World in 1492 of 53.9 million: "3.8 million for North America, 17.2 million for Mexico, 5.6 million for Central America, 3.0 million for the Caribbean, 15.7 million for the Andes, and 8.6 million for lowland South America."[7] Others have *guessed* that there were as many as 8 million people living north of the Rio Grande. Douglas H. Ubelaker of the Smithsonian Institution, however, believes there were only 2 million.[8] The anthology edited by Denevan, *The Native Population of the Americas in 1492*, shows just how sprawled the estimates are, how questionable is the evidence on which they are based, and how ideology elbows in. Denevan is straightforward in acknowledging that his estimate is simply a doubling of Ubelaker's, which he considers too conservative.[9] Although I think Ubelaker's population estimates are more accurate, I will follow Denevan's here so I won't be so readily accused of undercounting.

How widespread were native people?

Without question, nearly 23 million people in Mexico and Central America would have been a large, often dense population. However, for North America north of the Rio Grande, Denevan's estimate is a mere 3.8 million. Keep in mind that the combined population of Canada and the United States today is over 330 million. Even by Denevan's reckoning, the pre-Columbian population was little more than 1 percent of that. Nor were these fewer-than-

4-million people evenly spread across the landscape. There were large regions rarely visited by humans—much less hosting permanent settlements—because of the inhospitality of the environment, the small total population of people at the time, uneven distribution, limited technology, lack of horses, and constant warfare and raiding. Archaeology backs my point. Moreover, some areas, like the Colorado Plateau in the U.S. Southwest and the greater Yucatan area of Central America, had been depopulated centuries before Columbus because of drought and farmers overshooting the carrying capacity of the land, and their wilderness character had largely recovered.

University of Wisconsin geographer Thomas Vale, after carefully considering the various population estimates, wisely concludes that "much of the area of the West was only lightly inhabited." Vale uses archaeology, ethnology, ecology, and paleoecology to estimate both the actual area used by natives north of the Rio Grande for living space and agriculture and how much land was affected by their other activities, such as vegetation modification and tree cutting, to further prove his point. He shows that vast areas remained largely unaffected by Indians.[10]

As for the stronghold of wilderness in the contiguous United States today—the Rocky Mountains—William Baker, a geography professor at the University of Wyoming, calculates that "the population in the Rockies itself in A.D. 1500 may have been about 32,000."[11] That's a smaller population than the single town of Missoula, Montana. Spread over the Rockies, it was far from crowded, to say the least.

In the long view of half a billion years of complex animal life on Earth, human presence has existed for an extraordinarily short time, and our impact until very recently was scattered and light.[12] What went on during the vastness of the epochs before we showed up? Extreme postmodern deconstructionists and their supposed political opposites, theoretical free-marketers, seem to think nothing—or at least nothing that matters. I've come to suspect that such self-centered humanists are actually incapable of imagining a time or a place without humans present. They are hard social constructionists and can be unyielding foes of protecting nature except for the direct benefit of people and with Disneyland-type hordes all over.

How widespread were the impacts of native peoples?

What was the level of impact indigenous people had in the Americas? The plain answer is that no one knows for sure. The conventional wisdom until recently was that natives north of Mexico had done very little to the landscape. New England's Puritans argued as much in order to justify their taking of "unused" land from the Indians.[13] The pendulum has swung the other way in recent years, with claims that even tiny populations transformed pre-Columbian ecosystems—especially through burning. The "Myth of Pristine America" has been replaced with the "Myth of the Humanized Landscape."[14]

The issue is not whether natives touched the land, but to what degree and where. Even if certain settled and cropped places were not self-willed land due to native burning, agriculture, and other uses, it does not follow that this was the case everywhere. Because Los Angeles is paved, does this mean that everywhere in the United States is paved? Because most of Illinois is a human-created landscape, is the Bob Marshall Wilderness Area in Montana a human-created landscape? Of course not. Those early explorers and later colonists who, on the basis of the wilderness they encountered, extrapolated that all of the Americas was a wilderness before Europeans are now imitated by their deconstructors who, on the basis of native-modified spots, extrapolate that all of the Americas was domesticated. Both views are unfounded—and silly.

The first wave of skilled hunters who came into the Americas roughly thirteen thousand years ago quickly caused the extinction of dozens of species of large mammals unschooled with such a predator. The Pleistocene-Holocene Extinction had profound effects that still may be reverberating through American ecosystems.[15] In certain areas of the pre-Columbian Americas, high human population density and intensive agriculture led to severely degraded ecosystems and extermination of wildlife. But it is outlandish to assert that 2 to 4 million people north of the Rio Grande had thoroughly domesticated the place. According to University of Kansas historian Donald Worster, "Two million people spread over what is now Canada and the United States, a people armed with primitive stone tools, simply could not have truly 'domesticated' the whole continent. By comparison, 300 million Americans and Canadians today, armed with far more powerful technology, have not wholly domesticated the continent yet."[16]

A key plank in the domesticated landscape floor is that natives set fires throughout North America. More than ten years ago, however, Reed Noss, a top expert on North American ecosystems and the former editor of *Conservation Biology*, pointed out that lightning-caused fires better explained the presence of fire-adapted vegetation than did Indian-set fires.[17] Ecologist Craig Allen of the U.S. Geological Survey confirms this for northern New Mexico:

Widespread fires occurred about every 5–20 years wherever ponderosa pine grew, with somewhat lower frequencies on the order of 15–40 years in the bracketing piñon-juniper woodlands below and mixed conifer forests above. . . . Given our dry spring climate and frequent thunderstorms, lightning is believed to have caused the vast majority of these fires. This view is supported by the records of about 4,000 lightning caused fires documented by firefighters in the Jemez Mountains from 1909–1996, and by the over 160,000 lightning strikes recorded over the Jemez country by a lightning detection system between 1985 and 1994.[18]

Forest ecologist, paleoecologist, and director of Harvard University's Harvard Forest, David Foster has also pondered the claims that Indians in New England created the vegetation patterns there through burning. He writes that "the paleoecological record provides no support for these visions and when coupled with other historical data instead paints a very different picture of the broad landscape. Sites from the central Massachusetts uplands do record fires and associated vegetation dynamics, but only at intervals of centuries to millennia. . . . In the Berkshires and the uplands of northern Vermont an even lower frequency of fire is recorded."[19] Foster adds that "the charcoal record does not support the notion of widespread and frequent Native American management of the land with fire [in New England]."[20]

Thomas Vale has taken perhaps the most careful look at the claims of the humanized landscape. "The desire to visualize humanized landscapes in the pre-European era derives from social ideologies," he writes, "rather than from careful assessment of ecological facts."[21] I think Vale has hit the nail on the head for understanding the entire deconstructionist salvo against wilderness. Social *ideology* fires those guns, not assessment of ecological *facts*. Social ideology also powers the advocates of commercial logging and livestock grazing who argue for the Myth of the Humanized Landscape as justification for exploitation.

Using archaeology, history, ecology, and logic, Vale looks at claims of a humanized landscape in a specific place—Yosemite National Park—in his article, "The Myth of the Humanized Landscape." He suggests that a place can be called "natural, or 'in a wilderness condition' if the fundamental characteristics of vegetation, wildlife, landform, soil, hydrology, and climate are those that result from natural, nonhuman processes, and if these conditions would exist whether or not humans are present."[22] Michael Soulé makes a like argument: "To claim that *Homo sapiens* has produced or invented the forest ignores the basic taxonomic integrity of biogeographic units: species today still have geographic distributions determined largely by ecological tolerances and geological history and climate, rather than by human activities."[23]

Vale explains that claims of a humanized Yosemite should not be applied outside the inhabited Yosemite Valley to include the entire national park, and that minor modification of vegetation or use of plants does not mean that even the valley was completely humanized in native times. Finally, he considers the sweeping assertions made about Indian burning. He writes, "A more precise assessment should ask whether the human-induced ignitions were in addition to, rather than a substitution for, natural ignitions and whether or not, moreover, any fires set by American Indians changed the landscape from that which otherwise would have existed."[24] After weighing what science now knows about fire frequency and behavior in Yosemite, he judges that "these fire frequencies varied temporally, with burning closely tracking weather conditions—an indication that natural factors, not humans, determined fire occurrence."[25] According to University of Georgia geographer Albert J. Parker, who specializes in coniferous forest disturbance, "the preponderance of evidence from fire-prone ecosystems . . . suggests that fuel accumulation patterns are far more influential than ignition source in governing the timing and spatial extent of fires."[26]

Vale also reviews the literature on other regions in the United States to learn how widespread heavy human impact was. He concludes:

The general point, then, is that the pre-European landscape of the United States was not monolithically humanized, not a 'managed landscape, much of its look and ecology the product of the human presence' (Flores 1997). Rather, it was a patchwork, at varying scales, of pristine and humanized conditions. A natural American wilderness—an environment fundamentally molded by nature—did exist .[27]

Vale's 2002 anthology, *Fire, Native Peoples, and the Natural Landscape,* builds on his argument with evidence and careful analysis throughout the western United States. His contributors, including some of the foremost biological geographers and fire ecologists, demolish the romantic (and, as they show, imperialistic) case for widespread Indian burning. The regions covered in the book are the Rocky Mountains, Northern Intermountain West, Southwest Lowlands, Southwest Uplands, Pacific Northwest, Sierra Nevada Forests, and California Chaparral. Their book is essential for understanding the whole question of whether Indians had domesticated the United States at the time of European settlement. Anyone who wishes to intelligently discuss the pristine-humanized (or pristine-profane as Soulé puts it) problem needs to read this book. Its contributors know what they are talking about; the humanized-landscape wilderness deconstructionists—left and right—are woefully muddled.

Throughout the West, these experts show that lightning-caused fires ran the fire regime, not human-ignited fires. The advocates of Indian burning root much of their argument in historical accounts. But William Baker, Craig Allen, and other contributors to *Fire, Native Peoples, and The Natural Landscape* show how ignorant these early observers were of lightning-caused fires. For example, Aldo Leopold wrote in 1920, "As is well known to all old-timers, the Indian fired the forests with the deliberate intent of confusing and concentrating the game so as to make hunting easier."[28] Leopold's old-timers didn't know what they were talking about, and the ecological role of fire remained a blurred spot for Leopold throughout his life. Historian Stephen Pyne, widely seen as an expert on fire in America and someone who has done much good work, repeats the same misunderstanding, claiming that the most widespread Indian use of fire was probably fire for hunting. Fire and landscape-change ecologist Craig Allen, however, counters with "in the Southwest, the idea of landscape-scale hunting fires is based upon an insubstantial foundation of minimal documentation . . . Primary evidence for landscape-scale burning for hunting is nearly nonexistent in the Southwest, and supporting rationales are weak."[29] Pyne, Charles Kay, and other believers in native firebugs uncritically draw on a few unsubstantiated claims by Leopold's old-timers to create an ecologically garbled history and prehistory of fire.

Although writing specifically about the Southwest, Allen neatly summarizes the situation for the whole West: "Modern claims of extensive aboriginal burning of southwestern landscapes are shown to be based upon broad overgeneralizations and uncritical acceptance from a few historical reports of localized fire use."[30] Before Spanish conquest and colonization in the early 1600s, what is now northern New Mexico was well populated by Pueblo Indians. Allen, who probably understands the paleoecology and current ecology of this region better than anyone else, shows that even here lightning caused the fires. For example, the Jemez Mountains, west of Santa Fe, have an extensive array of automated lightning detection devices. This system "recorded 165,117 cloud-to-ground strikes . . . during the period 1985–1994."[31] I am not the least surprised by this barrage as it has come close to taking me out a few times. (One of the best meals of my life was under a Jemez spruce tree in a terrible lightning storm—my wife Nancy grilled fresh-picked boletes in olive oil on our camp stove while we waited it out.) In the Sierra Nevada, a lightning detection network "reported that lightning struck in the region of Yosemite National Park approximately 2,000 times per year in the 6-year period from 1985 to 1990 (65 strikes per 100 square km per year)."[32]

While many of those arguing for Indian domestication of the West are well-meaning, social-justice liberals, there is a darker side as well. As Craig Allen notes, "perhaps the late-1800s prejudice that Indians set many fires was also related to a 'Manifest Destiny' mind-set that sought to justify removing some tribes from their native forest lands."[33]

According to Pyne, "together lightning and people made the elastic matrix that defined the fire regime." Fire ecologists Tom Swetnam and C. H. Baisan rebut that with, "We contend that, even if humans had never crossed the land bridge from Asia to North America, historical fire regimes in most Southwestern forests would still have been similar in most respects to the fire regimes that we have documented."[34] And Allen summarizes his exhaustive research (much of it on the ground unlike that of advocates for Indian burning) as follows: "Multiple lines of evidence from this region overwhelmingly suggest that in A.D. 1850, as in A.D. 1580, most mountain landscapes were 'natural' and 'wild' with regard to fire regimes and associated vegetation patterns."[35]

What really runs this debate? Albert Parker clearly lays it out:

Discord over the role of indigenous humans in shaping the landscape is fueled by contrasts in the academic roots and ideological affinities of the principal voices in this debate . . . Evidence that argues against a pervasive role for aboriginal humans in shaping the Sierra Nevada landscape comes primarily from physical and biological scientists, foresters, and fire ecologists, who have addressed issues of late Quaternary paleoenvironments, precontact fire regimes, and the geography of lightning and lightning-caused fires. Their evidence is principally physical, and taken in aggregate, it provides a

logically consistent history of climate/vegetation/fire linkages that have oper-
ated to structure the Sierran landscape over the last twenty thousand years,
primarily without significant human alteration. Evidence favoring the view
that humans have domesticated the Sierran landscape comes primarily from
human geographers and cultural anthropologists. . . . Most of the evidence
presented to support this position is ethnographic, based on interviews of
past and present living elders descended from Sierran tribal communities.[36]

Parker further points out that these folks have "a strong urge to atone for past sins of aggression and transgression, both cultural and environmental," and have a "political agenda" to "put the Sierra back in the hands of native peoples, who, in the image of the Noble Savage, were excellent stewards of the land." He concludes, "nostalgia and political agendas are no substitute for valid evidence."[37] Amen.

Do ecosystems recover from human impact?

As Arturo Gomez-Pompa and Andrea Kaus assert: "New evidence from the Maya region suggests that the seemingly natural forests we are trying to protect from our version of civilization supported high densities of human populations and were managed by past civilizations. . . .[T]he Maya population of southeastern Mexico may have ranged from 150 to 500 people per km² in the Late Classic Period, contrasting sharply with current population densities of 4.5 to 28.1 people per km² in the same region. . . .These past civilizations apparently managed the forests for food, fiber, wood, fuel, resins, and medicines."[38]

This is probably partly true, but the rest of the story conveniently ignored by Gomez-Pompa and Kaus is that the highly overpopulated Mayans grossly overexploited the forests, and, when drought hit, their warlike, totalitarian civilization collapsed.[39] For one thousand years, however, those forests have been recovering. This ecological reality also explains the differences in population densities. Jared Diamond discusses the Mayan breakdown in his book, *Collapse.* He writes, "the population of the Central Péten at the peak of the Classic Maya period is variously estimated at between 3,000,000 and 14,000,000 people, but there were only about 30,000 people there at the time that the Spanish arrived."[40] In other words, the population dropped by over 99 percent. These population figures show that the Mayan collapse was due not to Spanish-brought diseases or Spanish conquest, but to how the Maya "managed" their forests and were thus unable to deal with drought. Gomez-Pompa and Kaus base their claims on social ideology, not ecological facts.

Common to the writings of the wilderness deconstructionists is a New Pristine Myth: Once touched by humans in any way, wilderness has evaporated and cannot be restored; therefore, there is no need to protect it from further human exploitation. This is the Forest Service's outdated and bogus purity view, which the agency used after the Wilderness Act's passage to try to minimize the amount of land protected as wilderness (I discuss this more fully in *Taming the Wilderness*). Michael Soulé warns against this "virgin metaphor," "because virginity, like pregnancy, knows no degrees," and is an excuse, then, "to justify further material reshaping" of wildlands.[41] Soulé calls this the pristine-profane dichotomy. In just one example of this, a free-market theorist in *PERC Reports* used the fallen-virgin notion to argue for weakening the Endangered Species Act.[42]

In answer to the question, then, ecosystems often can recover from human impacts over periods of time, depending on the level of impact. This resilience should never be used as justification for further intrusions into wilderness, but it does provide a valid rationale for the concept of wilderness recovery and rewilding.

And, finally, is the Pristine Myth important to the Wilderness Area Idea?

"The pristine view," according to Denevan,[43] "is to a large extent an invention of nineteenth-century romanticist and primitivist writers." I somewhat agree, but I do not believe that Denevan's "pristine view" has much to do with the wilderness idea that led to the National Wilderness Preservation System or with the motivation of wilderness conservationists during the last eighty-some years. In 1925, Aldo Leopold observed that "the wilderness idea was born after, rather than before, the normal course of commercial development had begun."[44] Thus the father of wilderness area protection makes it clear that his wilderness area idea was a new one, coming after "motor cars" began to invade the national forests following World War I. It had little to do with the Pristine Myth of "nineteenth-century romanticist and primitivist writers."

Nor does the New Pristine Myth carry water with wilderness area protection today. Places do not have to be pristine to be designated as wilderness; the Wilderness Act never required pristine conditions.[45] Leopold ·

wisely explained that "in any practical program, the unit areas to be preserved must vary greatly in size and in *degree of wildness*" [emphasis mine].[46] Senator Frank Church of Idaho was the floor manager in 1964 when the Wilderness Act passed. Ten years later, when the Forest Service "would have us believe that no lands ever subject to past human impact can qualify as wilderness, now or ever," Church countered: "Nothing could be more contrary to the meaning and intent of the Wilderness Act."[47]

The definition of wilderness in the Wilderness Act fully acknowledges that there are few if any places untouched by human influence; the Act does not require proposed wilderness areas to be untouched; and time and time again, conservationists have had to overcome anti-wilderness arguments based on lack of purity. There are now more than 600 areas totaling more than 107 million acres in the National Wilderness Preservation System. Most of these wilderness areas were designated despite the claims of foes that they were not pure enough.

William Cronon is among those who seemed to misunderstand the Wilderness Act when he wrote in the early 1990s, "If you follow the federal government's definition, there is no wilderness in Wisconsin."[48] Wrong, wrong, wrong, wrong, wrong, wrong—on six counts: At the time Cronon wrote there were in fact five designated national forest wilderness areas and one national wildlife refuge wilderness area in Wisconsin—Wisconsin Islands, Blackjack Springs, Headwaters, Porcupine Lake, Rainbow Lake, Whisker Lake. They total 44,170 acres. (In 1978, I testified before Congress on behalf of The Wilderness Society in favor of Blackjack Springs and Whisker Lake.) They meet the federal government's definition of wilderness and have been so designated. And conservationists have proposed additional wilderness areas in Wisconsin; since Cronon wrote, Congress established the Apostle Islands National Lakeshore Gaylord Nelson Wilderness Area. The wilderness area idea embodied in the 1964 Wilderness Act comes from post-designation management rules rather than from a romantic ideal. I further discuss the wilderness purity myth in *Rewilding North America* and in my forthcoming *Taming the Wilderness*.

Neither conceptualization of the "pristine myth"—one, that the Americas were pristine before Europeans and, two, that only pristine areas can be considered for wilderness designation—has much to do with the wilderness area idea. I hope I have beaten up on this dead horse enough so that no one will try to get it back up on its feet!

I'll close this essay with wise words from Thomas Vale:

Natural wildernesses, pristine landscapes, existed at the time of European contact. . . . Not occurring everywhere, surely, they did exist in places; they did exist somewhere. This conclusion will not strike many people as novel, but it will be resisted by those for whom 'wilderness' seems a politically incorrect challenge to social justice or a strategically unwise ideal for conservation goals, or by those who argue that 'nature' is merely a socially constructed category, an artifact of the human mind and human language.[49]

The Future of Conservation: An Australian Perspective

BRENDAN MACKEY

GEOLOGICALLY, AUSTRALIA IS a continent comprising mainland Australia, Tasmania, New Guinea, and neighboring islands. Australia, the nation state of the mainland and Tasmania (plus some small islands), has a surface area of around 7.7 million square kilometers (roughly 84 percent that of the United States). Biologically, Australia is a megadiverse nation continent, replete with an abundance of unique species, ecosystems, and human cultures. Since the Australian continent broke free from Antarctica around 60 million years ago, much of Australia's terrestrial biota has been evolving largely in geographical isolation, with the exception of a few rodent species who migrated during the Pliocene (between 2 and 5 million years ago) and the dingo (*Canis lupus dingo*, a top predator)—a wild dog that turned up about four thousand years ago. Humans arrived some fifty thousand years ago; and European colonization (and with it the modern era), in 1778.

Australians are known for being laid back, for being friendly, and for loving their natural environment. By and large this is true, as many tourists will vouch, and as our poets have celebrated:

> *I love a sunburnt country,*
> *A land of sweeping plains,*
> *Of ragged mountain ranges,*
> *Of droughts and flooding rains.*
> *I love her far horizons,*
> *I love her jewel-sea,*
> *Her beauty and her terror—*
> *The wide brown land for me!*
> (Dorothea Mackellar, "My Country"[1])

But, behind this projected tourist-friendly exterior, dark shadows lurk. Like all colonized nations, Aboriginal Australians continue to suffer the legacy of two hundred twenty-five years of dispossession and mistreatment, with a majority remaining underprivileged.

The second dark shadow of modern Australia is its sorry record of species extinctions, ecological degradation, and ecocide (the destruction of entire ecosystems[2]). Australian society is testimony to the fact that a relatively few wealthy people can cause immense ecological harm. Australia holds the world record for the number of terrestrial mammal extinctions in the modern era (27), and its landscapes are being degraded by widespread and pervasive pressures: invasive animals, especially cats, foxes, pigs, goats, donkeys, camels,[3] and water buffalo; changed fire regimes; diverted water flows; prospecting and mining; industrial logging; and commercial grazing by sheep and cattle (pastoral leases cover about 50 percent of the continent). Around 20 percent of Australia has been subject to broadscale land clearing, and while land clearing is slowing, it still averaged around 1 million hectares (close to 2.5 million acres) per year between 2000 and 2010.[4]

Much of the biodiversity loss and environmental degradation which is so obvious to the naturalist and conservationist is hidden from the casual eye of the city dweller or international tourist. The ecological disruption from weeds and other invasive species and the loss of genetic diversity from extirpation of populations are two examples of cryptic biodiversity losses. Even extreme disruptions such as deforestation can remain invisible to those without knowledge of a landscape's natural history and land use. However, the ecological loss is deeply felt by many Aboriginal Australians. As has been noted for people in other countries, the dispossession and alienation of individuals along with environmental degradation and the erosion of biodiversity are deeply connected and have common causal roots:[5]

The scrubs are gone, the hunting and the laughter.
The eagle is gone, the emu and the kangaroo are gone from this place.
The bora ring is gone.
The corroboree is gone.
And we are going.
(Oodgeroo Noonuccal, last five lines from "We Are Going"[6])

And now, after two and a quarter centuries of extinctions, loss, and degradation, Australia's species and ecosystems face the megapressure of human-forced rapid climate change. This is not to say that climate change is anything new in the ecology and evolution of the continent's flora and fauna. On the contrary, climate changes naturally (albeit in complex ways) and species have always responded through a diversity of mechanisms or faced extirpation.[7] However, greenhouse gas emissions from humans burning fossil fuels are now disrupting Earth's climate system rapidly and in ways that will continue for thousands of years.[8] All life processes—biological, ecological, evolutionary—are directly or indirectly affected by climatic conditions. Climate (the typical weather conditions experienced at a location) determines the patterns in the distribution of light, heat, and water—the primary environmental resources—along with the mineral nutrients needed for plant growth and, in turn, ecosystem productivity.[9] Climatic conditions also directly determine: rates of biochemical reactions; gross primary productivity (often measured by the rate of photosynthesis); respiration; the rates at which life cycles are completed; and the timing of phenological responses (for example, flowering). Indirect climate change impacts are also felt by species and ecosystems including through altered patterns of wildfire or flooding. With climatic disruption being layered over the suite of existing pressures, the prognosis for biodiversity is grim. Unfortunately, prospects look even grimmer in face of the potential for negative environmental impacts from ongoing technological innovation and the new land uses these enable, including energy developments like coal seam gas mining, hydro fracking, and tar sands extraction (occurring in Canada).[10]

Do we need a new compass bearing?

In the midst of what is now considered to be the sixth mass extinction in the approximately 4.5-billion-year history of Earth,[11] knowing that the primary agent of biodiversity loss (the aggregate impacts of human activities) is increasing in its reach and intensity, it is perhaps understandable that some conservationists have lost their way, have given up hope, or are now suggesting that the goal of conservation be abandoned and reinvented. The argument goes something like this: There is no longer any wild land, what we have left is in a seminatural state (the product of human management and impacts), so we should think of ourselves more as gardeners who have to manage the planet carefully, ensuring that ecosystems remain healthy and providing people with food, water, and other ecosystem services; in brief, we need to "domesticate nature more wisely."[12]

Resetting the conservation goal to one of "wise gardening" is tempting in that it enables us to focus on manipulating species and biophysical processes as circumstances suit us, without reference to or regard for evolutionary and ecological legacies and processes. Such a reorientation of conservation promotes actions that are more conducive to working with those governmental and private sector interests driving land development and natural resource exploitation. It also appeals to human hubris and vanity, suggesting it is people who are now in control of Earth and that we can manage our way out of this environmental crisis.

Geoscientists have proposed that because humans are now the dominant force of global environmental change, this current epoch should be called the "Anthropocene."[13] However, it is foolish and dangerous to confuse *force* with *control*. The Anthropocene, while an empirical fact, does not mean that humans "run the show." Rather, it means only that we can be powerfully disruptive. This power to disrupt does not translate into a power to control the Earth system. As the result of human impacts, natural planetary boundaries are now being breached, and we are taking Earth's environmental conditions outside the safe Holocene conditions, thereby threatening critical life-support systems.[14] Therefore, the Anthropocene should not so much mark the "end of nature" but the opposite: the end of "human exceptionalism"—the idea that humans, unlike every other species on Earth, can live outside the laws of nature .

The planetary boundaries noted above represent global environmental conditions related to biogeochemical cycles that reflect deeply coupled and complex interactions between species and ecosystems together with the atmosphere, geosphere, and hydrosphere.[15] Like all complex systems, higher-level behavior is the result of reinforcing and stabilizing feedbacks and synergistic interactions that are not predictable through knowledge of the component elements.[16] Complex systems are typically unmanageable in the conventional "command and control" sense. Rather, their patterns of response need to be understood, the key levers identified, and important lagged responses recognized, among other things. The Earth system exhibits such complex behavior as do its component ecosystems. At a local level too, we operate more as powerful disruptors of these complex ecosystems rather than as some kind of über-wise managers. Our attempts at ecosystem management inevitably result in their simplification—taxonomically, structurally, and functionally—and the elimination of evolutionary and ecological processes (including genetic diversity, natural selection, microevolution, coevolutionary adaptations, and strong, interspecies interactions[17]) which naturally provide these systems with their self-regeneration, resilience, and adaptive capacities.[18]

Nature conservation and traditional obligations to country

One version of the "wise gardener" argument with particular currency in Australia relates to the fact that people have lived here continuously for around fifty thousand years. This argument proceeds along the lines that Australia's biodiversity is primarily the result of this long history of Aboriginal land management achieved mainly through the use of fire to manipulate the vegetation cover.[19] Furthermore, the argument goes, as hunter-gatherers Aboriginal Australians functioned as the apex terrestrial predator and must have influenced trophic interactions. It would therefore follow that Australian landscapes are more accurately viewed as cultural landscapes, lending support to the idea that the goal of conservation should become more aligned with what we might call the "traditional gardener paradigm." There can be no denying that Aboriginal Australians over the course of fifty thousand years have become integrated with the native flora and fauna species and ecosystems. However, an evolutionary perspective is essential if we are to understand their role and the implications for conservation in the coming decades and century.[20]

Australia hosts an ancient biodiversity with a flora whose origin can be traced back to when Australia was part of the supercontinent Gondwanaland, over 100 million years ago.[21] Exceptions are the alpine and desert floras that both speciated and recruited in the Pliocene (from 5.3 to 2.6 million years ago) with the advent of cold or extensive dry climates.[22] Also during the Pliocene/early Pleistocene drying and cooling event from some 4 to 1 million years ago there occurred the last great vertebrate animal speciation event: the explosion of songbirds and the appearance and radiation of rodents on the Australian continent;[23] whereas most extant marsupial mammal species are derived from groups that appeared in the mid- to late Miocene, around 20 million years ago.[24]

In the period between Aboriginal people being established in Australia and the British first settlement in 1788, the dingo was the only known introduced mammal species. It was probably introduced by humans and is thought to have displaced the native thylacine, or Tasmanian tiger (*Thylacinus cynocephalus*), as the apex (nonhuman) predator.[25] Otherwise, to our knowledge, every species that was present when the British explorer Captain Cook arrived in 1770 had persisted through the fifty thousand years of Aboriginal influence, notwithstanding the evidence that Aboriginal people may have been implicated, albeit indirectly, in the extinction of some megafauna species around forty thousand years ago. We can thus conclude that Aboriginal Australian cultural practices and land use were conducive to the persistence and flourishing of much of Australia's evolved biodiversity. Aboriginal Australians prior to 1788 did none of the following: engage in broadscale clearing of native vegetation; introduce large numbers of invasive species; spread new diseases; build dams and irrigation systems to divert water from environmental flows and alter hydrological regimes; exploit forests for industrial-scale logging; or degrade rangelands by importing cloven-hoofed livestock. Nor did they burn fossil fuel contributing to human-forced, rapid climate change. All of these threats to biodiversity began with the first British colony in 1778.

The presence of humans altered fire regimes both through conscious efforts to use fire as a land management tool in some landscapes and presumably also unintentionally through accidently starting wildfires. However, fire has been part of Australia's ecology for tens of millions of years, with fire events increasing in frequency and intensity as the continent broke free from Antarctica and drifted north. Fire regimes change across the continent depending on bioregional characteristics.[26] The entry of northern Australia into the influence of the tropical convergence zone led to the onset of a monsoonal climate in that region with a long dry season leading to development of an open grassy savannah woodland biome. The grassy ground cover provides a seasonally abundant fuel, and tropical storms and lightning strikes provide ignition opportunities. In other biomes, such as the tall wet forests of southern Australia, the big fires which naturally occurred infrequently were not amenable to human manipulation.[27]

Pre-European Aboriginal burning practices varied between and within bioregions because climatic conditions, along with landscape and vegetation characteristics, regulated human ability to start and control fires. We also know that the Australian flora is remarkably adapted to dominant fire regimes through the evolution of a rich diversity of life-history traits that enable species to survive fire events or successfully reproduce in their aftermath.[28]

Within these natural constraints, and in some biomes more than others, Aboriginal Australians regularly burnt sections of landscapes as part of what they refer to as "traditional obligations to country." These land practices are grounded in Aboriginal cosmology and law and consequently are culturally regulated acts.[29] Given the long coexistence of Aboriginal Australians and the biodiversity present with the onset of Europeans, there is merit in the suggestions that the breakdown in the practice of "traditional obligations to country" over the last two hundred twenty-five years has contributed to the loss of biodiversity.[30] There is certainly abundant documentation of the extraordinary ecological knowledge held by Aboriginal people who are the traditional inhabitants of their ancestral lands.[31]

Toward an Earth community conservation goal

Given the sheer enormity of the current pressures on Earth's environment and biodiversity and the challenges ahead, we do need to reflect upon our conservation goals for the twenty-first century. A conservation goal defined by the gardening metaphor, however, takes us down the wrong path. It would have us abandon the sublimely rich legacies of evolution and perversely celebrate the unraveling of well-tested and ancient ecological relations. It would replace natural selection with human decision-making dominated by the desires to optimize for efficiency and maximize short-term gains.

An overreliance on the utilitarian value of species and ecosystems to humans would be a feeble foundation for a new conservation goal. Humans are dependent on species and ecosystems for food, fiber, freshwater, and other benefits, many of which are being replaced by technology. Whatever the wisdom and costs of this technology-dependent trend, it is inevitable as the human population grows and societies are increasingly urbanized.[32] And it is true that we are dependent on planetary boundaries—globally scaled conditions that characterize Earth's environment during the Holocene.[33] The relationship between planetary boundaries and biodiversity, however, has yet to be scientifically established. Two of the planetary boundaries directly relate to biodiversity:[34] one, the rate of species extinctions; and two, the percentage of land that is converted from its natural ecosystem cover to intensive agriculture. We currently do not have the scientific understanding to know what level of loss leads to significant and irreversible harm to biodiversity and undermines the regulatory capacities of the Earth system by affecting the climate system and the hydrological cycle; nor do we know if these thresholds have already been breached.

We need to challenge an anthropocentric paradigm grounded in the philosophy of human exceptionalism that requires support for conservation to be contingent upon the benefits it brings to people. If we are to leave room on Earth for other species and life-supporting processes, then the scope of our moral responsibility needs to be extended beyond classic ethical principles of justice and freedom where people are the only agents with moral standing. To say something has moral standing means that its well-being *counts* and is the basis of a presumptive duty to that thing.[35] There is no universally accepted philosophical foundation of environmental ethics, and a diversity of perspectives co-exists—spanning from anthropocentrism (humans beings alone are moral agents)[36] to biocentrism (moral standing expanded to nonhuman subjects who have inherent value)[37] to ecocentrism or holism (ecosystems and the biosphere as the ultimate reference of moral value).[38] Accepting the limitations of anthropocentrism does not mean rejecting the need for humanity to reduce its environmental impacts in order to protect planetary boundaries. Nor does it mean ignoring the many benefits we gain from healthy ecosystems. Rather, an environmental ethic is needed that encompasses rather than excludes this range of perspectives.

Leopold's land ethic[39] points in the right direction, as it acknowledges the ecological realities of human existence along with the intrinsic value of life in all its human and nonhuman expressions and the complex web of interactions that are implicated. The intrinsic value of other species is a key concept and is recognized by international environmental law in the Preamble to the Convention on Biological Diversity,[40] where it is stated that the 193 countries who are party to the convention are:

Conscious of the intrinsic value of biological diversity and of the ecological, genetic, social, economic, scientific, educational, cultural, recreational and aesthetic values of biological diversity and its components.

The ethical position of the Earth Charter[41] is also helpful here. The Earth Charter is a declaration of fundamental ethical principles for building a just, sustainable, and peaceful global society in the twenty-first century. The Earth Charter is a product of a decade-long, worldwide, cross-cultural dialogue on common goals and shared values. The Earth Charter project began as a United Nations initiative, but it was carried forward and completed by a global civil society initiative. The Earth Charter was finalized and then launched as a people's charter in 2000 by the Earth Charter Commission, an independent international entity. Of particular relevance here are two principles, Principle 1a:

Recognize that all beings are interdependent and every form of life has value regardless of its worth to human beings,

and Principle 2:

Care for the community of life with understanding, compassion, and love.

The Earth Charter ethic frames the claims made by anthropocentrism, biocentrism, and holism in terms of an ethic of responsibility and care which extends beyond concerns for human justice to encompass the Earth Community and the integrity of the Earth system—an Earth Community ethic. The final principle (Principle 16f) in the Earth Charter gives expression to this all-encompassing set of caring relationships:

Recognize that peace is the wholeness created by right relationships with oneself, other persons, other cultures, other life, Earth, and the larger whole of which all are a part.

The key to conservation in the twenty-first century is to recognize the overarching role played by evolutionary and ecological processes in the self-regeneration, resilience, and adaptive capacity of species and ecosystems. Conservation management is less about managing biodiversity and more about managing *humans* and the impacts that flow from their activities. Australia's biodiversity is the product of tens of millions of years of evolution. The genomes found within and between species represent the success stories from the long-term sieving of genetic diversity by natural selection: life history traits tuned to survival in the nutrient-poor landscapes that dominate most of the continent; coevolved relationships between plants and insects;[42] and ancient genetic lineages that science is only beginning to reveal,[43] among other things. The emergent landscape ecosystems have proven themselves to be extraordinarily resilient and adaptive, with remarkable powers of self-regeneration on a continent characterized by high year-to-year variability in rainfall and extreme weather events.

The conservation challenge for the twenty-first century is to avoid introducing threats to intact landscapes and to reduce or eliminate threats to species and ecosystem integrity in landscapes suffering loss and degradation. Some threats can be avoided when they are the direct result of a specific land use and it is possible to prevent its introduction. For example, altered hydrological regimes can be avoided by preventing new infrastructure developments that impound and divert water for human use and away from environmental flows. However, such action will typically require concerned citizens to mount a political and legal campaign to oppose the vested interests behind the development.[44]

While some land uses are simply incompatible with conservation, others can be made compatible depending on how they are designed and managed. Modifying land use to avoid or minimize biodiversity threats is essential if conservation outcomes are to be achieved on private, indigenous, and leasehold land, as well as crown land (that is, public land held by the government). We have the basic ingredients needed—when deployed in a complementary way with a network of protected areas, and keeping in mind the multiple scales over which key natural processes operate—to protect and restore Australia's biodiversity. The future of conservation resides in these complementary conservation actions being undertaken in a coordinated way between government, landowners, and civil society and implemented on a landscape-wide basis spanning regions and continents. In Australia, this approach, called "connectivity conservation,"[45] has taken root through a marvelous, synergistic combination of grassroots- and government-initiated projects that include continental-scaled corridors supported by federal government policy.[46]

Conclusion

While an anthropocentric perspective is useful because it highlights the very real and practical dependencies humans have on ecosystems and planetary boundaries, a utilitarian attitude toward nature is an insufficient foundation for conservation in the twenty-first century. Alone, this attitude inexorably results in ecosystems becoming depauperate and simplified to the point where they are no longer, among other things, self-organizing and resilient. Adopting an ethic of respect and care for the greater community of life is essential because this is the only way to protect the evolutionary processes and ecological relations that are essential to the flourishing of life on Earth.

Conservation needs to embrace a goal grounded in an Earth Community ethic—an ethic of responsibility and care that extends to all life and life-processes. Perhaps, just as Aboriginal Australians learned to do over millennia, we need to develop a deeper understanding of natural processes and constraints, including ecological and evolutionary systems, working *within* rather than *against* them, and adopt a more biocentric and more ecocentric land ethic. However, appeals to reason and morality are doomed to be ignored unless matched with supportive public policies, regulatory regimes, and resources.[47] Doing so will help navigate the way across contested landscapes and seascapes and support efforts to achieve more effective and sustainable conservation outcomes in the face of ever-increasing pressures and threats.

If there is a lesson to be learned from what is being called the Anthropocene, it is that *Homo sapiens* now has responsibility to Earth our home and for so changing human civilization that it sustains not only human well-being but also the greater community of life.

Mine the face on which you trample.
Mine the bones by which you live.
(Mark O'Connor, "XII. Earth," final stanza from "The Rainbow Serpent"[48])

The section on environmental ethics draws upon material from an unpublished paper co-written by Brendan Mackey and Dr. Vittorio Falsina (1962–2001) and presented at Environmental Justice: Global Ethics for the 21st Century; *International Academic Conference of the University of Melbourne, Australia, October 1–3, 1997. This essay is dedicated to the memory of Dr. Falsina and to his contributions to environmental philosophy. The essay benefited from helpful and insightful comments on a draft version received from Steven Rockefeller, Ron Engel, Bridget Mackey, and Michael Soulé.*

Expanding Parks, Reducing Human Numbers, and Preserving All the Wild Nature We Can: A Superior Alternative to Embracing the Anthropocene Era

PHILIP CAFARO

RECENTLY, THE CLAIM has been made that Earth has entered a new geological era. The Holocene has ended and the Anthropocene has begun, in which humans have become an important geochemical force, and perhaps the dominant ecological force on the planet. Moreover, conservationists are advised to *embrace* the Anthropocene era, in which humanity not only dominates, but *rightfully* dominates, the biosphere.

Now that we have entered the Anthropocene, according to prophets of this new dispensation, conservationists should give up outdated goals that no longer make sense or are no longer possible. These include trying to protect all Earth's species from anthropogenic extinction; ridding wildlands of invasive species; designating wilderness areas or parks that are off limits to most human economic activities (in order to minimize human interference in relatively wild ecosystems); and managing parks with the goal of meeting ecological baselines that reflect wilder, less human-influenced ecological conditions.

Truly wild nature is over, we are told, if it ever existed at all. Any baseline we choose is arbitrary. "A historic moment in the past" is not "the holy moment that we always have to return every piece of land to," according to Emma Marris: "Not just because it's getting more and more difficult with climate change and so on, but because those baselines we have grown up with are somewhat arbitrary. . . . The more we learn about how much people have changed the earth over the centuries and over the millennia, the more we know that 1491 in the Americas or 1776 in Hawaii were just moments between two different human landscapes."[1]

Besides, such goals reflect a foolish desire to keep nature "pure," a misanthropic dislike of humanity, and an outmoded metaphysics that sees a sharp line between humanity and the rest of nature. *We* are just as much a part of nature as bluebirds or buffalo; a vacant lot or an agricultural field is just as natural, or "natural," as a remote Arctic river.

So conservationists need new goals. According to Peter Kareiva and Michelle Marvier in their article "What Is Conservation Science?" conservationists' main goals should be to protect ecosystem services for a growing human population and to do our part to accelerate economic development in a world where so many people are poor.[2] We should avoid "fencing people out" of wildlands; that is old school. Instead, we must find creative "win/win solutions" where people use resources while preserving nature. We should learn to tolerate and even appreciate invasive species, which in many cases *increase* local biodiversity. Similarly, we should make our peace with the extinction of species that are maladapted to the new conditions of the Anthropocene. Rather than try to save every species on Earth, or even as many as possible, we should content ourselves with preserving whatever biodiversity 10 or so billion people find useful or interesting, and which can muddle through in the new conditions humanity is creating.

I believe that conservationists should reject this bold call to selfishness and human racism. Preserving wild nature is still the heart of conservation. Sharing the landscape generously with other species remains a necessary part of any reasonable, morally justifiable land ethic. But that necessarily involves setting *limits* to human demands on nature, not endlessly accommodating them. It involves setting *limits* to the degree of human influence that is acceptable in national parks and other wildlands. This, in turn, limits the degree to which real conservationists can accept the dominant trends of the Anthropocene.

Rather than embrace the Anthropocene era, conservationists should act to rein in its excesses. Among our key goals, we should work to expand parks and protected areas; work to increase the acreage kept free from intensive human resource extraction; and work to lessen the human impacts that degrade wildlife habitat, such as air and water pollution and the continued transfer of exotic species into new areas. Conservationists should advocate for humane measures to reduce human numbers, gradually and noncoercively. Recognizing that humanity is bumping up against ecological limits to economic growth, conservationists should avoid any temptation to make our peace with the current endless growth economy. Instead, a central part of our agenda should involve creating a truly sustainable economy: one that recognizes limits to growth.

Above all, conservationists should affirm the right of every species on Earth to pursue its unique destiny, free from human-caused extinction. I believe such a course is both more prudent and morally superior to embracing or adapting to the Anthropocene era.

Acceptable and unacceptable change

I disagree with much that Anthropocene proponents have to say. However, I do agree with them that Earth has entered a human-dominated era. We can debate the finer points. But our world now has huge dead zones at the mouth of many of its rivers. Summer sea ice in the Arctic is rapidly shrinking and perhaps soon will be completely gone. Meanwhile, every square meter of soil and every cubic meter of the atmosphere show trace amounts (or more) of artificial chemicals. Such a world is indeed generally and in many places decisively influenced by human activities. Where I begin to part company with cheerleaders like Kareiva, Marvier, and Marris is in their embrace of the Anthropocene.

Sometimes, the Anthropocene is seen as a positive good, as when Marris rhapsodizes over how much more biodiverse Los Angeles is today than it would have been two hundred years ago—before people came and planted so many different kinds of exotic trees—or about the many opportunities we have today to *create* new nature. According to Marris, embracing the Anthropocene is:

a much more optimistic and a much more fruitful way of looking at things. . . . If you only care about pristine wilderness . . . you're fighting a defensive action that you can never ultimately win, and every year there's less of it than there was the year before. . . . But if you're focused on the other values of nature and goals of nature, then you can go around creating more nature, and our kids can have a world with more nature on it than there is now.[3]

At other times, the Anthropocene is presented as regrettable, but inevitable.[4] Look, I don't like this brave new world any more than you do, some Anthropocene proponents say. But you are just kidding yourself if you think this juggernaut can be stopped, or even slowed. It is a new reality to which we have to adjust, if we hope to achieve as much conservation as possible.

Again, there is some truth to this: Conservationists do have to make our shifts with "the way things are," as anyone involved in practical land management decisions or political campaigns knows very well. But conservation also involves *changing* the way things are, or raising the alarm when the way things are will lead to great losses. Too often, proponents of the Anthropocene seem more interested in normalizing these losses than in stopping them.

For example, in 1973, the U.S. Congress, looking at "the way things were," passed the Endangered Species Act (ESA). The ESA affirmed a national commitment to prevent any and all native species from going extinct due to human activities. Crucially, this legislation specified that economic goals were not to be allowed to trump the very existence of other species (although it was subsequently amended to allow for such a possibility, in rare cases, through the decisions of the so-called "God squad").

Today, according to the U.S. Fish and Wildlife Service, the polar bear, *Ursus arctos,* is threatened with extinction, due to the effects of climate change. In fact, many species around the world are threatened by global warming. According to the Intergovernmental Panel on Climate Change: "Approximately 20–30 percent of species assessed so far are likely to be at increased risk of extinction if increases in global average warming exceed 1.5–2.5°C (relative to 1980–1999). . . . As global average temperature increase exceeds about 3.5°C, model projections suggest significant extinctions (40–70 percent of species assessed) around the globe."[5] To many people, the polar bear has come to symbolize both the threat of climate change to wild nature and the need for humanity to rein in greenhouse gas emissions in order to limit climate change.

What do Anthropocene proponents have to say about species extinctions? Here is Kareiva and coauthors, in an article titled "Conservation in the Anthropocene" that is worth quoting at some length:

Ecologists and conservationists have grossly overstated the fragility of nature. . . . In many circumstances, the demise of formerly abundant species can be inconsequential to ecosystem function. The American chestnut, once a dominant tree in eastern North America, has been extinguished by a foreign disease, yet the forest ecosystem is surprisingly unaffected. The passenger pigeon, once so abundant that its flocks darkened the sky, went extinct, along with countless other species from the Steller's sea cow to the dodo, with no catastrophic or even measurable effects.[6]

About the polar bear in particular, Kareiva et al. have this to say:

Even that classic symbol of fragility—the polar bear, seemingly stranded on a melting ice block—may have a good chance of surviving global warming if the changing environment continues to increase the populations and northern ranges of harbor seals and harp seals. Polar bears evolved from brown bears 200,000 years ago during a cooling period in Earth's history, developing a highly specialized carnivorous diet focused on seals. Thus, the fate of polar bears depends on two opposing trends—the decline of sea ice and the potential increase of energy-rich prey. The history of life on Earth is of species evolving to take advantage of new environments only to be at risk when the environment changes again.[7]

Note the way this account equates past extinctions due to natural causes with the possible extinction of the polar bear due to human-caused climate change. That is just "the history of life," adapting or failing to adapt to changing conditions. Note the disappearance of any sense of *human agency* for the current threat to the polar bear: The polar bear's fate depends on "two opposing trends" as "the environment changes," not on whether or not humanity ratchets back greenhouse gas emissions. Finally, note the glibness with which the authors talk about the extinction of this magnificent beast ("seemingly stranded on a melting ice block"). Elsewhere in the article, they contemplate with equanimity the relentless conversion of Earth's greatest reservoir of terrestrial biodiversity, the Amazon rainforest, to sterile, shit-caked cattle ranches.[8]

Extinguishing species through the continued expansion of human economic activities appears to be okay with Kareiva and his coauthors, at least as long as we do not harm the "ecosystem services" upon which humanity depends for its own well-being. Well, it's not okay with me.[9] I say that if our actions or institutions threaten to extinguish the polar bear and a large fraction of the other species on Earth, then we need to *change* our actions or institutions. And it seems to me that any real conservationist would agree.

When people take or ruin so much habitat or so many resources that another species is driven extinct, they have taken or ruined too much. Natural species are the primary examples and repositories of organic nature's order, creativity, and diversity. They represent thousands of millions of years of activity and achievement. They show incredible functional, organizational, and behavioral complexity. Every species, like every person, is unique, with its own history and destiny. Our fellow travelers on this beautiful blue-green planet deserve our appreciation and our restraint.

Conservation without such restraint threatens to render conservationists little more than a supporting division in a vast human army devoted to ecological imperialism. We can do better.

We have a choice

The problem with embracing the Anthropocene epoch is that it accepts a morally unacceptable status quo. Thankfully, we have a choice here. It is just not true that our only path is ever further into the Anthropocene. We can instead work to ratchet back the current, excessive human footprint on Earth and make a place (hopefully, many places) for other species to also flourish on our common home planet.

Question: Does talk about ratcheting back the human footprint mean that "people are bad"? That they make natural areas "impure" by their very presence? That conservationists want to return to an imaginary, Edenic past of unsullied innocence?

Answer: Of course not! People are great. Human culture, with all its achievements, is great. Cities can be great. But all of this is great only *within limits*.

Culture must be balanced by nature, in the life of a well-rounded person or on the landscape of any nation that is fit to live in. And it isn't just all about us. People need to limit how much habitat and other resources we engross, in order to leave enough for other species to flourish. An appreciation of limits and recognition of the need for this balance are the key differences between those who embrace the Anthropocene and those who seek to create something better.

In any case, I insist that we have a choice about all this. We can choose whether or not to further the human domination of the world. Consider the conservation goals I suggested earlier.

We can work to expand the number and size of parks and protected areas, or not. We can try, where possible, to keep biodiversity protection rather than resource extraction or other human economic uses, as the primary mission of these areas. Similarly, we can work within mixed-use, "working landscapes" to prioritize biodiversity protection over commodity production. All these are choices.

We can work to lessen the human impacts that degrade wildlife habitat, such as air and water pollution, or climate change. We know that Everglades National Park is not "pristine," but still, we can take steps which will significantly decrease the phosphates running into the park, or not. We can work to limit greenhouse gas emissions, or accept that rising sea levels will inundate and destroy large parts of the park. Again: choices.

We know that international trade will continue to transfer species around the world. But we can take steps to limit the transfer of exotic species into new areas, such as establishing and enforcing rules regarding acceptable ballast in ships, and prohibiting the trade in certain exotic animals. Or, we can just throw up our hands. Once again: choices.

Then there are the two primary forces driving ecological degradation in the world today: demographic and economic growth. Anthropocene proponents advise us to either accept or ignore population growth as a given, and to embrace economic growth as one of the main goals of conservation. Given the environmental costs of growth, these are their most perverse and self-defeating suggestions. But again, we are free to reject their advice.

We know that it is very likely that the human population will continue to grow over the next few decades.[10] But conservationists can and should work to help stabilize and then reduce human numbers, gradually and noncoercively. The U.N. Population Fund estimates that 215 million women around the world have an unmet need for contraception; meeting that need could help reduce the world population in 2060 from a medium or "most likely" projection of 9.4 billion to 8.2 billion people instead. Many conservation goals would be facilitated if we could achieve this lower number. Conservationists can engage with population policy debates, or continue to neglect them. It is a choice.

Similarly, we know that maximizing economic growth will continue to be the primary organizing goal for most politicians in most countries of the world in the short term. But this approach is not sustainable in the long term, so once again conservationists have choices to make. We can sound the alarm about the costs of growth, work to redefine personal success and social progress in less materialistic terms, and join our more progressive fellow citizens in exploring practical alternatives to the endless growth economy.[11] Or we can get with the Anthropocene program, redefine conservation in service to economic growth, and cut our goals to fit what the current, life-destroying system will give us. With the evidence building that humanity is bumping up against ecological limits, even those who care only about people would seem to have good reasons to begin to look into alternatives to the economic status quo. Those of us who also care about wild nature have even more reason to do so.

Consider the prognosis for several U.S. national parks under "business as usual" economic policies and their accompanying climate change:[12]

- ▶ Glacier National Park is losing its glaciers, the last of which may melt away by 2030. Loss of glacial runoff and reduced snowpack will decrease stream flows, possibly driving native bull trout (*Salvelinus confluentus*) extinct. Iconic wildlife species such as grizzly bears, wolverines, and mountain goats are likely to decline due to drier, warmer conditions.

- ▶ Rocky Mountain National Park and surrounding wilderness areas contain hundreds of thousands of acres of dead or dying pine forests. As the National Park Service Climate Change Response Program website explains: "Pine beetles are natural to this system, but normally the harsh Colorado winters are cold enough to kill off many of these beetles. However with warming winter temperatures it has allowed the beetle population to explode, causing the devastation of lodgepole pine trees in the park." In addition, like Glacier, Rocky Mountain could lose rare wildflower species as alpine habitats shrink or are degraded.

- ▶ In Everglades National Park, climate change–induced sea-level rises of only a few meters threaten to submerge large areas of the park, including most current mangrove stands, key nurseries for ocean fishes. Wading bird populations, already greatly decreased since the park's establishment in 1947, due to excessive water withdrawals, will decline even further due to habitat loss and introduced species. Coral reefs at nearby Biscayne National Park will probably be lost due to higher temperatures and ocean acidification. American alligators, at the southern edge of their distribution, may disappear from Everglades, as may pikas from Rocky and Harlequin ducks from Glacier.

It is up to those of us who care about wild nature to sound the alarm about all this and to try to specify alternatives. We need to affirm that it is *wrong* for humanity to displace and dominate nature; wrong to drive other species extinct for our own economic benefit; wrong to tame or displace Earth's remaining wildlands. Aldo Leopold said it well, sixty-five years ago, in *A Sand County Almanac*: "A land ethic cannot of course prevent the alteration, management and 'use' of these 'resources' [wildlands and other species], but it does affirm their right to continued existence, and, at least in spots, their continued existence in a natural state."

The flourishing of the diversity of life is a great good, while the anthropogenic extinction of species, ripping large holes in the tapestry of life, is a great and preventable evil. Given these moral imperatives, we need to move away from economies premised on the goal of ever-more-stuff-for-ever-more-people toward economies designed to provide a sufficiency for a limited number of people.

What truly sustainable economies will look like, in detail, is difficult to say. However, there is no long-term future for wild nature under the economic status quo. Along with our current work, then, conservationists need to begin working on the transition to a sustainable economy that respects ecological limits.

Would Aldo Leopold have been "optimistic" about the prospects for polar bears or jaguars today or about the prospects for wild nature generally in the twenty-second century and beyond? I do not know. But I doubt that he would have jettisoned his commitments to wild nature in order to feel more comfortable and optimistic in the Anthropocene era. And neither should we.

Green Postmodernism and the Attempted Highjacking of Conservation

HARVEY LOCKE

CONSERVATIONISTS ARE ACCUSTOMED to having a clear foe—the exploiters who would use up this beautiful world and then move on to use up
the next planet. The exploiters are hubristic and interested only in what
they can exploit for personal gain. Their core philosophy was captured
succinctly by Robert Bidinotto: "Nature indeed provides beautiful settings
for the work of man. But unseen and unappreciated the environment is
meaningless. It is but an empty frame, in which we and our works are the
picture. From that perspective, environmentalism means sacrificing the
picture to spare the frame."[1]

We know their arguments well, and we understand that with them we
debate an essentially moral issue. Conservationists are humble in the face
of creation and evolution and believe in the intrinsic value of all life regardless of its usefulness to us. Most of us know that we must use the Earth
to meet our needs, but we also believe that we must live responsibly by
practicing self-restraint. This includes a duty to preserve life on Earth in
all its beautiful manifestations. We feel morally armed by this altruism toward nature and contrast it with the exploiters' self-serving greed. It is hard
work. While we have had some major successes at creating park and wil-

derness areas to protect wild nature, overall we know we are losing ground. Nevertheless, we carry on, armed by the confidence that we are doing the right thing, optimistic that eventually a critical mass of humanity will rally with us to save the wild world and all the myriad benefits it confers on us.

In the last twenty years a more subtle and perhaps equally dangerous group has snuck up on conservationists. They come in stealth, professing to be allies with a fresh approach. They come armed with altruism—concern for the poor and disenfranchised humans around the world. Sharing this moral value, we conservationists listen to them, strive to accommodate their concerns, and then learn to our dismay that they don't share our basic goal of conserving wild nature. In reality their approach is about exploiting nature for the exclusive purpose of human gain. They would convert wild nature to a garden managed for the benefit of local communities in service of the cause of helping the world's poor and vulnerable.[2] They share with the exploiters a common core ideology: that the Earth is there to serve people; only their focus is the poor instead of the rich. And they now threaten to undermine the basic approach to conservation rooted in park and wilderness protection and in laws that protect wildlife which have proven successful worldwide.

Some call this group the "new environmentalists."[3] But I think that is not the right label. I prefer to call them "green postmodernists" because their ideas are rooted in the non-ideology of postmodernism. Unrecognized and unaddressed, they may become as problematic to the cause of the survival of wild nature as the exploiters.

If you have read this far and are over fifty, you might just be asking yourself: What the hell is he talking about? You may never have heard of *postmodernism*. If you care to read on, you are in for a surprising intellectual ride. In case you doubt whether it is worth your time, ask anyone educated between 1990 and 2005 at a liberal arts college in North America whether they have heard of postmodernism. They have. They just haven't told you about it. They might even delight in your ignorance. And you simply cannot understand the appeal or the danger of the green postmodernists without understanding at least enough of postmodernism to recognize it when you see it.

Postmodernism

Postmodernism is elusive to understand. One of its core elements is that it defies definition.[4] It has laudable origins. In Europe, after World War

II, several intellectuals surveyed the wreckage of the preceding hundred years and saw the devastating effects of the "Isms": colonialism and the destruction, including enslavement, of non-European cultures; fascism and the horrors of excessive nationalism, including genocide; capitalism, which benefits the rich and makes the poor poorer, including dangerous working conditions and even the exploitation of child labor; communism, which suppresses freedom, sometimes to the point of forced internment camps and mental reprogramming; and, finally, the appalling collision of all the "Isms" in the form of two ideologically driven World Wars. They also studied who holds power and how it is exercised in both apparent and hidden ways in Western society. All the big theories of history, progress, and knowledge are viewed as ways of trying to produce conformity. When one ideology is privileged over another it carries with it power over others. This led to a theory that all ideologies are tools of oppression and therefore the only way to be free of tyranny is to be free of ideologies. Postmodernism expresses mistrust of any centralizing thought or action.[5]

The skepticism toward ideologies includes even those ways of thinking designed to mitigate the worst effects of the "Isms." In their view, modernism, animated by the belief that we could have a humanitarian world using social tools, is just another form of oppression by the social engineers. The scientific worldview is a form of oppression too, tyrannical for excluding other ways of knowing, such as traditional ecological knowledge of aboriginal people. Indeed any coherent approach to a problem based on ideas can be deconstructed to expose the powerful group it was designed to serve. This in turn requires us to be skeptical of metanarratives, which means we should refuse to participate in the coherent stories by which societies function. There are no core truths or facts, for they are all devices that serve some group at the expense of others. This includes Western science and the discipline of history.

Faced with the inherent tyranny of ideologies, the postmodernist concludes that the only proper course is to tear down all of them. The only goal should be the relief of human suffering. Thus, attacking power by attacking the core beliefs on which it is based, exposing the elite group that is served by those beliefs (often the "dead white men" from colonial empires who first espoused them), and demanding the elimination of such power concentration by distributing all control to the "community" level is the only valid course in the postmodern worldview. It is expressed with great clarity in David Mitchell's *Cloud Atlas*, which is considered a postmodern "classic." The thirty-something lead-female character who is an investigative reporter says: "I ask three simple questions. How did he get that power? How is he using it? And how can it be taken off the sonofabitch?"[6]

The postmodernist has no plan to make a better world, he or she just engages in an effort to make it less oppressive.[7] The thing to do is to challenge power on a day-to-day level rather than engage in grand utopian schemes to improve human destiny.[8] This is the core non-ideology of postmodernism. And now green postmodernists have set their sights on challenging conservationists.

The postmodern approach to conservation

True to postmodernism's European origins, the first critics of conservation's basic tool of parks and wilderness protection came from Europe. This was aided by a cultural predisposition toward anti-Americanism,[9] because parks and wilderness conservation have often been called "American ideas." I first experienced postmodernism's entry into conservation at a NATO conference—held in Kraków, Poland, in 1995—on the topic of national parks and their contribution to sustainable development. In his talk, the British head of the International Union for Conservation of Nature's (IUCN's) World Commission on Protected Areas, Adrian Phillips, referred to wilderness as a "discredited concept." He and others promoted a "new paradigm" of people-centered conservation and called for a rejection of "Yellowstone's children," meaning the national-park-as-nature-reserve approach to conservation.[10] This approach came to have a big presence on the agenda at the 2004 IUCN World Park Congress in Durban, South Africa. In some corners, conservation based on scientific findings was squarely attacked. In a pamphlet made available in Durban, the French Institute of Biodiversity took the postmodern position against a scientific approach: "We call this science 'conservation biology' and the people making these arguments are still biologists, ecologists, and population geneticists. This creates a harmful bias which leads to exclusion and close-mindedness . . . This cultural bias is already impeding the implementation of a sustainable biodiversity management strategy in some developed countries."[11]

The human-dominated approach to conservation highlighted at Durban provoked an intense international debate when defenders of the traditional approach to conservation spoke up.[12] We said that if we want to save nature, then traditional parks and wilderness areas devoted to protecting wild species and natural processes work well, and we need more of them, interconnected across the landscape. We should not think of human-dominated landscapes as protected areas if they are primarily serving the needs of people instead of nature conservation. We urged respect for conservation biology and called for action on their findings, which would enable us to prevent extinction, establish viable populations of species, and maintain natural processes. "Sustainable development" is what we do outside protected areas.

At the core of the debate was whether protected areas exist to protect the ecological needs of biodiversity as determined by science (with the incidental benefits that flow to people), or whether they should serve as gardens managed for the benefit of people (with biodiversity protection as a hoped-for by-product of local management by traditional means). One is focused on the needs of nature, the other on meeting the needs of people with nature only potentially an incidental beneficiary. The World Commission on Protected Areas addressed the controversy by facilitating a global consultation that culminated in a summit in Almeria, Spain, in May of 2007, where park experts from around the world debated these ideas. A thoughtful paper, intended to counter ours, was produced that illustrated the challenges of conservation in crowded and long-settled areas like the Mediterranean Basin.[13] Importantly, the authors moved toward reconciliation with conservationists by expressing fundamental agreement about the need for protected areas to focus on nature first regardless of where they are. They also agreed that wilderness conservation should not be eliminated in favor of a people-centered approach to conservation, but it should be supplemented by it. While their focus was on biodiversity conservation in more human-affected landscapes, they acknowledged the importance of wilderness: "Wilderness, where it exists, should also be protected where possible, since the presence of naturally occurring ecological processes in those areas are most likely to be resilient in the face of increasing disturbance, natural or otherwise."[14]

The Almeria Summit's participants concluded that protected areas should remain focused on nature conservation as the primary objective, and new guidelines were issued to make that clear.[15] A recent article from the United Kingdom (UK) demonstrates the widespread international agreement with the outcome of this process and calls for its implementation in the UK's protected areas.[16] The authors recognize the primacy of nature conservation as the key outcome: "The most important [outcome of the Almeria process and new guidelines] . . . is recognition of the multiple roles for protected areas but with nature conservation (broadly defined) as the ultimate priority."[17]

Green postmodernism in America

In spite of the long-standing global conservation and the reasonable reconciliation reached at the international level through IUCN's process, we now find the emergence of green postmodernists in the United States. Predictably, they argue for a human-centered approach to conservation; support the rejection of wilderness; and do not make any reference to the global debate that preceded them.

It is useful to review the history of the American engagement with the postmodern approach to conservation. It first surfaced in the United States in the 1990s. Historian William Cronon's book *Changes in the Land* suggested that aboriginal people were farming everywhere and that there was no wilderness when the pilgrims arrived in New England. In a subsequent essay Cronon argued: "If wildness can stop being (just) out there and start being (also) in here, if it can start being as humane as it is natural, then perhaps we can get on with the unending task of struggling to live rightly in the world—not just in the garden, not just in the wilderness, but in the home that encompasses them both."[18] Historian Baird Callicott subsequently edited a book, *The Great New Wilderness Debate*, which contained essays infused with a postmodern worldview (such as his own in that volume), juxtaposed with essays defending the traditional value of wilderness conservation.[19] In 2004 Mac Chapin called into question the presumption that biological science should be the sole guiding principle for biodiversity conservation in protected natural areas: "This notion has produced a running debate between those who do not see human inhabitants as a part of the ecological equation, and those who argue for partnerships and the inclusion of indigenous and traditional peoples in protected area plans, both on human rights grounds and for pragmatic ecological reasons."[20] While these arguments caused controversy in professional circles in the United States, they did not really undermine the conservation movement. They were taken into account in the international discussions. They also had the salutary effect of making conservationists think more about how to include local people's needs in their efforts. But these postmodernist-inspired debates did not widely seep into broader culture.

That has begun to change. The coauthored 2011 essay by Peter Kareiva, Robert Lalasz and Michelle Marvier, "Conservation in the Anthropocene: Beyond Solitude and Fragility," published on the website of the Breakthrough Institute, has presented to a broader audience the postmodern approach to conservation. It no doubt garnered attention because the lead author is the chief scientist for the Nature Conservancy, a well-known conservation organization in the United States that also has global programs. This essay was not published in a peer-reviewed journal where factual assertions would be scrutinized; it was published online which made it easy to circulate. Its tearing down of the traditional approach to conservation has been praised by the exploiters and their intellectual allies who hail the authors as "new environmentalists."[21]

Deconstructing the postmodern "Conservation in the Anthropocene"

It is important to scrutinize the postmodern approach to conservation advocated by Kareiva and his colleagues. My concern lies with the authors' central point that "instead of pursuing the protection of biodiversity for biodiversity's sake, a new conservation should seek to enhance those natural systems that benefit the widest number of people, especially the poor."[22] Such an approach is dangerous to the survival of wild nature.

In classic postmodern style, Kareiva et al.'s essay deconstructs the conservation of wild nature through parks and reserves. Their critique is not limited to examining ideas; it also endeavors to discredit the source of the ideas. They prove a point made by British writer George Monbiot, who recently wrote: "So those of us whose love of the natural world is a source of constant joy and constant despair, who wish to immerse ourselves in nature as others immerse themselves in art, who try to defend the marvels which enthrall us, find ourselves labelled—from the Mail to the Guardian—as romantics, escapists and fascists."[23] Kareiva and coauthors first endeavor in the article to deconstruct nature as a cultural concept, stating: "One need not be a postmodernist to understand that the concept of Nature, as opposed to the physical and chemical workings of natural systems, has always been a human construction, shaped and designed for human ends."[24] This and the related idea that wilderness is a human construct as well are common postmodern assertions. I will address them in more detail below.

Then the authors attack the thinkers who have most persuasively exposited the ideas on which nature conservation has been based. Henry David Thoreau, who spoke of wildness as the preservation of the world, is mocked for living close enough to town so "that he could frequently receive guests and have his mother wash his clothes."[25] Ralph Waldo Emerson and other nature writers are marked as hypocrites for their concern about the impacts of cities and human development, because they were "mostly urban intellectuals." Wilderness writer Edward Abbey is chastised because he "pined for companionship in his private journal even as he publicly exulted in his ascetic life in *Desert Solitaire*." Rachel Carson, they say, "wrote plaintively in *Silent Spring* of the delicate web of life." They accuse conservationist John Muir of having been a colonial oppressor: "Muir had sympathized with the oppression of the Winnebago Indians in his home state, but when it came time to empty Yosemite of all except the naturalists and tourists, Muir vigorously backed the expulsion of the Miwok. The Yosemite model spread to other national parks, including Yellowstone, where the forced evictions killed 300 Shoshone in one day."[26]

This Yellowstone story is egregiously inaccurate (which will be discussed further below) as well as a slur on a man who is a hero to many conservationists.

The authors also attack the moral underpinnings of traditional conservation. Conservation, they argue, may look like altruism, but it isn't; it is a tool of oppression: "Conservation is widely viewed as [an] innocent practice. . . .In truth, for 30 years, the global conservation movement has been racked with controversy arising from its role in expelling indigenous people from their lands in order to create parks and reserves. The modern protection of supposed wilderness often involves resettling large numbers of people, too often without fair compensation for their lost homes, hunting grounds, and agricultural lands."[27]

The authors go on to declare that park and wilderness conservation is "controversial," which apparently is bad in and of itself: "Conservation will be controversial as long as it remains so narrowly focused on the creation of parks and protected areas, and insists, often unfairly, that local people cannot be trusted to care for their land."[28] And they further suggest that parks with visitor facilities are "no less human constructions than Disneyland." The article culminates with this inconsistent one-liner: "None of this is to argue for eliminating nature reserves."[29] This is a transparent attempt by the authors to insulate themselves from the force of their own words. One is reminded of Mark Antony's eulogy in Shakespeare's *Julius Caesar*.

Science and history: casualties of postmodernism

A cavalier attitude toward the findings of science is a hallmark of post-modernism. Ian McEwen's humorous novel *Solar* chronicles the astonishment of his protagonist Michael Beard, a Nobel prize–winning scientist, when he encounters the ideas of postmodernism: "Beard had heard rumours that strange ideas were commonplace among the liberal arts departments. It was said that humanities students were routinely taught that science was just one more belief system, no more or less truthful than religion or astrology. He had always thought that this must be a slur against his colleagues on the arts side."[30] Devaluing science has become so acute among postmodernists that physicist Alan Sokal was able to publish a deliberately satirical article in the "Science Wars" issue of the postmodern journal *Social Text* in which he glibly declared that "physical reality" is a social and linguistic construct. The editors of *Social Text* didn't get the spoof and published it as a bona fide, serious article.[31] In a review of Curtis White's *The Science Delusion*, philosopher Mark Kingwell highlights the postmodernist's skepticism of science: "Good science can shade itself into the self-aggrandizing ideology of scientism," which has "ties to financial and social power." He continues: "Refusing to accept its status as one imaginative discourse among many, claiming the key to all intellectual doors as well as the lion's share of grant money, this kind of science has aligned itself with 'the broader ideology of social regimentation, economic exploitation, environmental destruction, and industrial militarism.'"[32]

Kareiva and his colleagues talk of the resiliency of nature. They maintain that "the trouble for conservation is that the data simply do not support the idea of a fragile nature at risk of collapse." There is unquestionably good news that components of ecosystems, if protected soon enough, can rebound.[33] But the assertion that nature is not fragile does not follow. Extinction is permanent. The IUCN Red List chronicles the alarming number of species at risk of disappearing forever.[34]

Perhaps the most astonishing assertion the authors make to support their view that nature is not fragile is that cod on George's Bank, off the coast of Newfoundland, have recovered to "pre-collapse levels," and that this is not celebrated because conservationists are "somehow addicted to stories of collapse and environmental apocalypse." This assertion of cod recovery is farcical. The George's Bank cod populations are an extension of those found off the coast of Newfoundland which have not rebounded at all, and in fact cod populations are a shadow of what they were even in living human memory.[35] Jeff Hutchings, a coauthor of a study on the status of cod, published in a 2013 *Science* article,[36] said in a press interview: "Looking at the size of the [cod] stock today compared to what it was in the [19]60s, it's still miniscule. So while there's been some positive signs over the last decade, really, at the end of the day, the stock is so far below what's called its limit reference point, it isn't funny."[37] This assessment is not limited to cod. According to the authors of the aforementioned *Science* article, current harvest levels render recovery improbable for the majority of the world's depleted stocks. Just as troubling as these inaccurate assertions is the authors' omission of other, pertinent information. Kareiva and his coauthors fail to mention either important research chronicling the unsustainability of fishing in most fisheries or the remarkable success of no-take marine sanctuaries where they have been established.[38]

The authors anchor their attack on conservation reserves by pointing out a few of them where management failures have resulted in degradation within the areas protected. This is fallacious. The failure to implement a good idea well does not invalidate the idea. It speaks only to the failure of implementation.

All of this is very curious for an essay that begins by professing a concern for wild tigers and apes that "will be lost forever if current trends continue." It is crystal clear that mountain gorillas in East Africa and tigers in India currently persist only in parks and protected areas.[39] Kareiva et al. never circle back to talk about how we can conserve and protect those species from extinction without such reserves.

In her deeply insightful essay, "Postmodernist History," historian Gertrude Himmelfarb describes the skepticism postmodernists show toward the discipline of the professional historian: "Where modernism regards the obstacles in the way of objectivity as a challenge and makes a strenuous effort to attain as much objectivity and unbiased truth as possible, postmodernism takes the rejection of absolute truth as a deliverance from all truth and from the obligation to maintain any degree of objectivity."[40]

The deliverance from the obligation to remain objective in relation to history is highlighted in the slur made by Kareiva and coauthors against John Muir as quoted above. There simply was no slaughter of 300 Shoshone people in a day to create Yellowstone. This is a fabrication. Even the most postmodern history of the park and native people makes no such reference.[41] It is also grossly unfair to infer that American attitudes to aboriginal people in the nineteenth century had to do with park imperialism in Yosemite, Yellowstone, or anywhere else. Such attitudes were pervasive in the culture and rooted in the idea of Manifest Destiny and the related colonization and agricultural conversion of the West, and not specific to national parks at all. As Ferdinand Hayden—the man who surveyed Yellowstone in 1872—put it: "The present Indian policy, which doubtless looks forward to the localization and settlement of these roving tribes, is ultimately connected with agricultural development of the West. Unless they are localized and made to enter upon agricultural and pastoral pursuits they must ultimately be exterminated. There is no middle ground between these extremes. . . . If extermination is the result of non-compliance, then compulsion is an act of mercy."[42]

It is widely known that this society-wide policy has had many tragic consequences for Native Americans,[43] but it is wrong to blame it on parks and other protected areas.

Wilderness is real

For people like me who have done multi-week wilderness trips that involve travel by foot, horse, canoe, or raft hundreds of kilometers from the nearest road or human settlement, the assertion that there is no such thing as wilderness is patently absurd. Kareiva and his colleagues, however, boldly assert that wilderness doesn't exist at all. "The wilderness so beloved by conservationists—places 'untrammeled by man'—never existed, at least not in the last thousand years and arguably even longer."[44] To counter these assertions it is useful to examine Anthropocene proponent Erle Ellis's findings, published in his coauthored paper "Used Planet: A Global History."

Ellis and his colleagues challenge a widely used HYDE model that indicates that, except for developed regions of Europe, transformative human use of the land was insignificant before 1750. Their new KK10 model suggests human transformative use was much earlier and more widespread than that: "Regionally, KK10 predicts that 20% of Europe and Asia were already used significantly by 3000 BC and most other regions by A.D 1000 . . . HYDE suggests that no other region than Europe reached these levels before A.D. 1900."[45]

While their findings may challenge the HYDE model's, they are a far cry from supporting the assertion that there was no wilderness in the world over the last one thousand years. At least 80 percent of the terrestrial world was in a wilderness condition in 1900, according to their own KK10 model. In fact, the maps in Ellis et al.'s "Used Planet" article show vast areas of the world that even today remain unaffected by significant human use or dense settlements. And the oceans are not even included in their analysis. They were in a largely wild condition before the industrial revolution and the demand for whale oil emerged in the early 1800s.

Ellis's coauthored terrestrial analysis corresponds well with the findings of another global analysis, "The Human Footprint and the Last of the Wild" and several other surveys done using different metrics that show the remaining wild places on terrestrial Earth.[46] These places are roadless; are still dominated by natural processes; have never been cultivated; have very few or no permanent human settlements; and are still roamed by animals that can eat you. I and other adventurous people have seen these wild places firsthand. The fact that both human-made aerial toxins and climate change impact the wilderness does not make it cease to exist. Simply put, the assertion that wilderness does not exist, and has not existed for the last one thousand years, is unsupportable.

To those of us who have experienced such primeval places, claims of the non-existence of wilderness are absurd and offensive, for there is more to it than the physical reality of wilderness. I feel a spiritual connection to wild nature.[47] Writers like Emerson, Thoreau, and Muir were masters at capturing our feelings in the presence of nature; they were not inventors of idealized places. I remember being surprised as a young adult when I first read the work of these authors, for they expressed something I had felt all my life but which I had not known others had described. These great American nature writers should be honored, not mocked. And they do not express a uniquely American phenomenon but rather a *human* experience that defies national boundaries and cultural differences. I am Canadian, and people of many other cultures experience these feelings too, for this spiritual connection is a response to the power of wild places—like mountains, forests, and rivers—and not the invention of any particular culture.[48] Many countries around the world are engaged in wilderness and wild nature protection,[49] and the numerous individuals invested in these protection efforts include aboriginal people.[50] For the sake of both wild nature and the human spirit, we need to protect wilderness, restore it where it has been damaged, and not deny its existence.

What is really animating the postmodernist approach of denying the very existence of wilderness is an effort to privilege its people-oriented approach over a wild nature–oriented approach to conservation. This is well captured by Nigel Dudley: "It would be fair to say that conservation is to some extent divided into two camps: those who focus primarily on wilderness or some similar concept and the need to preserve what is left of mainly natural habitats, and those predominantly interested in nature as an aspect of culture, whose focus is primarily in places where humans and nature co-exist. The very word 'wilderness' has become a battle ground between people who view it as positive or negative term."[51]

Non-conservation "Conservation"

Freed from the scientific evidence that parks and wilderness reserves have been enormously effective and essential to the survival of many wild species, and with complete disregard for the permanent consequences of extinction, the green postmodernists feel at liberty to advocate for the dissolution of conservation as a coherent enterprise: "If there is no wilderness," they ask, "if nature is resilient rather than fragile... what should be our new vision for conservation?"[52] To them the goal of conservation should not be a conservation goal at all. It should be about something else, namely relieving the suffering of poor people; as referenced earlier, the green postmodernists envision a new conservation, one that focuses on providing optimal benefits for the greatest number of *people* possible, in particular poor people, rather than an effort to protect biodiversity for the sake of biodiversity itself. In their view: "Protecting biodiversity for its own sake has not worked. Protecting nature that is dynamic and resilient, that is in our midst rather than far away, and that sustains human communities— these are the ways forward now."[53] One must ask: Where did the concern for wild apes and tigers go? Poof! Vanished!

Apes and tigers, grizzly bears and wolves, and elephants and lions are all inconvenient to people. Natural processes like fire and flooding are also inconvenient, but they are critical to the health of biodiversity and the structure of ecosystems.[54] Large, even continental-scale landscapes unfragmented by roads, industrial agricultural fields, large resource extraction projects, and human settlements are inconvenient to some people (though inspiring to others like me) but necessary for the preservation of wildlife migratory paths and habitat for large, keystone carnivores and herbivores. The wealth or poverty of humans is not a factor for these species and processes.

Inconvenient species survive only if we make concerted efforts to protect them. Conservation reserves, managed intentionally for their benefit, are essential. Of course more is needed than just reserves, but reserves are the indispensable prerequisite to their survival in all but the most remote places. Inconvenient species will not survive as an incidental side effect of local people's preference for biodiversity that serves only their needs. The concerted efforts that have been required to protect large carnivores like brown bears and lynx, and to try to return them to viable population levels in Europe, illustrate these points clearly.[55]

To begin an essay with professed concern for apes and tigers, which are surviving only in conservation reserves, and to end the same essay with no reference whatsoever to those species highlights the basic flaw inherent in the postmodern approach to conservation. Notwithstanding the fact that these inconvenient species need interconnected nature reserves with natural processes to survive and thrive, the green postmodernists don't care. It is all about people and what they want.

The close kinship of exploiters and green postmodernists

The exploiters' worldview is fundamentally aligned with the green postmodernists' worldview—the only material difference being that the former are concerned with protecting the wealthy, and the latter, with empowering the poor. To both, wild nature is neither a priority nor even a worthy concern. "Instead of trying to restore remote iconic landscapes pre-European conditions," Kareiva and his colleagues write, "conservation will measure its achievement in large part by its relevance to people, including city dwellers. Nature could be a garden." A recent Facebook post, attacking the Yellowstone to Yukon Conservation Initiative, illustrates the striking similarity between the postmodern perspective and the more familiar exploiter worldview:

Sounds to me like as long as humans stay indoors and don't have a life or job (building roads for logging, mining, fishing and hunting, fuel exploration) you are all ok with this. Well, I live in the Y2Y area and am not an environmentalist. God made this earth for us to inhabit and populate and rule over the animals; not the other way around. Forests are for us to manage, like a big garden you have to weed it, protect it from disease, replant if necessary (God made it to rejuvenate itself). I love wildlife but I think you go too far in the name of conservation.[56]

The exploiters and the green postmodernists equally reject the idea that humans must practice self-restraint in order to return to a healthy and more humble relationship with nature. Right-wing editorial writer Margaret Wente celebrates the union of these two groups in her Earth Day 2013 column. After praising Kareiva and his colleagues for their pragmatism, and after citing their assertion that nature is not fragile, she points out that there is no point in addressing carbon emissions at all:

Peter Kareiva and his fellow enviro-optimists are the key to saving environmentalism from terminal irrelevance. Global warming is the biggest case in point. The challenge is far too great to solve with carbon treaties... or restraint. . . . The fixes for global warming will require dramatically different new technologies, and will only be available in the long term.

Meantime, the planet may indeed be more resilient than we thought. . . . And cheer up, the Anthropocene Age might be better than you think.

The Anthropocene and our ethical responsibility toward nature

The Anthropocene concept is an interesting effort at a novel description of a geological phenomenon of profound change to the Earth's natural systems, comparable to some of the great events of the Earth's deep past, but this time caused by humans. We can agree with the claim that the driving force behind the global changes we are experiencing is human behavior, particularly in social, political, and economic spheres.[57] This, however, does not call for us to abandon tried-and-true methods of conservation, which will continue to be the most effective for protecting nature in light of global change.[58] Rather, the Anthropocene raises the ethical question of what behavior is appropriate for one species with the power of life and death over millions of others.

The approach to conservation in the Anthropocene advocated by the green postmodernists would ensure that we all live in a world diminished by extinction, haunted by the loss of wildness, and managed to the lowest possible standard, if it is managed at all. Even worse, the visionless non-ideology of green postmodernism deprives us of hope—the hope of reconciling humanity with the rest of wild nature in an ethical way that allows all of nature to flourish along with us.

We can have a more beautiful and fulfilling relationship with the wild world, even on a planet where we have become a geological force. We just have to have a positive dream, work hard, and make it so using the tried-and-true tools of conservation. To this we add the need for connectivity.[59] Moreover, we must scale-up our thinking to protect at least half of the natural world, including land and water, in an interconnected way.[60] We can be gentle and thoughtful while we do so and work with local people to take into account their needs. But we cannot abandon apes and tigers or other inconvenient species and processes.

Those of us who love wild nature must stand up to the green post-modernists as vigorously as we do to the exploiters. Even if we are to credit them with an altruistic motive, the road to extinction will be paved with their postmodern intentions. If we have the moral courage to work passionately for the survival of wild nature, and create more interconnected parks and wilderness reserves, our grandchildren will thank us for the Earth they inherit.

Why the Working Landscape Isn't Working

GEORGE WUERTHNER

WORDS INFLUENCE HOW we think about issues. We use euphemisms to hide or modify the perception of what might otherwise produce negative reactions to more honest terminology. Saying "collateral damage," for example, sounds more innocuous than announcing civilian deaths of non-combative women, men, and children. "Coercive interrogation," to provide another example of alternative language, became a convenient phrase for the Bush Administration, when it had stated unequivocally that "this government does not torture people." In George Orwell's *1984*, the Ministry of Peace waged war.

George Lakoff, author of *Don't Think of an Elephant*, suggests that conservatives and industry have spent decades defining ideas and carefully choosing enticing language to best present those ideas. One of the more insidious terms used to promote a pro-development agenda is *working landscapes* and its derivations, such as "working ranches," "working forests," "working lands," or "working rivers" (with hydro dams). The ultimate Orwellian spin-off of the "working landscape" is "working wilderness," used to describe domestic livestock ranching operations in the Southwest.[1] Extractive industries have succeeded in capturing the values debate through the frequent use of the phrase "working landscape," putting a positive spin on domesticated lands that are logged, grazed, farmed, or otherwise human-modified.

"Working landscapes" was first coined by the timber industry in New England seeking to put a happier face on the wreckage and ruin it imposed upon the natural landscape and to counter a then-popular and far more accurate characterization of logged lands as "Paper Factories" or "Paper Colonies." The notion of working landscapes was adopted to counter the negative connotations of "factories" and "colonies" in the public's mind, with the former suggesting smokestacks and the latter conjuring imperialism.

For instance, the brochure "Keeping Maine's Forest," put out by a collection of unidentified timber companies and conservation and environmental interests, trumpets the merits of the "working forest" for its ability to provide timber and environmental values. The brochure states: "The Maine Woods has long been a working forest, producing lumber for boats and buildings, pulp for paper, firewood and chips for heat and electricity. The Maine Woods supports thousands of jobs for Mainers and contributes billions of dollars to the state's economy—all while providing critical environmental services like water quality, wildlife habitat and carbon storage."[2]

The phrase "working forest" subsequently has been widely adopted across America, deployed to describe natural resource-based economic activity including farming,[3] ranching,[4] and logging.[5] Indeed, a Google Search turns up 70 million hits for the term *working landscape* alone, not including working forests, working ranches, working farms, and other variations on the theme.

Disconcertingly, the phrase "working landscape" has even been adopted by many people in the environmental movement or with conservation leanings—even though "working landscapes" connotes and heralds the domestication of natural systems. In particular, boosters of the "Anthropocene" idea—the conceit that humans now control and should intelligently manage the Earth—have embraced the "working landscape" as the centerpiece of their conservation agenda.[6] Even the Nature Conservancy's chief scientist says that conservation's task is no longer to "preserve the wild, but to domesticate nature more wisely."[7]

The concept of working landscapes resonates with America's Puritan work ethic. The implied message of working landscapes is that these lands—controlled, modified, tamed, and put toward so-called productive human ends—are somehow more valuable, more functional, than natural lands. In fact, there is often a perspective that if we don't manage lands, they become degraded. For instance, the Working Forest website suggests that the biggest threat to America's forests is a lack of management:

"Wealthy countries such as the United States are loving many of their forests to death with a lack of active stewardship."[8] Another comment, issued online by Idaho's Forest Products Commission under the topic heading of Working Forests, echoes this same attitude: "Harvest is also an essential part of good forest management that can improve forest health and keep our forests growing."[9]

It would be one thing if advocates of so-called working landscapes merely asserted that lands are still capable of providing limited conservation value even if used for human ends, but supporters of working landscapes often promote them as "superior" and/or desirable alternatives to natural landscapes.[10] In a recent video on Iowa Public TV, for instance, the narrator asks the question: "How do we sustain our mountainsides, ocean-sides, and countryside ecosystems for future generations?" And then answers it: "By turning them into working landscapes."[11]

Lands developed or put to use for human purposes are promoted as adequate alternatives to natural wildlands, because they are often characterized as a "win-win," with people getting to exploit natural systems for utilitarian benefit, while nature purportedly also benefits from this exploitation.[12] This justification is akin to how southern plantation owners rationalized slavery by claiming their chattel benefited from their enslavement by having a job, housing, and food provided.[13]

Subtly appealing to the American Protestant ethic, the implied subtext of the phrase "working landscape" is that natural, self-willed landscapes outside of human manipulation and control are shiftless, lazy, unemployed, and not operating at their full "potential." To the devotees of "working landscapes," these self-willed wildlands are not contributing to human health and happiness—or at least not to economic prosperity. Such wildlands certainly are not, in their view, producing economic gains for corporations, individuals, or society.

By contrast, "working landscapes" are linked to economic benefits. In a special issue on working landscapes in *Rangelands*, the authors defined areas deemed to be working landscapes in terms of economic production: "'Working' means, first, that there is *productive* activity on the land—such as farming, ranching, or forestry [emphasis added]."[14]

A recent report on the topic notes, "When most people talk about the 'Working Landscape' they are referring to the land actively used in productive agriculture and forestry."[15] In yet another example, the Idaho Forest Products Commission notes, "Working forests fuel Idaho's economy. Wood and paper businesses employ over 15,000 Idahoans. These are good, solid jobs that pay better than many other industries. And these employees pay more than 20 million dollars in state income taxes each year." Yet in the same publication the authors noted that many national forests were "unhealthy" because they were not being actively "managed" for productive purposes.[16]

Promoting themes that valorize the "working landscape" delegitimizes wildlands protection and green-washes Nature exploitation. In truth, human manipulation of the land generally leads to biological impoverishment. Compared to natural ecosystems, "working landscapes" tend to have lower overall productivity and to suffer losses in biological diversity, soil health, and other ecological attributes.[17] Maintaining these areas also usually requires substantial energy subsidies.[18] Finally, "working landscapes," as a conceptual model for conservation, skews values toward human uses while ignoring the intrinsic value of Nature.

Working landscapes diminish evolutionary processes and are not ecologically benign

Working landscapes, because they manipulate species composition and production toward human ends, tend to disrupt natural evolutionary processes. A tree farm managed for timber fails to maintain natural elements and processes like insects, disease, and wildfire, which are threats to maximizing wood fiber production. A landscape grazed by livestock, which often consume the bulk of native plant production, suffers numerous negative consequences for native plants and animals. Native herbivores depend on the same plants that the cows or sheep are eating for food, and other animals depend on natural vegetation for cover. Compared to the original grassland it supplants, a prairie plowed up and reworked into a monoculture of corn or soybeans becomes, biologically speaking, bankrupt. Promoters of working landscapes have usually been tied to industrial or exploitative economic interests, but increasingly proponents include politicians, media, and social justice advocates (and even many land trusts) who espouse "working landscapes" to protect perceived cultural traditions.

Acknowledging that human activities have modified vast portions of the world's natural ecosystems, and *celebrating* this fact, as advocates of the "working landscape" often appear to do, reflect profoundly different attitudes. We can clearly do better in managing a forest so as to preserve more natural function, or in designing a farm to promote more wildlife-friendly habitat, but we should not be fooled into thinking that such exploitative schemes are superior alternatives to natural ecosystems.

Given our current global population and dependence on technology, humanity may have no choice but to "work the landscape." At the same time, though, we should remain aware that many working-landscape activities are ultimately unsustainable (if only because of heavy reliance on fossil fuel energy subsidies) and that, sooner or later, they impoverish and diminish the natural world.

Indeed, in most instances, "working landscapes" are biologically impoverished compared to the natural landscapes they have replaced.[19] Just to give one example, a comparison between old-growth unlogged forests and a managed forest in Ontario showed a 50 percent reduction in genetic diversity in the logged forest.[20] Biodiversity preservation involves more than maintaining native species. It also requires preservation of ecological and evolutionary processes that shaped biodiversity in the first place. Unfortunately, most active management deliberately minimizes natural ecological/evolutionary processes. For instance, a great deal of forest management in the western United States is now justified to preclude and slow the effects of native pine beetles, which kill some trees, and/or to reduce wildfires which are among the major evolutionary forces in forest ecosystems.[21] Similarly, even the best-managed livestock operations tend to support the killing of large predators like wolves, who are important for their trophic cascade effects on native herbivores and plant communities.[22]

The flawed assumption of the working-landscape proponents is that farms, ranches, or managed timberlands are ecologically benign and help promote conservation. Indeed, after years of hearing working-landscape propaganda, many people now think protecting working landscapes preserves "open space" and assume that open space is the same as good wildlife habitat. Too few realize that due to the emphasis on bending natural systems toward economic goals, working landscapes may be "open" but they are far from wild or natural.

Agriculture, by definition, is the conversion of native plant and animal communities into simplified operations dominated by a few select domestic species. Short of pavement or stripmining, nothing tops agriculture in terms of all-out destructiveness to natural processes and systems. Indeed, in much of the world the major cause of habitat fragmentation and degradation is farming.[23] Society depends upon agriculture to feed ourselves, but we should also understand and acknowledge that farming is the antithesis of wild nature.

Ranching and livestock grazing are somewhat less destructive than cropland farming because the native vegetation is usually retained to some degree, but their physical global footprint affects at least 25 percent of the ice-free surface of the Earth.[24] Thus the overall effect of livestock on biodiversity is substantial.[25]

Domestic species such as cattle or sheep typically replace the native herbivores. Around the world, native animals are forced to compete for forage with domestics. Further, domestic animals raised on relatively arid lands often require irrigated pasture or hay operations that dewater streams and rivers, thereby harming aquatic ecosystems and fish populations. Dewatering of southwestern Montana's Big Hole River for irrigation, for example, has been the primary factor leading to the Montana Arctic grayling (*Thymallus arcticus*) being on the brink of extinction. And depending on how they are managed, domestic animals can trample stream banks and pollute water, and the fences required to contain them become barriers to animal migration.[26] Livestock can also transfer disease to native species. Domestic sheep, for example, are known to carry diseases that are lethal to wild bighorn sheep.[27] Because domestic animals are unable to fend off predators, governments and ranchers often kill bears, wolves, lions, cougars, tigers, and other native predators to protect domestic livestock. In addition to the questionable ethics of such killing, the loss of these predators has serious consequences for the ecosystem.[28]

Although commercial forestry often maintains native tree species, and thus is less destructive than farming, forestry also has significant ecological affects. First, most forestry requires roads for access. Both roads and logging fragment forested landscapes and provide pathways for the invasion of weedy species; sedimentation sources that pollute rivers; and hunters who may adversely impact natural plant and animal community numbers and relationships.[29] Logging also changes the age structure of forests. In presettlement times, large-scale disturbance was rare in many forest communities, and thus forests were older and many were what we now term *ancient* or *old growth*.[30] Such older forests have a greater abundance of snags, tip-up mounds, and large-diameter down woody debris (DWD)—all of which ecologists now recognize as biological legacies that are critical to long-term forest ecosystem function.

The antithesis to landscapes dominated by human resource exploitation are wildland ecosystems, or what I call "working ecosystems." Working ecosystems are productive irrespective of human aspirations. They are the home for most of the world's species, the fountainheads for pure water, and the places where ecological and evolutionary processes operate with minimum interference from humans.

Father-knows-best syndrome

When I was a child, I used to watch a television show called "Father Knows Best," about the Anderson household, an idealized middle-class family. Father was the patient patriarch who distributed wise advice to his wife and three children. There was never a crisis that Dad couldn't solve, and in a way, the show reflected the optimistic attitudes of America in the 1950s and 1960s of my childhood.

Those who advocate greater domestication of the Earth as "working landscapes" have a lot in common with the mythical Anderson family. There is a Father-Knows-Best attitude held by working landscape proponents that, at best, demonstrates a lack of caution regarding human manipulation and exploitation of the Earth. Indeed, the overriding philosophical assumption behind the "working landscape" is that humans are intelligent and wise enough to manage and manipulate landscapes without causing significant harm to the biosphere.

There is no doubt that humans have tremendous influence over the Earth's land, sea, and atmosphere. By some accounts more than a third of the global land area is under cultivation,[31] and an even greater amount of land is used for livestock production.[32] Add to these facts the logging of forests, the overfishing of the oceans, the fossil-fuel burning by humankind that is driving climate change, and a growing human population demanding ever more of the Earth's resources, and it is easy to see why humans may be considered a geological force shaping evolution. And yet, there's a critical difference between documenting and acknowledging human impact and accepting it as inevitable and even desirable.

Industry and others seeking to benefit by capturing the Earth's resources for private profit have long framed exploitation of the natural world in a positive light. What is new about the working-landscape advocates is their promotion of the same exploitation and manipulation in the name of "saving" nature. Be these advocates corporate representatives or the new environmentalists, they lack humility and fail to acknowledge how much we don't understand about how the Earth works. Unlike the positive-outcome-tending mythical father in the TV show, every time we believe we have solved a problem or have figured out how to exploit nature more efficiently, we likely have created a new, unintended consequence.

Many of the spokespersons for this new environmentalism seek to undermine or devalue time-proven approaches to conservation such as parks, wilderness areas, and nature reserves. For instance, Emma Marris, author of *Rambunctious Garden*, has argued that parks and wilderness advocates seek to preserve nature in its pristine, pre-human condition.[33] But no serious supporters of parks believe these places are "pristine" in the sense of being totally untouched or unaffected by humans. To make such a claim one would have to deny global warming, the global spread of pesticides and other chemicals, and a host of other well-known human impacts. Those involved in conservation are well aware of these human influences.

There are, however, hugely varying degrees of human influence. Downtown Los Angeles is a far more human-created and human-dominated environment than, say, the Arctic National Wildlife Refuge in Alaska. In the Arctic Refuge, natural forces continue to dominate the land. Preserving such places where natural forces operate with a minimum of human influence is still the best way to preserve nature and evolutionary processes.

Parks and wildlands are key to conservation

Parks, wilderness, and other reserves are well-established means of conserving natural ecosystems and species. Protected areas are the cornerstones of biodiversity conservation: They support species migration, provide refuges from exploitation, maintain important habitats, and—perhaps most importantly—maintain ecological and evolutionary processes. While few existing preserves and parks are adequate for protecting all native species and ecological/evolutionary processes, science has shown that large preserves do work to slow down or minimize species losses even if they cannot completely eliminate these losses.[34]

For instance, Harini Nagendra did a meta-analysis of 49 protected areas in 22 countries, looking at the rate of land clearing outside protected areas compared to lands within the reserves. Nagendra found that land clearing was "significantly lower" in protected areas compared to the surrounding unprotected areas.[35] A meta-analysis of marine reserves came to similar conclusions, finding that marine reserves had significantly higher numbers of species, biomass, and diversity than adjacent unprotected areas. Unsurprisingly, larger reserves had greater absolute differences than smaller ones, confirming that large protected areas are better for conserving biodiversity.[36]

At present, some 13 percent of the Earth is protected, yet species continue to decline toward extinction. The fact that extinction is not completely averted, however, does not mean that protected areas are useless in conservation efforts: On the contrary, it means that we need more, larger, and connected protected areas. The best conservation science has confirmed that we need larger core protected areas, linked together by wildlife corridors.[37] Of equal importance may be where those protected areas are located. For instance, a recent study found that protecting 17 percent of the Earth's land could conserve two-thirds of all plant species.[38]

A visit to any of Alaska's reserves, such as the Arctic Refuge, would confirm that restricting development and human impacts is indispensable for preserving species and ecological processes. Of course, the refuge is not immune to human impacts—global warming is melting permafrost, high levels of PCBs are found in polar bears, and so forth—but on the whole, the wild Arctic Refuge is less degraded than working landscapes around the globe. Ecological processes like floods, droughts, wildfire, winter storms, predation, and so on still function here relatively unimpeded by human manipulation. Even popular parks such as Yellowstone—which suffers from various intrusions such as the introduction of exotic lake trout into Yellowstone Lake, white pine blister rust killing whitebark pine (*Pinus albicaulis*), and various introduced weed species—are still healthier, ecologically speaking, than surrounding private lands and public lands managed by the Forest Service or Bureau of Land Management that are open to resource extraction and commodity production.[39]

The problem with many reserves is that they are too small and are set in a matrix of heavily compromised domesticated landscapes.[40] That is a problem created by humans and a problem that humans can solve by enlarging protected areas and reducing the portion of the Earth devoted to domesticated landscapes. Will this be easy? Certainly not. But it's also not impossible. We should not concede the argument that we have no choice but to accept further erosion of natural areas, because of human population growth or desires for more and more commodities.

Proponents of "working landscapes," who view them as the cornerstones of human-friendly conservation, are undermining public support for large protected and interconnected areas and substituting an alternative of questionable effectiveness. By simplifying conservation, they are making it trivial. For instance, Marris presents "designer ecosystems"—ecosystems shaped by humans to include domestic and alien species—as innocuous or "the new wild."[41] While one might submit that man-made nature can benefit people, such landscapes may only minimally support native species.

We have seen the consequences of this kind of impact, intended or not: for example, the highly flammable cheatgrass originally introduced into the western United States to improve cattle forage but which ended up changing fire regimes dramatically with dire consequences for native flora; or the numerous introductions of alien species into Australia (including European rabbit, red fox, camels, and feral cats), all of which brought devastating consequences for that continent's native species.

Loss of native species has serious consequences for ecosystem function. Compared to species moved to a new location, native species tend to have a far greater number of interdependent species. Douglas Tallamy, in his book *Bringing Nature Home,* provides numerous examples of how native trees, such as oaks, may have hundreds of insects associated with them, while nonnative trees, such as those typically used in suburban landscaping, may have only a half dozen or fewer.[42]

The elimination of native insect habitat cascades through the ecosystem by reducing the food for many insectivores, including numerous bird species. Many of these relationships we are not even aware of, and thus advocating the shifting around of plants and animals to satisfy human desires is risky business at best. Biodiversity losses and promoting ecosystem-manipulating practices (even if well-meaning) have inherent ecological hazards. Having such a cavalier attitude toward these matters demonstrates the arrogance of the Father-Knows-Best attitude.

While we may acknowledge that parks, reserves, and other protected areas will not completely halt the accelerating loss of biodiversity around the globe, protected areas are a time-proven means of preserving natural ecological function and evolution. Natural-area protection should be the first goal in any strategy for protecting global life-forms.

A looming issue, often dismissed out of hand if it is even discussed, is whether a human-domesticated Earth of 9 or 10 billion people is possible. Many advocates of the "working landscape" suggest that human technology and intelligence will save us from any limits to growth.[43] But given immense and rising energy requirements, the need for basic resources such as clean water and adequate food, and infrastructure requirements to support billions of people, it is highly questionable whether such a world is possible, let alone sustainable. It is thus a straightforward matter of prudence to reduce our global population and resource exploitation and, ultimately, to halt our domestication of the Earth. It is reasonable to advocate that at least half of the terrestrial Earth and the vast majority of the seas should be protected reserves where human exploitation is limited or excluded. However, this is feasible only through a substantial reduction in human population and consumption. That the Anthropocene supporters do not even acknowledge that we need to limit population and consumption is emblematic of their denial.

A key dimension of the support of protected areas is the philosophical implications of such decisions. Though it is almost never specifically acknowledged in the designations of such reserves, by setting aside natural areas, we are implicitly countering the human-centered worldview. We are affirming that at least a portion of the globe is not a cookie jar open for human resource extraction. Rather than exulting in the human juggernaut, setting limits on human exploitation becomes a statement of self-restraint and self-discipline. Parks, wilderness areas, and other reserves are thus a philosophical acknowledgement, at least in some fashion, that we don't know everything. Given that Father may not know what is best for the Earth, and to hedge our bets for our own survival and quality of life, we recognize that we must maintain significant portions of the globe where human influence is minimized.

Another practical reason for establishing parks and other reserves is that such places serve as gauges and reminders of how our collective actions have changed the natural world. Without protected areas, a kind of collective ecological amnesia can set in and distort our perspective. Without old-growth forests as a reference, for example, it is easy for people to think that tree plantations are forests. Without wild herds of bison or wildebeest, it becomes easier for people to believe domestic livestock are somehow a functional ecological analog. Without native predators to control populations of prey, it is all too easy to forget how a healthy landscape with the presence of predators functions. And, of course, without large wild natural areas, it becomes easier for people to believe that human domestication of the Earth is a neutral or even positive force.

Conclusion

Whatever may be their direct benefits (clean water, recreation, scenic beauty, etc.) to humans—parks, wilderness areas, and other ecological reserves are ultimately a clear moral statement that we recognize the need to safeguard natural processes, indigenous species, and native landscapes for their inherent right to exist. Establishing protected areas is a symbolic moral gesture that a Father-Knows-Best philosophical attitude is not a suitable guidepost for the human relationship with the natural world.

As previously stated, it is one thing to acknowledge human dominance over the landscape, and quite another to celebrate and promote it. The term *working landscape*—along with the proposed *Anthropocene* term for our geological epoch—expresses self-aggrandizement of the human impact on Earth. Such terms put a positive spin on what is ultimately a destructive process.

It's unlikely that all ranching, farming, and logging will soon disappear from rural parts of the country where the "working landscape" is idealized. Locally produced agricultural products, particularly fresh vegetables and fruits, can help meet the food needs of communities. Additionally, a reduction in export-oriented commercial farming and timber production, while simultaneously expanding the acreage of land devoted to natural ecosystem processes and wildlands, would go a long way toward creating "working ecosystems." And working ecosystems ultimately provide the most long-term benefits to human societies as well as to native plant and animal communities.

Valuing Naturalness in the "Anthropocene": Now More than Ever

NED HETTINGER

RECENTLY THERE HAS BEEN some serious hype about entering "the age of man." Popularized by a leading proponent of geoengineering the planet in response to climate change,[1] "the Anthropocene" has boosters among environmental scientists, historians, and philosophers, as well as the press. While a useful way to dramatize the human impact on the planet, the concept is deeply insidious. Most importantly, it threatens the key environmental values of "naturalness" (by which I mean the degree to which nature is not influenced by humans) and respect for nature. This essay is a critical assessment of the Anthropocene notion, arguing not only that it seriously exaggerates human influence on nature but also that it draws inappropriate metaphysical, moral, and environmental policy conclusions about humanity's role on the planet. Despite our dramatic impact on Earth, significant naturalness remains, and the ever-increasing human influence makes valuing the natural more, not less, important in environmental thought and policy.

Some geologists have been debating whether the human impact on Earth is significant enough to justify designating a new geological epoch named after us—*the Anthropocene*. There is no question that humans are a dominant species that affects nature on a global scale. Humans now consume between 30 and 40 percent of net primary production, use more than half of all surface freshwater, and fix more nitrogen than all other terrestrial sources combined.[2] Humans rival the major geologic forces in our propensity to move soil and rock around.[3] Overfishing has had massive effects on sea life; our dams control water flow in most major rivers; and human-assisted, nonnative species are homogenizing Earth's ecosystems. Our contribution to greenhouse gases is predicted to raise the planet's temperature 2°C–5°C, affecting climates, and thus organisms, globally.[4] Human-caused extinctions are said to be between 100 and 1,000 times the background extinction rate.[5] One study concluded that less than 20 percent of land surface has escaped direct human influence.[6] It appears likely that we are altering the planet on a scale comparable to the major events of the past that mark changes in geological epochs.

However, the idea that we now live in "the age of man" has moved well beyond the narrow geological claim that the fossil record thousands of years from now will bear a distinct difference that can be traced to human influence. Some proponents of the Anthropocene concept interpret the facts about human influence as justifying broad metaphysical and ethical claims about how we should think of the human relationship to nature. Our impact, it is argued, is now so pervasive that the traditional environmental ideals of preservation of nature and respect for it are passé. Naturalness is now either gone or so tenuous that the desire to preserve, restore, and value it are sentimental pipe dreams. The human virtues of humility and restraint toward the natural world are no longer possible or desirable, and we need to reconcile ourselves to a humanized world and adapt to it. Whether we like it or not, we have been thrust into the role of planetary managers who must engineer nature according to our values and ideals. Rather than bemoan or resist this new world order, we should celebrate "the age of man," for it offers us hope for a world in which humans take their responsibilities seriously and are freed from constraints grounded on a misguided desire to preserve a long-gone, pristine nature.

A recent op-ed in the *New York Times* titled "Hope in the Age of Man" illustrates this worrisome moral and metaphysical perspective.[7] Written by environmental professionals, it argues that viewing our time as "the age of man" is "well-deserved, given humanity's enormous alteration of earth." The writers criticize those who worry that the Anthropocene designation will give people the false impression that no place on Earth is natural anymore. They suggest that the importance placed by conservation biologists on protecting the remaining, relatively wild ecosystems depends on the fantasy of "an untouched, natural paradise" and a pernicious and misanthropic "ideal of pristine wilderness." They conclude with the absurd Promethean claim that "this is the earth we have created" and hence that we should "manage it with love and intelligence," "designing ecosystems" to instantiate "new glories."

Philosophers have also been seduced by the Anthropocene concept, and it has led them down a similar path. I focus here on some writings by Allen Thompson, an environmental philosopher from Oregon State University. Thompson claims to have found a way to "love global warming."[8] He argues that the anxiety we now feel in response to our new and "awesome responsibility for the flourishing of life on Earth . . . bodes well for humanity"[9] and should give us "radical hope" that we can find a new type of "environmental goodness . . . distinct from nature's autonomy."[10]

Like other proponents of the age of man, Thompson overstates the extent to which humans have influenced nature. At one point he claims that "we now know that the fundamental conditions of the biosphere are something that, collectively, we are responsible for."[11] But surely we are not responsible for the existence of sunlight, gravity, or water; nor for the photosynthetic capacity of plants, the biological process of predation, or the chemical bonds between molecules; nor, more generally, for the diversity of life on the planet or its spectacular geology! That we have influenced some of these conditions of life, and in some cases significantly, is a far cry from being responsible for them. That humans have obligations to avoid further undermining the life conditions that we have affected is not well put by claiming we are "responsible" for them. To propose that humans have an obligation, for example, to not destroy the beauty or biodiversity of a mountain by removing its top is not to say that we are responsible for the mountain's beauty or its biodiversity. On the contrary, nature is responsible for those values; humans are not. Even in those cases where we should restore these conditions to ones that are more friendly to the biosphere (perhaps by cleaning a river of pollutants), we cannot claim we are responsible for the river's ability to support life, even though we are responsible for degrading it and we have a responsibility to clean it up.

A charitable reading of Thompson's "responsibility for the fundamental conditions of the biosphere" language is that he is simply asserting a negative duty to avoid further undermining the naturally given, basic conditions for life on the planet and not claiming responsibility for their creation. But

Thompson, I believe, has more in mind than this. His language suggests a metaphysical claim about the power and importance of humans on the planet. He writes: "Once the planet was larger than us, but it no longer is."[12] But the reason given for this new importance of humans—that "there is no corner of the globe, no feature of our biosphere, which escapes the influence of human activity"[13]—is utterly insufficient to justify such a metaphor. It is undoubtedly true that humans have a greater causal impact on the planet than does any other individual species (and have for a while). Human influence may be so massive that future geologists will see our impact in the geological record. But this is a far cry from showing that human causal influence on Earth is greater than the combined causal contributions of the nonhuman geological, chemical, physical, and biological forces. Humans are a fundamental force shaping the planet, but we are one among many.

Like other Anthropocene boosters, Thompson finds in the "age of man" an enhanced authority for humans in our relationship with the planet. He asserts that "whether we accept it or not, human beings now shoulder the responsibility of planetary management."[14] Note that what Thompson rejects here is not only Leopold's "plain member and citizen" view of our place in the natural world, but also a number of other conceptions of humans' relationship with nature: We are not caretakers or restorers of Earth, not janitors charged with cleaning up the mess we have made, not those who repent and try to make restitution for our destruction, nor healers of a wounded Earth. Instead we are managers—we are in charge—of this place. Humans are boss. Rather than develop our human capacities for "gratitude, wonder, respect, and restraint"[15] with regard to nature, we should take control and handle the place. Rather than celebrate Earth, we humans, "like adoptive parents," need to "enable" the "flourishing" of life.[16] But as many have pointed out, Earth does not need us, and the nonhuman world as a whole would be far better off if we weren't around. Our responsibility toward nature is not mainly to enable nature, but to stop disabling it. Our responsibility toward the planet is not to control and manage it, but—at least in many ways—to loosen our control and impact.

For Thompson and other boosters, the Anthropocene means that the traditional environmentalism that places the value of naturalness at its center is dead. "My analysis supports that idea that environmentalism in the future . . . will hold a significantly diminished place for valuing the good of the autonomy in nature."[17] I think the opposite conclusion is warranted. It is true that there is a decreasing extent of naturalness on the planet and thus there is less of it to value. But it is also true that what remains has become all the more precious. If one starts with the assumption that nature's autonomy from humanity is valuable, and one then points out that humans control more and more dimensions of the natural world—thereby diminishing its naturalness and making its autonomy increasingly rare—then the remaining naturalness increases in value. Rarity is a value-enhancing property of those things antecedently judged to be good. Furthermore, if naturalness is a value, then the more it is compromised by human control and domination, the more (not less) important it is to take steps to regain it, as well as protect what remains.

The naturalness that persists in human-altered or human-impacted nature is a seriously important object of valuation. Unless one ignores a central point maintained by defenders of the natural—that naturalness comes in degrees—and accepts the discredited notion that in order for something to be natural it must be absolutely pristine, then dimensions of nature can be natural (that is, relatively autonomous from humans) and can be valued as such even when they have been significantly influenced by humans. Take urban parks as an example: Although significantly shaped by humans, they retain much naturalness, and these parks are valued (in large part) for their naturalness by those who enjoy them. They would, for example, be valued much less if the trees were plastic and the birds genetically engineered.

A central strategy of the Anthropocene boosters is to accuse their opponents of accepting an outdated ideal of pristine nature. In this view, nature must be virginal and untouched to really be nature. As a result, we have either reached the end of nature (à la McKibben)[18] or we bask in profound ignorance of widespread human influence. For the most part, this ploy attacks a straw man: Defenders of an environmentalism that prioritizes respect for the autonomy of the natural world are well aware of the demise of pristine nature, yet this does not undermine their commitment to respect, and—where possible—to enhance or reestablish, nature's autonomy.

Ironically, the Anthropocene boosters themselves frequently rely on the idea of nature as pristine and use it to invoke the false dichotomy: Either nature is pristine or it is created (or domesticated) by humans. Consider a few comments expressed by current Anthropocene proponents: "An interesting way to look at nature now in the Anthropocene is that nature is something that we create. . . .There is really nothing around that has not been touched by us. And if there is something that hasn't been touched by us that was a decision for the most part. . . . Nature is something you have to nurture yourself, *just* like your garden";[19] and, "There really is no such thing as nature untainted by people. Instead, ours is a world of nature domesticated, albeit to varying degree, from national parks to high-rise megalopolises."[20]

So while the Anthropocene boosters criticize the McKibben ideal of pristine nature (which led Bill McKibben to the absurd conclusion that "we now live in a world of our own making"[21]), they arrive at the same conclusion and for pretty much the same reasons! But as I've argued, significant naturalness remains and it is possible and desirable to value diminished naturalness. There is plenty left to value and defend for the advocates of traditional "naturalness" environmentalism.

Furthermore, Anthropocene boosters ignore the potential for humanization to *flush out* of human-impacted natural systems and the real possibility for greater degrees of naturalness to return.[22] That restoration, rewilding, and just letting naturalness come back on its own are desirable environmental policies (though certainly not the only environmental goals) is something else that the Anthropocene boosters seem to reject. Note that nature need not return to some original, baseline state or trajectory for naturalness to be enhanced; the lessening of human control and influence on the course of nature is sufficient. Even if, as proponents of the Anthropocene insist, it is true that there is "no going back," that does not mean that the only path forward is a thoroughly managed future increasingly devoid of naturalness. That leaving nature alone to head off into a trajectory that we do not specify is itself ostensibly a "management decision" does not show that this trajectory is a human-controlled or human-impacted one.

In conclusion, I see the recent focus on the age of man as the latest embodiment of human hubris. It manifests a culpable failure to appreciate the profound role nonhuman nature continues to play on Earth and an arrogant overvaluation of human's role and authority. It not only ignores an absolutely crucial value in a proper respect for nature but leads us astray in environmental policy. It will have us downplaying the importance of nature preservation, restoration, and rewilding and also have us promoting ecosystem invention and geoengineering. Further, by promoting the idea that we live on an already domesticated planet, it risks the result that monetary and public support for conservation will seem futile and dry up.[23] We should not get comfortable with the Anthropocene, as some have suggested, but rather fight it. Such comfort is not the virtue of reconciliation, but the vice of capitulation.

THREE

THE VALUE OF THE WILD

Wild World

RODERICK FRAZIER NASH

MY PURPOSE IS TO PERSUADE YOU that wilderness is a moral resource. Human cultures have seen an extraordinary intellectual revolution in recent centuries that has transformed their view of wilderness from a liability to an asset. That transformation has largely been promoted by anthropocentric arguments emphasizing the value of wilderness to civilization.

But, as Henry David Thoreau wrote, the point of wilderness is that it is the home of "civilizations other than our own." Or, as children's author Maurice Sendak put it more recently, it is "where the wild things are." Conceived as the habitat of other species, not as a human playground, wilderness is the best environment in which to learn that humans are members in, and not masters of, the community of life. And this ethical idea, working as a restraint in our relations with the environment, may be the starting point for saving this planet.

In the beginning, civilization created wilderness. For nomadic hunters and gatherers, who have represented our species for most of its existence, everything natural is simply habitat, and people understood themselves to be part of a seamless living community. Lines began to be drawn with the advent of herding, agriculture, and settlement. Distinctions between controlled and uncontrolled animals and plants became meaningful, as did the concept of controlled space: corrals, fields, and towns.

The unmastered lands—the habitat of hunter-gatherers—came to seem threatening to settled folk. Ancient Greeks who had to pass through forest or mountain dreaded an encounter with Pan, the lord of the woods—who combined gross sensuality with boundless sportive energy. Indeed, the word *panic* originated from the blinding fear that seized travelers on hearing strange cries in the wilderness and assuming them to signify Pan's approach.

The origins of the English word *wilderness* reflect this trepidation. In the early Teutonic and Norse languages, the root seems to have been "will," with a descriptive meaning of self-willed, willful, or uncontrolled. From "willed" came the adjective "wild." By the eighth century, the *Beowulf* epic was populated by *wildeor*—a compound of "wild" and "deor," meaning beast—savage and fantastic beasts inhabiting a dismal region of forests, crags, and cliffs.

The Judaeo-Christian tradition constituted another powerful formative influence on Europeans' attitude toward wilderness, perhaps especially those who colonized the New World. When the Lord of the Old Testament desired to threaten or punish a sinful people, he found the wilderness condition to be his most powerful weapon.

So the dawn of civilization created powerful biases. We settled down, developed an ecological superiority complex, and bet our evolutionary future on the control of nature. Now there were survival-related reasons to understand, order, and transform the environment. The largest part of the energy of early civilization was directed at conquering wildness in nature and disciplining it in human nature.

For the first time humans saw themselves as distinct from—and, they reasoned, better than—the rest of nature. They began to think of themselves as masters, not members, of the community of life.

Civilization severed the web of life as humans distanced themselves from the rest of nature. Behind fenced pastures, village walls and, later, gated condominiums, it was hard to imagine other living things as relatives, or nature as sacred. The remaining hunters and gatherers became "savages." The community concepts, and attendant ethical respect, that had worked to curb human self-interest in dealings with nature declined in direct proportion to the "rise" of civilization. Nature lost its significance as something to which people belonged and became something they possessed: an adversary, a target, an object for exploitation.

The resulting war against the wilderness was astonishingly successful. Today we have fragments of a once-wild world, together with the wholesale disappearance of species. The ark is sinking—and on our watch.

Of course humans remain "natural." But somewhere along the evolutionary way from spears to spaceships, humanity dropped off the biotic team and, as author and naturalist Henry Beston recognized, became a "cosmic outlaw." The point is that we are no longer thinking and acting like a part of nature . Or, if we are a part, it is a cancerous one, growing so rapidly as to endanger the larger environmental organism. Our species has become a terrible neighbor to the 30 million and more other species sharing space on this planet. Our numbers and our technology are wreaking ecological havoc. We have become the latter-day "death star," with the same potential for destruction as the asteroid that ended the days of the dinosaurs.

This is not really an "environmental problem." It's a human problem. What needs to be conquered now is not the wilderness, but ourselves. We need to understand that it is civilization that is out of control.

Mind-pollution is more serious than chemical pollution. It is time to understand that there is no "good life" without a good environment and that it is a false prosperity that cannot be sustained over the long ecological haul. Growth must be dissociated from progress. Bigger is not better if the system is destroyed. As the deep ecologists recognize, we must now emphasize wholes over parts, and pursue justice at the level of entire ecosystems. A new valuation of wilderness is an excellent place to start.

The transformation that led some to view wilderness as an asset probably began with the Romantics. For example, Lord Byron wrote in 1817 in the fourth canto of his poem "Childe Harold's Pilgrimage":

> *There is a pleasure in the pathless woods,*
> *There is a rapture on the lonely shore,*
> *There is society, where none intrudes,*
> *By the deep sea, and music in its roar:*
> *I love not man the less, but Nature more . . . .*

But this insight developed into a largely anthropocentric justification of wilderness, as something to be valued and preserved for people. Recreational, spiritual, and scenic values all used humanity as the measure. And so did the early ecological arguments for wilderness, with their utilitarian emphasis on protecting species that possibly held the cure for cancer. More recently, wild ecosystems have been praised as resources capable of providing environmental "services" and supporting human health. These are the arguments that, sometimes, sell nature protection on the political stage.

But wilderness is not for people at all. It is where the wild things, the self-willed things, are.

From this ecocentric perspective, wilderness preservation becomes a gesture of planetary modesty and a badly needed exercise in restraint on the part of a species intoxicated with its power. Seen this way, wilderness preservation expresses a belief in the rights of nature.

Rightly seen, wilderness is the best demonstration that we are not the only, or even the primary, members of the biotic team. It is a living reminder of the gross limitations of our definitions of "society" and "morality." Our real society is coterminous with life on this planet, a fact that our ethical sensibilities have as yet failed to recognize.

In the biblical past people went to the wilderness to receive the commandments with which to restructure society. We need to do so again. Right now we desperately need a "time-out" to learn how to be team players in the biosphere. We need to learn how to live responsibly in the larger community called the ecosystem. The first requirement for this is to respect our neighbors' need for habitat.

We should try to define an "ecological contract" that widens the circle of morality beyond the limits of the "social contract" proposed by the seventeenth-century philosopher John Locke. Aldo Leopold, a founder of conservationism in America, would have understood this to give priority to what he called the "land community." The challenge is to advance morality from natural rights to the rights of nature.

And this is where wilderness assumes critical importance. What it provides is precisely this "time-out" from the juggernaut of civilization. Wild places are uncontrolled. Their presence reminds us of just how far we have distanced ourselves from the rest of nature.

We did not, after all, make wilderness. In it we stand naked of the built and modified environment, open to seeing ourselves once again as large mammals dependent not on our technological cleverness but on the health of the ecological community to which we belong. Writing in a preecological age, Thoreau was more correct than he could have imagined about the importance of wildness to the preservation of the world.

The actuality of wilderness reminds us that when we enter it we enter someone else's home. Recall your parents' admonitions: Courtesy is called for; so is respect. Stealing is wrong (but think of the past few thousand years of human relationship to nature). Wild places deserve respect not for what they can do for us but for what they mean to our fellow evolutionary travelers.

The concept of wilderness is just as important. It instructs us in the need for a more embracing, environmental ethic. The fact that wilderness is nature we do not own or use can open us to perceiving its intrinsic value. By definition we do not dominate or control wild places, and so they suggest the importance of sharing—which was, after all, the basis of the ethic of fair play that we did not learn very well in kindergarten. A species whose technological cleverness has made it the schoolyard bully desperately needs the ethical discipline that wilderness provides.

Ethics are concepts of right and wrong that work as restraints on freedom in the interest of preserving communities. It is easy to think of the kind of ecocentric ethic that I propose as being "against" human interests and freedoms. But most basic interests of human beings are inextricably linked to those of the greater environmental whole.

From this perspective, less, in the way of human impact on the Earth, can indeed be more. Growth is a good thing that has been carried too far. We spend our ecological capital as if there were no tomorrow and run an environmental deficit. In the relatively near future, some feel, the notes will come due. Our self-interest is very definitely involved. If we sink that ark, we go down too.

Respecting wildness, then, is prudent as well as ethically enlightened. Its instrumental and intrinsic values converge on the distant perspective point of evolutionary biology. Evolutionists increasingly recognize that species coevolve—in communities.

In respecting wildness, we forgo economic advantages. Lumbering, farming, and mining stop. Roads and buildings stay outside. We even limit our recreational options: limiting the use of mechanized transport, for example. Indeed the power of "recreation" as a justification for keeping land wild is in its twilight years; the sun is rising on the new moral and ecological arguments.

Wilderness is the best place both to learn and to express ecological limitation. Its value as a moral resource is not in the least diminished by our staying out altogether. Properly managed and interpreted, designated wilderness could give us the inspiration to live responsibly and sustainably elsewhere. In wildness is the promise of both biological and ethical repair.

Living Beauty

SANDRA LUBARSKY

IN HIS ESSAY, "Goose Music," Aldo Leopold admits to having "congenital hunting fever," and that, coupled with the fact that he has three sons to train in its virtues, keeps him shivering in his jacket at daybreak, fingers so frozen that the geese have nothing to fear from his aim. It's not clear how many shots he fires, but they are all wide of their mark. The hour is early and the cold is intense, and Leopold has just missed what he describes as a "big gander."

But Leopold gives no indication of aggravation or disappointment. Almost as quickly as that big gander veered away from his gunfire, he rejoices in the morning's outcome. "[M]iss or no miss, I saw him, I heard the wind whistle through his set wings as he came honking out of the gray west, and I felt him so that even now I tingle at the recollection."[1]

Hunting, it turns out, is not only about the pursuit of game. It is also about the pursuit of beauty. "Poets sing and hunters scale the mountains primarily for one and the same reason—the thrill to beauty."[2] Whether with weapon or recorder, game hunters, fishermen, "field-glass hunters," "rare plant hunters," "nature-loving poets," and "professional conserva-tionists"[3] all hunt for "living beauty."[4] To be fully *human*, Leopold declares, we must participate in the natural world; to be fully *alive*, we must experience the living beauty of the natural world.

Leopold's notion of beauty exceeds the conventional confinement of beauty or aesthetics to art or art history. If we think of beauty only as having to do with appearance or pleasure or art, we won't understand the new philosophical territory on which Leopold planted the science of ecology. Leopold's allegiance to the standards of careful observation led him to trust his direct experience of nature as evidence that there was something more at work in the world than either scientific or economic materialism could measure. When he invited his readers to enjoy the early spring sky dance of the woodcock or to sip a cup of coffee as field sparrows, robins, orioles, and wrens welcomed the new day, he was beckoning readers toward a way of experiencing the world that presupposed a sweeping metaphysical shift. And when he sat out after sunset next to the Rio Gavilan in northern Mexico, listening to the music in the river, he knew there was a grandeur and richness to wilderness that exceeded its usefulness and monetary value.

Leopold's reference to beauty as essential to land health is the most important signifier of this new worldview. He understood nature as a network of social relations between incalculable varieties of beings, all filled with resident vitality and intrinsic value—and yielding beauty. For Leopold, beauty was the "key-log" in unjamming the whole mess made by economic and scientific mechanism. Beauty, he maintained, is fundamental to an ecological worldview. Not to recognize this was to make a place of great aliveness into a mere repository of commodities.

The importance of Leopold's insight should not be underestimated. When it is, Leopold is made into a much more conventional thinker than he was. And we remain tied to an explanatory system that, no matter how well it explicates the ebb and flow of energy or the interdependencies of processes, explains away experience of the intrinsic, immediate worth of the natural world.

IN SHARP CONTRAST to Leopold's sensitivities to the wild world as a place limned with value is the assumption that beauty is simply a judgment that originates in the human mind. It appears in conventional wisdom as the claim that "beauty is only in the eye of the beholder." This assertion is the product of the modern philosophical tradition, particularly as shaped by René Descartes and Immanuel Kant.

In this tradition, objective reality is thought of as a landscape of "bare facts," fully describable in terms of its physical characteristics. According to Descartes, judgments of color, emotional intensity, ethical worth, and aesthetic value are like a brocaded silk cloth, overlaid on the material world that lies untouched beneath it. Any value that might be attributed to a fact is not intrinsic to the fact itself but is an embellishment of the fact by the individual experiencing it. For example, the sweet smell of an orange and its vibrant color are not fundamental to the nature of an orange; after all, over time brilliant color fades and sweetness dissolves. But though it may shrivel, an orange continues to have physical dimension and form. These are the properties that are considered to be primary qualities of the orange. All other qualities are secondary or tertiary and not part of the objective reality of the orange.

Beauty, like sweetness and orangeness, is a judgment formulated by a perceiver, descriptive of his or her unique experience. Just as an orange may be sweet to one person, bitter to another, so beauty is a personal sentiment. It is not an objective quality of the world, but a mental laminate, layered onto physical forms by our subjective experience.

Kant radically extended this anthropocentric approach. We cannot know the world in itself, says Kant. We can only know it as it is ordered by our minds. The world gives us raw data—the "thatness" of some world beyond our minds—but the "whatness" of the data is created almost whole cloth in our minds. All knowledge then, not just our judgments about beauty, is "in the eye of the beholder." And the beholder, the human subject, is the source of the rational order of the world. Filtered as it is through our mental lens, the world is made in the image of the human mind.

The assumption that beauty is a subjective production of the human mind implies the tacit and damaging proposition that the reason why there is no inherent value in the world (apart from that given to it by human beings) is because reality fundamentally consists of merely physical entities. The idea that beauty is entirely subjective is coincident with the idea of a valueless, lifeless nature. The exception, of course, is human experience. It is the human subject who endows lifeless nature with value. In this way, modernist philosophy continues the habit of making humans ontologically different from the natural world (even as it affirms that humans are genetic relatives of the great apes). Nature is physical, material, mathematically measurable, and mindless. It functions like a machine. Human life can be likewise described, with the one exception that countermands all else: Humans have minds. They are subjects in a world of objects, chess players in control of not only the board but also the rules of the game. The human project becomes a game of domesticating, controlling, and deliberately remaking nature to human benefit.

A world devoid of anything that makes an orange sweet, a berry bush dewy, a late fall day glorious or a summer morning glad, is a world without any value except what is given to it by an external source. That value is, more often than not, the value that comes with utility. Nature's value is as a useable resource for human purposes or enjoyment. All the many constituents of the natural world, whether as single lives or in relation with each other, have no aim of their own or capacity for feeling or freedom. They—and all of nature—are lifeless.

The word *mundane* literally means "belonging to the world." But in a world bereft of life and beauty, it connotes boredom and tedium, the dullness of a place stripped of the qualities that foster character and personality. The word *pedestrian,* too, bears this same stamp: to walk in such a world is "unexciting" and "unlovely." Together, these synonyms give etymological evidence of a devalued world.

In a deeply dug grave, somewhere in this unremarkable landscape, nature and beauty lie interned together, victims of the mechanism and materialism that define modern science and philosophy.

"NO WORD MEANS MUCH BY ITSELF," said Wendell Berry, talking about the word *sustainability.* "[Y]ou have to find a context for it in which it can mean something."[5] Our contemporary use of the word *beauty* is enmeshed in the philosophical and methodological assumptions of modern science that give primacy to the material and measurable aspects of reality. Where intrinsic value is denied to experience, as it is in Cartesian-Kantian metaphysics, aesthetics (and ethics) contribute nothing to our knowledge of reality. Under these conditions, beauty (and all aesthetic inquiry) was reduced to personal, unverifiable judgment. Aesthetics becomes peripheral, an unnecessary way of knowing. It took refuge in the realm of art and the philosophy of art as a way of inquiring into the meaning of cultural production but not of nature or reality itself. (Aesthetics eventually regained some power but only as a mercenary tool of commerce, with beauty as its most lucrative agent.)

But our modern context for the word *beauty* is strikingly different from the preceding two thousand years of western thought. Beginning with the sixth-century-B.C.E. Greek philosopher Pythagoras, and extending through the Renaissance, beauty was linked to meditations on the order and structure of the universe. The Greek word *cosmos* means "order," and the order that was discovered came from the relations of numbers and the harmony that resulted. Because beauty was assumed to be the consequence of harmonious order, the cosmic order was regarded as beautiful. This was a mathematical–aesthetic vision of the universe.

Out of this vision emerged what has been called "The Great Theory of Beauty." It is based on the idea that the structure of the universe can be expressed by a set of mathematical and musical proportions. These proportions are recapitulated throughout the cosmos, giving coherence to the arrangements of life, from microcosm to macrocosm. In the visual arts, the word *symmetry* was used to describe the goal of right proportion. In the aural arts, the word was *harmony*. In his text on architecture, the first-century-B.C.E. Roman architect and engineer Marcus Vitruvius Pollio (Vitruvius) showed that this theory could be applied architecturally as well, and he established what he believed to be right relationships of height-width-length in order to achieve structural symmetry. The Pantheon in Rome is often cited as an example of the Vitruvian ideal. In the mid-fifteenth century, Leone Battista Alberti applied Vitruvius' principle that beauty is "the harmony of all parts in relation to one another" to the magnificent Basilica of Santa Maria Novella. And in 1490, Leonardo da Vinci sketched his version of the *Vitruvian Man*—the now-iconic image of a male body inscribed within both a circle and a square, drawn so that the human figure's measurement from forehead to chin is one-tenth of the total height and the span between the outstretched arms is equal to the distance from heel to head. "Man," Leonardo declared, "is the model of the world," a replication of the geometric beauty of the cosmos.

The Pythagorean inheritance is a philosophical system in which the entire universe participates in harmonious relations. Thus beauty abounds. So compelling was this image of the cosmos and of human life—of an intelligible world that, despite all the vagaries of human existence, was harmonious and beautiful—that it was sustained throughout the Middle Ages and into the Renaissance. Johannes Kepler (1571–1630) embraced it, and he titled his 1619 work describing the new calculations of planetary orbits *Harmonice Mundi* ("harmonies of the world"). When Kepler found that the celestial orbits were elliptical rather than circular and thus, according to the Pythagorean system, harmoniously imperfect, he first reacted with aversion to his own discovery. Eventually, he became convinced that an even greater order was present, one that preserved the principal Pythagorean values of mathematical order, ratio, harmony, and beauty.

Some have interpreted Kepler's loyalty to a universe in which fact and value are interlaced, in which the empirical structure of the universe can be declared beautiful, as nothing more than a holdover of the medieval mind, a psychological and intellectual handicap he needed to overcome in order to cross cleanly and completely to the side of modern science. But to contend that the genius Kepler was either more naive than we moderns or that his mystical inclinations were the result of knowing-not-enough about reality is quite obviously a modern conceit. The same must then be assumed of Plato, Plotinus, Cicero, Augustine, Boethius, Aquinas, and Copernicus, all of whom upheld the idea of harmonic proportion and cosmic beauty as unapologetically as we assume the law of gravity. Surely, their desire for an intelligible universe was as strong as ours. And surely they were at least as aware as we of the ruthless and heart-breaking ills that relentlessly shadow our lives. Yet, they believed that in its deepest structure, the universe was so ordered as to yield harmony and beauty.

THE FACT THAT IN the modern era we have tried to understand both the world and ourselves apart from beauty is neither an oversight nor a minor philosophical decision. And the fact that we have lived as if beauty doesn't matter in the "real world" is not unrelated to the callous ways in which we have uprooted places of great beauty and life.

We need a more accurate way of seeing the world. The natural world refutes the position that reality is a dull affair, devoid of meaning and value. Our encounters with nature are neither mundane nor pedestrian. These facts are a signal that some philosophical mistake has been made by those who portray the natural world as bare and lifeless matter.

Mechanism, says the philosopher Alfred North Whitehead, is true under certain general abstractions but false as a fully explanatory model of experience. In spite of the fact that mechanistic explanations of reality have been immensely useful in expanding human technological abilities, there remains much of importance they cannot account for—life, feeling, freedom, purpose, consciousness, moral worth, and beauty. Quantum physics and relativity theory can be added to the list. Despite these inadequacies, we cling to the modern scientific worldview as if it were the whole truth about reality.

Whitehead set out to correct the exaggerations of the modern worldview, with its roots in seventeenth-century physics and its commitment to a metaphysics based primarily on what can be seen and measured. In Whitehead's view, a more accurate philosophy addresses all experience, not just physical experience. "The various human interests which suggest cosmologies are science, aesthetics, ethics, religion," he wrote.[6] Each inquiry discloses something important about the nature of reality. The task of philosophy, Whitehead argues, is not to deny or neglect one aspect over another but to coordinate the partial truths vouchsafed by each. Since the seventeenth century, the dominant cosmology has been the one derived from science. This has constituted both real gain and real loss. A more adequate metaphysics would not discard the whole range of experiences that occur in our lives. Philosophical adequacy (and honesty) requires an appeal to lived experience. Aesthetic experience is without doubt a part of our experience of the world. Explaining it away is bad metaphysics.

Whitehead built a new philosophy, one that reversed the judgment reached by mechanistic philosophy. "It is the essence of life that it exists for its own sake, as the intrinsic reaping of value."[7] This was Leopold's intuition as well. Leopold's description of ecological "rightness" was meant as a guide for a new kind of science, one that involved vitality and value and recognized values beyond utility and profit margin. Whitehead's metaphysics, which he called a philosophy of organism but which is now better known as process philosophy, begins where Leopold's empirical studies led him: with the insistence that the world is best understood as a marvel of *relations*, suffused with a worth and creativity that cannot be reduced to dead, valueless matter or figured in dollars and cents. "How do we add content to the notion of bare activity?" Whitehead asked. "This question can be answered only by fusing life with nature." Nature is alive, and because it is alive, it is imbued with value and aesthetic worth.

For both Leopold and Whitehead, the value most associated with livingness is beauty. Beauty refers to the quality of aliveness and the vivacity that inheres in living beings and is intensified in the relations between beings. It is descriptive of the way things organize themselves, a measure of the degree of life present throughout a living structure. Beauty contributes to the success of life and the enjoyment of being alive. It is what we name those experiences of life that affirm our own vitality in relation to the vitality of other beings.

Beauty is the value that arises from an innumerable number of finely tuned adjustments of actuality-to-actuality, adjustments that enable and sustain life. This means that it is not a quality—blue or shiny or well-proportioned, or a composite of these—overlaid on a substance. It is not owned by the world of art or fashion or cosmetics. It is not "skin deep." Nor is it simply "in the eye of the beholder." It is embedded in life, part of the dynamic, relational structure of the world created by the concert of living beings. And it is what we name those relational structures that encourage and support freshness and zest so that life can continue to make life.

To conceive of beauty in this way, as both aim and consequence of life, involves a very different metaphysics from the Cartesian-Kantian narrative, one that connects livingness with feeling and value. In an aesthetic-organic metaphysics, the aim of life is be alive in ways that affirm the full measure of life beyond mere survival. To be sure, this worldview requires a detailed exposition. But beauty is so clearly a part of our experience of being alive and encountering the livingness of other beings that it is astounding we have relinquished this plain fact.

NATURE, LIFE, AND BEAUTY cannot be untangled. The philosophical attempt to do so has done great harm to the world. What makes wilderness wild is the great "willful" effort exerted by the abundance of life residing in relation. And where there is much life, there is the potential for great beauty. Indeed, beauty and biodiversity are concurrent, the multiplicity of life yielding patterns of living vibrancy.

Neither wilderness nor wild beauty is something humans can make. They are the production of many life-seeking creatures in relationship, adjusting life to life, often over durations that exceed human history. Because the natural world is not constructed like a machine, once it is dismantled all the power tools in the world cannot reassemble it. If there are no more woods or wolves, they cannot, at a later date, be retrofitted back into the contraption of nature. The beauty they generated, the invaluable issue of millions of life events, is likewise irreparable. Life, wilderness, biodiversity, and beauty are an interlaced knot; when the cord is cut, the intricacies are lost, the entire weave undone.

Leopold's essay, "Goose Music," begins with the gander's getaway but ends with the haunting question, "What if there be no more goose music?" In an anthropocentric narrative, the loss of goose music would mean the end of a valued game bird. For Leopold and Whitehead and any who believe that every living being is a storehouse of value, it would mean much more: the loss of a unique form of life, the loss of its unique beauty, and reverberations of loss throughout the whole elegant symphony of life. "We do not live *on* the earth," says Wendell Berry, "but *with* and *within* its life."[8] Absent the goose and its distinctive voicing of life, its V dance of migration, and its willful presence, the community of life-within-life is literally *dis*membered. We fall downward—as if shot by a marksman who cares little for the whistle of wind through pinioned feathers—into a wasteland of our own making.

Wilderness: What and Why?

HOWIE WOLKE

A FEW YEARS AGO, I led a group through the wilds of northern Alaska's Brooks Range during the early autumn caribou migration. I think that if I had twenty lifetimes I'd never again experience anything quite so primeval, so simple and rudimentary, and so utterly, uncompromisingly wild. If beauty is in the eye of the beholder, this beheld my eye above all else. Maybe that trek—in one of the ultimate terrestrial wildernesses remaining on Earth—is my personal yardstick, my personal quintessence of what constitutes real wilderness among a lifetime of wilderness experience. The tundra was a rainbow of autumn pelage. Fresh snow engulfed the peaks and periodically the valleys, too. Animals were everywhere, thousands of them, moving across valleys, through passes, over divides, atop ridges. Wolves chased caribou. A grizzly on a carcass temporarily blocked our route through a narrow pass. It was a week I'll never forget, a week in an ancient world that elsewhere is rapidly being engulfed by the frightening nature-deficit technophilia of the twenty-first century.

Some claim that wilderness is defined by our perception, which is shaped by our circumstance and experience. For example, one who has never been to the Brooks Range but instead has spent most of her life confined to big cities with little exposure to wild nature might consider a farm woodlot or a small state park laced with dirt roads to be "wilderness," or, for that matter, a cornfield, though this seems to stretch this theory of wilderness relativity to the point of obvious absurdity. According to this line of thought, wilderness, like beauty, is in the eye of the beholder.

Yet those who believe that perception defines wilderness are dead wrong. In our culture, wilderness is a very distinct and definable entity, and it can be viewed on two complementary levels. First, from a legal standpoint, the Wilderness Act of 1964 defines wilderness quite clearly. A designated wilderness area is "undeveloped" and "primeval," a wild chunk of public land without civilized trappings that is administered to remain wild. Section 2c of the Wilderness Act defines a wilderness area as "untrammeled," meaning "unconfined" or "unrestricted." It further defines wilderness to be "an area of undeveloped Federal land retaining its primeval character and influence, without permanent human improvements or habitation." The law also generally prohibits road building and resource extraction such as logging and mining. Plus, it sets a general guideline of 5,000 acres as a minimum size for a wilderness. Furthermore, it banishes to non-wilderness lands all mechanized conveniences, from mountain bikes and game carts to noisy fume-belching all-terrain vehicles and snow machines.

Written primarily by the late Howard Zahniser, the Wilderness Act creates a National Wilderness Preservation System (NWPS) on federally administered public lands. All four federal land management agencies administer wilderness: the U.S. Forest Service, National Park Service, U.S. Fish and Wildlife Service, and the Bureau of Land Management. In order to designate a wilderness, the United States Congress must enact a statute, and the President must sign it. Also, under the Wilderness Act, the NWPS is to be managed uniformly as a system.

In addition to viewing wilderness as a legal entity, we also have a closely related cultural view, steeped in mystery and romance and influenced by our history, which yes, includes the hostile view of wilderness that was particularly prevalent during the early days of settlement. Today, our cultural view of wilderness is generally positive. Today's cultural view of wilderness is greatly influenced by the Wilderness Act, which means that when people simply speak of wilderness, without regard to legal definitions, they speak of wild country that's big, wild, and undeveloped, where nature rules. And that certainly isn't a woodlot or cornfield.

In summary, then, wilderness is nature with all its magic and unpredictability. It lacks roads, motors, pavement, and structures but comes loaded with unknown wonders and challenges that at least some humans increasingly crave in today's increasingly controlled and confined world.

Untrammeled wilderness, by definition, comes with fire and insects, predator and prey, and the dynamic unpredictability of wild nature, existing in its own way and in its own right, with utter disregard for human preference, convenience, and comfort. And perception. As the word's etymological roots connote, wilderness is "self-willed land," and the "home of wild beasts." It is also the ancestral home of all that we know in this world, and it spawned civilization, although I'm not convinced this was a good thing.

Neither the Wilderness Act nor our more general cultural perception of wilderness require that wilderness landscapes be pristine. The authors of the Wilderness Act wisely recognized that, even in 1964, there were no remaining landscapes that had completely escaped the imprint of humanity. Consider acid rain, global air pollution, and the anthropogenic climate crisis. That's why they defined wilderness as "*generally* appearing to have been affected *primarily* by the forces of nature with the imprint of man's work *substantially* unnoticeable" [emphasis mine]. Indeed, those who cite humanity's ubiquitous impacts to wrongly claim that wilderness no longer exists fail to grasp the difference between wild and pristine. Absolute pristine nature may be history, but there remains plenty of wildness on this beleaguered planet. As the mushrooming human population continues its malignant growth into the globe's shrinking domain of wild habitat, the value of wildness—and of protecting wilderness—increases.

So wilderness isn't just any old unpaved undeveloped landscape. It isn't merely a blank space on the map. For within that blank space might be all sorts of human malfeasance that have long since destroyed the essence of wilderness: pipelines, power lines, water diversions, overgrazed wastelands, and off-road vehicle scarring, for example. No, wilderness isn't merely a place that lacks development. It is unspoiled and primeval, a sacred place in its own right. It might not be entirely pristine, but it's still a functional storehouse for evolutionary processes, by far the best one remaining. Wilderness designation is a statement to all who would otherwise keep the industrial juggernaut rolling: Hands off! This place is special!

Nor is wilderness simply a political strategy to thwart bulldozers from invading wildlands. That's one valid use of our wilderness law, yes, but when we view wilderness only—or even primarily—as a deterrent to industry and motors, we fail to consider all of the important things that really differentiate wilderness from less extraordinary places. Some of those things include tangible physical attributes such as native animals and vegetation, pure water, and minimal noise pollution. But in many ways, the intangible values of wilderness are equally important in differentiating wilderness from other landscapes. Wonder and challenge are but two of them. For many of us, the simple knowledge that some landscapes are beyond our control provides a respite of sanity. Solitude and a feeling of connectedness with other life forms are also best attained in wilderness.

Wilderness also provides us with some defense against the collective disease of *landscape amnesia*. I began to use this term in the early 1990s while writing an educational tabloid on wilderness and roadless areas. It had begun to occur to me that, as we continue to tame nature, each ensuing generation becomes less aware of what constitutes a healthy landscape because so many components of the landscape gradually disappear. Like someone watching the proverbial frog in a pot of water being slowly brought to a boil and missing the point when the frog goes from thrashing to dead, society fails to notice before it's too late that the surrounding landscape is slipping away.

For example, few individuals today remember when extensive cottonwood floodplain forests were healthy and common throughout the West. So today's generations view our currently depleted floodplains as "normal." Thus there's no impetus to restore the ecosystem. This principle applies to wilderness. Wilderness keeps at least some areas intact, wild and natural, for people to see. We don't forget what we can still see with our own eyes. When we keep wilderness wild, there's little danger that as a society we'll succumb to wilderness amnesia and forget what real wilderness is.

What sets wilderness apart is that it is dynamic, always in flux, never the same from one year or decade or century to the next, never stagnant, and entirely unconstrained—despite unrelenting human efforts to control nearly everything. Natural processes such as wildfire, flood, predation, and native insects are (or should be) allowed to shape the wilderness landscape as they have throughout the ages.

It has been said that wilderness cannot be created; it can be protected only where it still persists, and there is some truth here. But there's a big gray area, too. Even though most new wilderness units are carved out of relatively unspoiled roadless areas, the U.S. Congress is free to designate as wilderness any area of federal land, even lands that have been impacted by past human actions, such as logging and road building or off-road vehicles. In fact, Congress has designated such lands wilderness on numerous occasions. Once designated, agencies are legally required by the Wilderness Act to manage such lands as wilderness. Time and the elements usually do the rest. For example, most wildernesses in the eastern United States were once heavily logged and laced with roads and skid trails. Today, they have reattained a good measure of their former wildness.

Perhaps the most crucial but overlooked sections of the Wilderness Act deal with caring for designated areas. The Wilderness Act quite clearly instructs managers to administer wilderness areas "unimpaired" and for "the preservation of their wilderness character." This means that *the law forbids degradation of wilderness areas.* Therefore, you would assume that once an area is designated as wilderness, all would be right with at least a small corner of this world. But you would be wrong.

That's because, despite the poetic and pragmatic brilliance of the Wilderness Act, land managers routinely ignore the law, and thus nearly all units of the National Wilderness Preservation System fail to live up to the promise of untrammeled wildness. To be fair, agency wilderness managers are often under tremendous pressure—often at the local level—to ignore abuse. Sometimes their budgets are simply inadequate to do the job. On the other hand, we citizens pay our public servants to implement the law. When they fail to properly maintain wilderness character, they violate both the law and the public trust.

Throughout the National Wilderness Preservation System, degradation is rampant. Weed infestations, predator control by state wildlife managers (yes, in designated wilderness!), eroded multilane horse trails, trampled lakeshores, bulldozer-constructed water impoundments, the proliferation of structures and motorized equipment use, overgrazing by livestock, and illegal motor-vehicle entry are just a few of the ongoing problems. Many of these problems seem minor in their own right, but collectively they add up to systemic decline, a plethora of small but expanding insults that I call "creeping degradation," although some of the examples seem to gallop, not creep. External influences such as climate change and chemical pollution add to the woes of the wilds as we head into the challenging and perhaps scary decades that lie in wait.

In addition to wilderness as both a cultural idea and a legal entity, there's another wilderness dichotomy. That's the dichotomy of designated versus "small *w*" wilderness. America's public lands harbor perhaps a couple hundred million acres of relatively undeveloped, mostly roadless, wildlands that—so far—lack long-term congressional protection. These "roadless areas" constitute "small *w*" or "de facto" wilderness. Here's a stark reality of the early twenty-first century: Given the expanding human population and its quest to exploit resources from nearly every remaining nook and cranny on Earth, we are rapidly approaching the time when the only remaining significant natural habitats will be those we choose to protect—either as wilderness or as some other (lesser) category of land protection. Before very long, most other sizeable natural areas will disappear.

In order to get as many roadless areas as possible added to the National Wilderness Preservation System, some wilderness groups support special provisions in new wilderness bills in order to placate wilderness opponents. Examples include provisions that strengthen livestock grazing rights in wilderness, that allow off-road motor vehicles and helicopters, that grandfather incompatible uses like dams and other water projects, that exempt commercial users from regulations, and many others in addition to these examples. So we get legalized overgrazing, ranchers and wildlife managers on all-terrain vehicles, overzealous fire management, and destructive new water projects—just to mention a few of the incompatible activities sometimes allowed in designated wilderness. These and other such activities de-wild both the wilderness system and the wilderness idea. And when we allow the wilderness idea to decline, it is inevitable that society gradually accepts "wilderness" that is less wild than in the past. Again, it's the disease of landscape or wilderness amnesia.

An equally egregious threat to wilderness is the recent tendency to create new wilderness areas with boundaries that are drawn to exclude all potential or perceived conflicts, also in order to pacify the opposition. So we get small, fragmented "wilderness" areas, sometimes with edge-dominated amoeba-shaped boundaries that encompass little core habitat. Or, large, otherwise unbroken areas without roads get transformed into small fragmented "wilderness" units because Congress legislates motor-vehicle corridors that slice through them. These trends alarm conservation biologists, who are concerned with biological diversity and full-ecosystem protection. If we fail to demand and work for real wilderness, then we'll never get it. That's guaranteed.

To some, particularly those who equate motors or resource extraction with freedom, wilderness designation seems restrictive. But in truth, wilderness is more about freedom than is any other landscape. I mean the freedom to roam, and yes, the freedom to blunder, for where else might we be so immediately beholden to the physical consequences of our decisions? Freedom, challenge, and adventure go together, and wilderness provides big doses of each—"Should I try to cross here?" "Can I make my way around that bear?" "Is there really a severe storm approaching?" When we enter wilderness, we leave all guarantees behind. We are beholden to the unknown. Things frequently don't go as planned. Wilderness is rudimentary and fundamental in ways that we've mostly lost as a culture. This loss, by the way, weakens us. Wilderness strengthens us.

Freedom. In wilderness we are free to hunt, fish, hike, crawl, slither, swim, horse-pack, canoe, raft, cross-country ski, view wildlife, study nature, photograph, and contemplate whatever might arouse our interest. We are free to pursue our personal spiritual values, whatever they might be, with no pressure from the proclaimed authorities of organized church or state. And we are generally free to do any of these things for as long as we like. Wilderness is also the best environment for the underutilized but vitally important activity of doing absolutely nothing—I mean nothing at all, except perhaps for watching clouds float past a wondrous wilderness landscape.

Wilderness provides an essential antidote for civilization's growing excesses of pavement, pollution, technology, and pop culture. Wilderness provides clean water and flood control, and it acts as a clean air reservoir. It provides many tons of healthy meat, because our healthiest fisheries and game populations are associated with wilderness (Who says "You can't eat scenery"?). And wilderness reduces the need for politically and socially contentious endangered species listings. When we protect habitat, most species thrive.

By providing nature a respite from human manipulation, wilderness cradles the evolutionary process. It helps to maintain connectivity between population centers of large wide-ranging animals—especially large carnivores. This protects genetic diversity and increases the resilience of wildlife populations that are so important to the ecosystem. We are beginning to understand that without large carnivores, most natural ecosystems falter in a cascade of biological loss and depletion.

Wilderness is also our primary baseline environment. In other words, it's the metaphorical yardstick against which we measure the health of all human-altered landscapes. How might we ever make intelligent decisions in forestry or agriculture, for example, if there's no baseline with which to compare? Of course, wilderness acts as a real baseline only if we really allow it to be wild and untrammeled.

Wilderness is also about humility. It's a statement that we don't know everything and never will. In wilderness we are part of something much greater than our civilization and ourselves. It moves us beyond self, and that, I think, can lead only to good things. Perhaps above all, wilderness is an acknowledgement that nonhuman life forms and the landscapes that support them have *intrinsic value,* just because they exist, independent of their multiple benefits to the human species. Intrinsic value is a tough concept for some to grasp, especially when it pertains to nonhuman life or habitat. So no, I cannot absolutely prove the idea of the intrinsic value of wilderness (nor can I prove the intrinsic value of Grandma); its validity depends upon one's basic values and the cultivation of receptivity and listening. Few who spend much time in wilderness would argue against it.

Most emphatically, wilderness is not primarily about recreation, although that's certainly one of its many values. Nor is it about the "me first" attitude of those who view nature as a metaphorical pie to be divvied up among user groups. It's about selflessness, about setting our egos aside and doing what's best for the land. It's about wholeness, not fragments. After all, wilderness areas—despite their problems—are still the healthiest landscapes with the cleanest waters, and they tend to support the healthiest wildlife populations, particularly for many species that have become rare or extirpated in places that are less wild.

Having made a living primarily as a wilderness guide/outfitter for thirty-five years, I've had the good fortune to experience many wild places throughout western North America and occasionally far beyond. Were I to boil down to one succinct statement what I've learned, it would probably be this: *Wilderness is about restraint.* As Howard Zahniser stated, wilderness managers must be "guardians, not gardeners." When in doubt, leave it alone. For if we fail to restrain our manipulative impulses in wilderness, where on Earth might we ever find untrammeled lands?

Finally, when we fail to protect, maintain, and restore real wilderness, we miss the chance to pass along to our children and grandchildren—and to future generations of nonhuman life—the irreplaceable wonders of a world that is too quickly becoming merely a dim memory of a far better time. Luckily, we still have the opportunity to both designate and properly protect a considerable chunk of the once-enormous wilderness. Let's not squander that opportunity. We need to protect as much as possible, and to keep it wild.

Resistance

LISI KRALL

THERE WAS A TIME when Wyoming was infinite and wild. That was before the exponential growth curves began to shoot upward in the inevitable flight that took much of Wyoming with it. Wyoming's elevation and aridity were not sufficient sentinels to ward off energy development and its architecture of despair. Man-camps and half-abandoned trailer parks. Cities of gas wells lighting up the night sky. Ancient migration paths interrupted. Dust and ozone and water that ignites. Halliburton trucks endlessly pacing up and down the once-empty roads. Wyoming has become a restive place. Its legacy of deep time now in drawdown to provide the raw material of our civilization's experiment with domestication: endless economic growth. There seems no limit, as yet, to the demand for coal, oil, and gas.

My epiphany about the fate of Wyoming came in South America the day I drove through Chile's Chacabuco Valley and crossed into Argentina. I entered a vast space that went on for so long that I began to have flashbacks to a time whose memories came to me in fragments of pictures. I am a young child riding in a pickup truck with my father on a rainy June day; I can smell the sagebrush and see the endless expanse of the Wyoming steppe outside the windows. During that drive through Patagonia I realized what had happened to Wyoming. I wept for months after that, mourning the loss of my home landscape that registered for me on the other side of the equator.

Wyoming is a testament to the misguided belief that Earth's domestication can be relatively innocuous in a world of endless growth. The belief in domestication as a balanced Earth state is a dangerous elixir that pacifies our misgivings about the economic order of things—misgivings that we now ought to acknowledge and voice. It expresses how we carve hope out of convenience. It is the fantasy born of denial about the magnitude of our predicament. Granted, our circumstance is so daunting that we seem unable to grasp it. We fail to confront what is true: that our present economic system cannot be reconciled with a reverence for the wild impulse of the Earth or even with its biophysical limits. I utter this economic heresy without equivocation .

It is much easier to hold onto the illusion that reconciliation is possible. This illusion is reinforced by a seductive strain of our economic belief system, a strain that lacks the rancor of neoconservative free-market ideology. It is the belief that it is possible to reform and manage a capitalist economy to simultaneously generate jobs, eliminate poverty, grow ("green," of course), solve climate change, conserve biodiversity, and lead us to the promised land of progress and a more perfected point along the continuum of human development. This belief ignores the reality of our economic history.

If we peer into the black hole of economic progress and take a good hard look we will find an ambiguous progress at best: material well-being for some at the cost of a relentless assault on the Earth, entrenched poverty, economic instability, and excess that boggles the mind. In spite of all the institutional reforms to our economic system, from Keynesian monetary and fiscal policy to the reforms distilled from the sweat and blood of the many resistance movements (the labor and environmental movements, for example), the list of unacceptable outcomes continues to multiply.

It is unpopular to explore the dark recesses of economic reality. There is no surer way to discredit oneself than to question the promise of the global-market society to fulfill our economic possibilities and our human potentialities (with a little nudging from the right policies of course), while continuing to inhabit a livable planet. This is precisely what I question. I question whether it is possible to continue with a system structurally disposed to grow (and stagnate) and at the same time have a vibrant or even livable planet. But when I make this claim I am usually confronted with blank stares, as if the people I'm talking to have just discovered that I'm an invasive species, muddying the ecology of clear thought and compromising our ability to move forward.

I fear that avoiding any questioning of the structure and purpose of our economic system has become the deliberate strategy of the environmental movement. There is no doubt that many battles will be won following this strategy. Yet I am also certain the war against the wholesale domestication of the planet will be lost. The truth is that it is not easy to change the leopard spots of globalized capitalism as environmentalists who seek to partner with it seem to believe. If it were, I like to think we would have done it by now. It's not surprising, though, that faith is invested in a successful marriage between a market society and green domestication. The alternative is to question the foundational precepts of our economic system, and this is a daunting prospect. It is much more convenient to compromise.

We might take a serious look at the path we follow. It is a journey of diminished existence for humans and nonhumans alike after which there will be little redemption. Diminishment means *gradually lessening*: This is what's happening to our humanity and to the impulse of the Earth. We are pursuing and creating a dystopia of domestication. Species, languages, glaciers, cultures, predators, unencumbered vistas, human lives, animal lives, ecologies, magic—all diminished. And for what? For economic growth and the dream of global consumerism? For green growth? For the abrogation of democracy at the hands of the economically powerful? For the drone of motors instead of the cry of wolves and the silence of uninhabited spaces? Maybe a reality check is in order. Instead, we perfect our denial and circle the wagons.

We have settled into our domestication with the illusion that the Earth has already become a garden; our only challenge is to cultivate it well. In that spirit we make sure we step around the elephant in the room. We don't challenge the nature and logic of capitalism; it is more convenient to strike out at excessive greed and corporate irresponsibility. We argue about how to enact policies to redistribute income rather than work to discern why it is so skewed in the first place. We convince ourselves that putting a price on nature is a reasonable way to defend it and a valid substitute for changing our economic dynamic of accumulation and growth. We worship human ingenuity and technological change rather than call for moral restraint and the granting of freedom to the more-than-human world. We don't think about the rights of the Earth; we avoid thinking about the sixth extinction. Instead, we patronize nature by declaring it resilient in the face of humankind's manipulation. After all, haven't humans always manipulated nature? Yes, of course, but we haven't always *imperialized* it. There's a difference. It is one thing for humans to use nature to reproduce their material existence, it is quite another to construct human society around an economic dynamic of never-ending expansion. And still another to focus that dynamic on the production of exchange value or, in common parlance, profit.

For the long span of history, the nonhuman world existed without being dominated by humans and their economic preoccupation. For most of our natural history *Homo sapiens* existed as an embedded species in ecosystems that were not human-dominated. So the question of the human relationship with the natural world is not whether our species has always manipulated nature, but whether it has always colonized the forms and rhythms of the natural world for narrow economic purposes. The answer to this question is a thousand times no. For much of its natural history the human species has been able to feel the pulse of the Earth.

This changed with the onset of agriculture some ten thousand years ago. Agriculture ushered in a bioeconomic revolution, and the evolution of human society and the integrity of the Earth's ecosystems have never been the same. There is a complex story here that goes beyond the scope of these few pages. If we distill the importance of this revolution we might say this: With agriculture human society became economistic—centered on economic activity in a continuum of expansion and surplus production. With this revolution a wholly different dynamic for human society and its relationship with the nonhuman world was set in motion. The consequences for humans and their ecological impact are well-documented. Explosive population growth, diminished health and well-being, economic hierarchy, and ecological decay are the indelible marks of agricultural civilization.

The present economic system is derivative of this earlier revolution and continues in its spirit. The difference is that the results are more pronounced because a market system and its attendant profit imperative is a particularly powerful force in generating surplus production. And once market society was fertilized with the industrial revolution and its fossil fuel dependency, the metabolism of economic activity was profoundly altered. In little more than two centuries humanity has had the impact of a geological force.

Our exponential growth curves document this escalating force, which accumulates like compound interest. The most obvious expression can be seen if we look at human population growth. At the beginning of the nineteenth century there were about 1 billion people on Earth. This means it took all of human history until the early nineteenth century to get a total of 1 billion people on the planet. Between 2000 and 2012 alone, 1 billion people were added, bringing the total to 7 billion. The exponential growth in population is surpassed by economic growth with all of its attendant material manifestations and demands on the Earth. China's economy now grows somewhere between 7 and 8 percent per year, which means it will double in less than ten years, and the U.S. economy, with a much higher standard of living, now has a growth rate of between 2 and 3 percent per year. At this rate it will double in less than thirty-five years. The U.S. economy currently has an official unemployment rate of around 8 percent (and it's probably much higher). If it were to grow at a rate of 4 percent per year it would double in less than eighteen years, and under our present economic arrangements that level of growth will be necessary to bring our unemployment rate down to acceptable levels. Is this possible given the ecological imbalances and challenges now before us? This is not progress, it is devolution—it is the impossible economics of the undoing of the web of life.

Aldo Leopold wrote: "It of course goes without saying that economic feasibility limits the tether of what can or cannot be done for land. It always has and it always will."[1] In his own day Leopold correctly grasped the magnitude of this tether. But given the world that has unfolded since he wrote these words, he might have been inclined to rethink his concession to the demands of economic feasibility—which are unreasonable if not immoral in relentlessly pressing the natural world to yield to those demands. We should now challenge the concession to economic feasibility, but instead the economy's dominion over us is all too often conceded and rationalized with garden metaphors and ideologies of balanced domestication.

We need a line in the sand, affirming human dignity, and restraint in the face of the economic insanity that envelops us. This is why we practice conservation. It is why we rise up in defense of wolves and elephants, mountains and rivers, and the black night of the sagebrush steppe. Conservation is a tangible resistance, an expression of humility and reverence for the wild in a world ruled by madmen and the seemingly limitless tether of economic feasibility. Alone, conservation will come up short, but it will at least provide those who come after us with an accounting of what has been sacrificed in the name of economic progress.

Wyoming is a land where the imprint of civilization stands out like a proverbial sore thumb. Drive through its vast public lands, now dotted with "low-carbon" gas wells, and you'll see what I mean. The multiple-use mandate that governs the management of these lands embodies the belief in balanced domestication: All human constituents can be served while still preserving a modicum of the integrity of the nonhuman. This mandate first hit a wall with ranching; energy development has added a final nail to the coffin of this untenable proposition.

Wyoming, fortunately, has another legacy—a legacy of unadulterated, unapologetic conservation of the wild. This legacy puts the challenge of our historical moment in a different light. Instead of the promise of balanced domestication sprinkled with garden fairy dust, it demands a place for the wild pulse of this miraculous planet in this now zero-sum game.

An Open Letter to Major John Wesley Powell

TERRY TEMPEST WILLIAMS

4 July 2013

Dearest Major Powell:

I write to you on the banks of the Colorado River at a time when the landscape before me feels much like the political landscape in our nation's capital. Both are eroding. Both are experiencing a state of drought: One involves a lack of water; the other involves a lack of vision.

Almost one hundred fifty years ago, as a prophet overlooking the future of America's western lands, you recognized that the aridity in the desert southwest was a matter of identity. You adopted that identity as a man who was bathed and baptized in the wild waters of the Green and Colorado Rivers. Your lips were parched, your skin was dry, and your body was stretched by each mile you muscled through, rapid after rapid, as you explored the beauty and brutality of this unknown territory, these blank spaces on our country's evolving map. And in the process of your wanderings, you became even more passionate about "creating a society to match the scenery" as your biographer Wallace Stegner described the measure of your character in *Beyond the Hundredth Meridian*.

When you returned to the political mirage of Washington from the wilderness of red rock canyons and dry heat that animates the stone still-ness of the desert, you said courageously to minds accustomed to green, that rain does not follow the plow. And you advocated for the dissolution of state boundaries seeing them for what they were, a geometry of power that had little to do with the realities of nature, and you argued vocifer-ously for the adoption of boundaries based on rivers and watersheds. This was not just a pragmatic statement in your hope of creating an enlight-ened public policy regarding our public lands, your *Report on the Arid Regions of the United States, with a More Detailed Account of the Lands of Utah* written in 1876 was nothing short of a spiritual manifesto. Your vision was a call for connectivity in a country in love with compartmental-ism. You saw the need for cooperation within communities laced together through water. And you asked for less government bureaucracy and for more collaborative jurisdictions among the peoples who inhabited this "land of little water."

I can imagine your ire in 1893, as you put aside your planned speech and spoke from your radical heart to the International Irrigation Con-gress in Los Angeles, California, after hearing them proudly praise their delusional dreams of irrigating the millions of acres of federally owned lands in the arid West as though the myth of the garden could simply be reclaimed through water. You called them mad, you said, "I tell you gentlemen, you are piling up a heritage of conflict and litigation over water rights for there is not sufficient water to supply the land." And you were right, drought right, to the lost drops of water we find ourselves protecting a century later. But on that day, those in attendance and power heckled you, booed you, and disregarded your words.

In 1894, you resigned from your post of Director of the United States Geologic Survey after thirteen robust years of geographic reform. You not only led the geologic mapping of the American West, but you led an intel-lectual revolt in understanding a region where erosion and drought require a philosophy of restraint. You never forgot your fidelity to science and not only fought for but supported a myriad of disciplines such as history, an-thropology, and art to color our perceptions of what it means to be human.

No, you were not listened to then, but you are heralded now, revered by those of us living in the American southwest today. We honor your prudence and prescient intelligence born out of the fullness of your ex-plored experience of these vast wild spaces, still incomprehensible by dandies in Washington, still discounted by politicians who denounce and deplore science in favor of religion. Your lifelong project to integrate "the science of man" with "the science of the Earth" is ongoing in our colleges and universities and remains part of our public discourse be it in the value of wilderness or how our communities resist unbridled growth.

With my trembling pen, Major Powell, this is what I can tell you: Our rivers are shrinking. Our lands are blowing away. And our lawmakers from our president to our legislators, both federal and state, are in denial of this one hard fact: We must change our lives, our politics, our beliefs, our actions, if we are going to survive.

Three things you should know from the grave, Major Powell:

The planet is heating up. The level of carbon in the atmosphere, 400 parts per million and climbing, is a result of our exhaustive use of fossil fuels to support our human population of 7 billion people. As a result, seas are rising, storms are eroding fragile coastlines, and droughts are expanding. Extreme weather is now the norm. We can no longer call tornados, hurricanes, and forest fires "natural disasters." We are responsible. Glaciers are melting. Islands are disappearing. People are being displaced. The story of aridity in the American West is becoming the narrative of the planet.

A new epoch is upon us. The Holocene which you were so familiar with as a geologist and which began after the last ice age, some 11,500 years ago, is being replaced by a new epoch, marked by the force of our own species. Some scientists and geologists alike are coming to see our press on the planet as its own geologic force that will one day write its rapid and destructive history in the stratigraphy of the Earth. Surprisingly enough, it will not be just the laying down of our cities or the removal of our forests or even the plowed scars of agriculture that will mark this moment through time, the onset of the Anthropocene. It will also be the effects of what is currently invisible, the changing composition of our atmosphere that will describe the demise of diversity on the planet. The burning of coal, the fracking of natural gas, and the extended dependence on oil to heat our homes, fuel our cars, and run our factories that will blacken the record of our existence. Bleached corals in the increasing acidic seas will tell our story of this sixth extinction that is upon us.

The Grand Canyon appears to be much older than we thought. Data unearthed by researchers at the California Institute of Technology suggests that the conventional geologic models that have placed this wonder of the world to be 5 to 6 million years old are much too conservative.

Clarence Dutton's *Tertiary History of the Grand Canyon District*, so painstakingly researched and elegantly drawn one hundred thirty years ago by the hands of Thomas Moran and William H. Holmes, is now more of an aesthetic document than a scientific one. The Grand Canyon, Major Powell, that you, sir, put on the map, with all its blessed layers of deep time explored, expressed, and catalogued through your leadership of the U.S. Geologic Survey, may in fact, be 70 million years old.

What are we to do with these revelations? How do we integrate and incorporate the harsh and horrifying facts of today with the wisdom and beauty held and recorded in the stratigraphy of the Earth?

I return to your wisdom on the importance of "a home-grown education," of being wedded to a place through our wanderings and fighting for it. I have learned from your history, Major Powell, that it is only through the power of our own encounters and explorations of the wild that we can cultivate hope because we have experienced both the awe and humility in nature. We can passionately enter into the politics of place, even the realm of public policy, and change it, if we dare to speak from the authority of our own residencies.

Bernard DeVoto spoke of "the cult of action" associated with the frontier. You were part of that cult and transformed the culture of science in Washington, D.C. You mapped spaces with your curiosity and courage. Can we not also become part of this history of courageous engagement to fight for what we love—which is not just the imperiled arid lands in the American West now slated for an insane onslaught of oil and gas development, but also the sanctity of the Earth and all its wild places? May we also rise up and set our planned remarks to the side and speak from the heart, passionately, vociferously, to our leaders that they are mad and that the only way forward is to embark on the shared voyage of uncharted territory trusting the weight of science and the power of our collective imaginations.

My question, Major Powell, is this: Can we learn to love the Earth enough to change?

Respectfully yours,
Terry Tempest Williams

The Road to Cape Perpetua

KATHLEEN DEAN MOORE

IT TAKES A STRONG STOMACH to drive over the Coast Range from my house to the Pacific Ocean. The road goes the way of the rivers, following tight curves between the hills. Logging trucks crowd the turns, going the other way. They downshift to hold heavy loads against the grade. Over the crest of the range, in the green tumble of hills that form the headwaters for the coastal salmon streams, each curve uncovers another square of bare mountainside, clear-cut to the mud. There's hardly a green leaf left in the cut—only gray dirt, shattered tree trunks lying every which way, and root wads and dead branches bulldozed into muddy piles. Even the rivers are gray, muddied by rain that erodes the raw draglines.

When I reached this part of the range, I drove as fast as I could through it, keeping my eyes on the single row of alders that the logging company left along the road to hide the carnage. I knew that on the coast, just south of Cape Perpetua, I would finally come to remnant patches of ancient rainforest, somehow saved from the chain saws—six-hundred-year-old Sitka spruce and red cedars that grow, dark and mossy, down the slope to the edge of the sea. I pushed through the scarred hills, trying to concentrate on how the ancient forest would smell, all damp earth and cedar, and how the surf sounds, far away through deep ferns.

South of the Cape, I walked a trail under Sitka spruce to the edge of a cliff, where the forest cracks off into the sea. On the headland, the air was suddenly salt-thick and cold, the wind ferocious. In wild surf, scuds of sea foam sprang up like startled birds, and wave-tossed logs shot ten feet in the air. A few children ran shouting along the cliff edge, holding their hats against the gale, ducking under sheets of spray, changing course simultaneously, like sanderlings. I pulled my rain jacket tight around me and sat on a bench overlooking the sea.

The bench was a memorial. Someone who deeply loves the coast must have chosen the site, just above the wild collision of coastal stream and cobbles. I read the inscription on the brass plaque: *Mother, when you hear a song or see a bird, please do not let the thought of me be sad, for I am loving you just as I always have. It was heaven here with you.*

A living, grieving mother must have written this note, as if her child were not dead but was speaking to her through the sea of her pain. And the heaven they shared? It must have been here, in this exact spot, where the sea surges into the river at high tide and gulls stand hip-deep, shouldering fresh water across their backs, as they must have done for centuries.

I imagined a mother pulling rain-pants on a child already dancing to go. A last pat on his wool hat, and he runs across the grass in too-big boots. She pulls on her own raincoat and follows him down the trail. At the cliff edge, she stands beside him in the wind, looking out to sea.

How can she live with the sorrow?

We're told by psychologist Elisabeth Kübler-Ross that there is a pattern to grief: Everyone must make the same terrible journey, putting one foot in front of the other in air suddenly gone cold and thick. My friend Katherine, who knows many kinds of sorrow, agrees with Kübler-Ross and wonders if people who are mourning the loss of a beloved part of the world—a forest, a salmon run, a species, a stream—don't experience some of the same feelings as those who mourn the loss of a human being. The quality of the pain may be different, and its intensity, she says, but the sequence of steps is familiar.

Denial is often the first reaction to loss, Kübler-Ross says. Maybe the forest isn't really dead. All those seeds hiding in the bulldozed ground—they might grow into a forest eventually. And if it's too late to save this forest, isn't there still time to save the forests on the other side of the mountains? And maybe the salmon runs aren't extinct; the salmon might be waiting in the ocean until the rivers clear and silt washes off the spawning beds. "Look around," my neighbor says, trying to lift my spirits. "It's still a beautiful world. The environmental crisis is just a protest-industry fund-raising scam."

The next stage is anger. What kind of person can cut an ancient forest to bloody stumps, bulldoze the meadows to mud, spray poison over the mess that's left, and then set smudge fires in the slash? And when the wounded mountainside slumps into the river, floods tear apart the waterfalls and scour the spawning beds, and no salmon return, what kind of person can pronounce it an act of God—and then direct the bulldozers through the stream and into the next forest, and the next? I hope there's a cave in hell for people like this, where an insane little demon hops around shouting "Jobs or trees! Jobs or trees!" and buries an axe blade in their knees every time they struggle to their feet.

Step three. Bargaining. Look, we're rational people. Let's work this out. Destroy this forest if you have to, but plant new seedlings in the slash. Drain this wetland and build your stupid Wal-Mart, but dig a new swamp next to the highway. Let cattle trample this riverbank and plop into this headwater, but fence them from this spawning bed. Kill the smolts in your turbines, but buy new fish for another stream. Then let's create community and study the issue again in five years.

Step four. Depression. Hopelessness deep and dark enough to drown in.

And gradually, disastrously, grief's final step. Acceptance.

ON THE OREGON COAST, the children know mostly fish-poor, flood-stripped streams. Here, all estuaries are fouled, and no river water is safe to drink. That's the way it is. Why should they think it could be any different? Children who have never seen an ancient forest climb the huge, crumbling blood-red stumps as they might climb onto the lap of a vacant-faced grandfather. They look out over the ferns and hemlock seedlings, unable to imagine what used to be. They don't remember waking up to birdsong. How can they miss a murrelet if they've never seen one? It's not just their landscape that has been clear-cut, but their imaginations, the wide expanse of their hope.

And when their grandparents' memories of unbroken forests fade and the old stories grow tedious—the streams of red salmon pushing into the river—and the photograph albums hold dry images of some other place, some other time, then another opening in the universe slams shut, another set of possibilities disappears forever.

Ecologists call this the sliding baseline; what we accept as normal is gradually changing. This is what we must resist: finally coming to accept that a stripped-down, dammed-up, paved-over, poisoned, bulldozed, radioactive, impoverished landscape is the norm—the way it's supposed to be, the way it's always been, the way it must always be. This is the result we should fear the most.

I turned away from the ocean and hiked back into the forest. It was dark there, and noisy with wind and distant surf. Shadows sank into the whorls of maidenhair ferns and shaggy trunks of cedars centuries old. The decaying earth was a black granite wall bearing the names of all that had been lost and forgotten on the far side of the mountain: the footprints of cougar and elk, yellow-bellied salamanders pacing across dark duff, sword ferns unfurling, the flute of the varied thrush, the smell of cedar and soil, the wild coastal river—its headwaters buried in mossy logs, its waters leaping with salmon, its beaches dangerous with surf and swaying bears. Kneeling, I traced a heron's tracks engraved in black soil at the edge of the stream.

Into the shadows, light fell like soft rain. It shone on every hemlock needle and huckleberry, each lifted leaf of sorrel. A winter wren sang somewhere in the salal, and a raven called from far away. I leaned against an ancient Douglas fir that soared to great height and disappeared into the overcast.

The wilderness is a witness, standing tall and terrible in the storm at the edge of the sea. A wild forest confronts us with what we have done. It reminds us of what we have lost. And it gives us a vision of what—in some way—might live again.

ACKNOWLEDGMENTS

Conservation—its methods, objectives, and animating philosophy—is endlessly fascinating intellectual terrain, having a practical outcome for actual terrain, the body of the Earth. We're grateful first and foremost to this wondrous planet for giving us life and for the opportunity to engage in the vital discussions about how to restore and preserve its ecological integrity.

We are thankful to Don Weeden and his colleagues at the Weeden Foundation (and to that foundation's trustees) for organizing and sponsoring a meeting of conservationists to discuss the increasing prominence of voices who are promoting the "Anthropocene" and using it to frame conservation in terms of a human-dominated Earth. While too numerous to acknowledge by name here, all of the participants in that Denver meeting—and most especially Michael Soulé, who helped convene it—influenced our thinking. In large measure, this volume is the result of that gathering and the conversations it prompted. We're grateful also to the Foundation for Deep Ecology for helping underwrite *Keeping the Wild*, and to David Miller and the entire team at Island Press.

Several individuals have provided valuable editorial assistance on the project; they include Leonard Rosenbaum, John Davis, and Mary Elder Jacobsen, whose keen eye and indefatigable attitude when dealing with unruly endnotes or other editorial emergencies is laudable. Kevin Cross's work designing and overseeing production of the book was, typically, excellent.

Most importantly, we offer thanks to all of the volume's contributing writers. Their insights, so well articulated, have deepened our appreciation for the wild and, we believe, will contribute to the vital, sometimes spirited, debate about the future of conservation.

—TOM BUTLER, EILEEN CRIST, AND GEORGE WUERTHNER

CONTRIBUTORS

TOM BUTLER, a Vermont-based conservation activist and writer, is the board president of the Northeast Wilderness Trust and the former longtime editor of *Wild Earth* journal. His books include *Wildlands Philanthropy*, *Plundering Appalachia*, and *ENERGY: Overdevelopment and the Delusion of Endless Growth*.

CLAUDIO CAMPAGNA is a senior research zoologist with the Wildlife Conservation Society and National Research Council of Argentina. He holds an MD from the University of Buenos Aires and a PhD in Animal Behavior from the University of California, Santa Cruz, and he is a Pew fellow in marine conservation.

PHIL CAFARO is a professor of philosophy at Colorado State University in Fort Collins, Colorado. His research centers on environmental ethics, consumption, and population issues, and wildlands preservation. He is the author of *Thoreau's Living Ethics: Walden and the Pursuit of Virtue* and is coeditor of the anthology *Life on the Brink: Environmentalists Confront Overpopulation*. Cafaro is president of the International Society for Environmental Ethics, and board president of Progressives for Immigration Reform.

TIM CARO is a professor of wildlife biology at the University of California, Davis. He does basic research, applied research, and development work, principally in Africa, where he focuses on how anthropogenic forces are affecting large mammal populations in protected areas. He is the author of numerous articles and five books, including *Behavioral Ecology and Conservation Biology*, *Antipredator Defenses in Birds and Mammals*, *Cheetahs of the Serengeti Plains*, and *Conservation by Proxy: Indicator, Umbrella, Keystone, Flagship, and Other Surrogate Species*. The coauthors on his chapter were all students at UC Davis at the time of writing.

EILEEN CRIST teaches in the Department of Science and Technology in Society at Virginia Tech, where she is advisor for the Humanities, Science, and Environment undergraduate program. She is author of *Images of Animals: Anthropomorphism and Animal Mind* and coeditor of *Gaia in Turmoil* and *Life on the Brink: Environmentalists Confront Overpopulation*.

DAVID EHRENFELD is a professor of biology in the Department of Ecology, Evolution and Natural Resources at Rutgers University. He was the founding editor for the journal *Conservation Biology* and has authored eight books; among his best known are *Becoming Good Ancestors: How We Balance Nature, Community, and Technology* and *The Arrogance of Humanism*. He holds a PhD from the University of Florida and an MD from Harvard University.

DAVE FOREMAN is a scholar of wildlands philosophy and one of the most influential conservationists alive today. He has served as Southwest representative for The Wilderness Society, was one of the founders of the Earth First! movement, and later cofounded the Wildlands Project (now Wildlands Network). He has written numerous books, the most recent of which include *Take Back Conservation*, *Man Swarm*, and *Rewilding North America*. Foreman directs The Rewilding Institute.

DANIEL GUEVARA is a philosophy professor at the University of California, Santa Cruz, where he teaches environmental ethics, moral philosophy, and history of philosophy. He holds a PhD from University of California, Los Angeles. His most recent publication, coedited with Jonathan Ellis, is *Wittgenstein and the Philosophy of Mind* (forthcoming from Oxford University Press).

NED HETTINGER is a professor of philosophy at the College of Charleston in South Carolina. He teaches courses in environmental philosophy, aesthetics, and business ethics. He has written dozens of papers, including critiques of biotechnology and discussions of environmental aesthetics. Hettinger received his PhD from the University of Colorado in Boulder.

DAVID JOHNS is an adjunct professor of political science at Portland State University, where he teaches courses on U.S. constitutional law, politics and the environment, and politics and film. He was a founding coeditor of *New Political Science* and serves on the board of the Society for Conservation Biology. He is author of *A New Conservation Politics*. He was awarded the Denver Zoological Foundation Conservation Award in 2007. He earned his JD from Columbia University.

DAVID W. KIDNER worked as a process design engineer in the petroleum industry before turning to social science with a PhD in psychology from London University. For the past three decades he has taught critical social science and environmental philosophy in Britain and the USA, and his most recent book is *Nature and Experience in the Culture of Delusion*. He has recently retired from Nottingham Trent University, and continues to explore and write about wild nature.

PAUL KINGSNORTH is a writer and poet living in Cumbria, in northern England. He is cofounder and director of the Dark Mountain Project, a network of writers, artists, and thinkers. His essay in this volume was adapted from the third anthology of writing from the Dark Mountain project.

LISI KRALL is a professor of economics at the State University of New York, Cortland. Her areas of specialization include labor economics, the political economy of women, environmental and resource economics, and ecological economics. Her present research concentrates on U.S. land policies with an emphasis on the influence of those policies on the settlement and land use of the West. Krall received her PhD in economics from the University of Utah.

HARVEY LOCKE, a conservationist, writer, speaker, and photographer, is recognized as a global leader in the field of parks and wilderness and large landscape conservation. He is a founder of the Yellowstone to Yukon Conservation Initiative, with the goal of creating a continuous corridor for wildlife from Yellowstone National Park in the United States to northern Canada's Yukon Territory. In 1999 Locke was named one of Canada's leaders for the twenty-first century by *Time Magazine*, Canada.

SANDRA LUBARSKY is a professor and chair of the Sustainable Development Department at Appalachian State University in North Carolina, where she teaches courses on beauty and sustainability, environmental humanities, and strategies for reenchantment. She has worked to bring the issue of sustainability to higher education. She has authored three books and is now completing a manuscript on the importance of beauty as a public value. She holds a PhD from Claremont Graduate University in California.

BRENDAN MACKEY is director of the Griffith Climate Change Response Program. He received a PhD in ecology from Australian National University. Mackey's research addresses the interactions between climate change, biodiversity, and land use; the role of science in policy formation of environmental regulatory frameworks; and the nexus between climate change responses and sustainable development. He is a member of the International Council for the International Union for Conservation (IUCN), and serves on the science advisory group to the Climate Change Commission. He is the author of more than 150 academic publications.

CURT MEINE is a conservation biologist, historian, and writer. His biography *Aldo Leopold: His Life and Work*, published by the University of Wisconsin Press, was the first full-length biography of Leopold and was named Book of the Year by the Forest History Society. His other books include *The Essential Aldo Leopold: Quotations and Commentaries* and *Correction Lines: Essays on Land, Leopold, and Conservation*. Meine received a PhD in Land Resources from the Nelson Institute for Environmental Studies at the University of Wisconsin, Madison.

KATHLEEN DEAN MOORE, a professor of philosophy at Oregon State University, is cofounder of, and senior fellow with, OSU's Spring Creek Project. Her recent award-winning edited volume, *Moral Ground: Ethical Action for a Planet in Peril*, addresses the question: Do we have a moral obligation to the future to leave a world as rich in possibilities as the world we inherited? She is the author of *Wild Comfort: The Solace of Nature*, *Riverwalking: Reflections on Moving Water*, and *The Pine Island Paradox: Making Connections in a Disconnected World*, winner of the Oregon Book Award.

RODERICK NASH is a retired professor of history and environmental studies at the University of California, Santa Barbara. He is best known for his book *Wilderness and the American Mind*, which is one of the foundational texts for environmental history. Nash received his PhD from University of Wisconsin, Madison.

MICHAEL SOULÉ is a conservation biologist and professor emeritus of environmental studies, University of California, Santa Cruz. He is the cofounder of the Society for Conservation Biology and of the Wildlands Project. He is a fellow of both the American Association for the Advancement of Science and the American Academy of Arts and Sciences, and in 1998 he was named as one of the 100 Champions of Conservation of the 20th Century by *Audubon Magazine*. He has published over 170 scientific papers and 9 books on topics including evolutionary biology, island biogeography, biodiversity policy, nature conservation, and ethics.

HOWIE WOLKE is a longtime wilderness advocate, author of two books, columnist, public speaker, university instructor, and, for more than 35 years, a professional wilderness guide. Wolke is well known in the conservation movement for his expertise on public lands and wilderness. After working as the Wyoming representative for Friends of the Earth in the mid-1970s, he cofounded the original Earth First! in 1980. He is a past president of the national conservation group Wilderness Watch.

TERRY TEMPEST WILLIAMS is an author, teacher, conservationist, and activist. Her writing is rooted in the American West and has been influenced by the arid landscape of her native Utah and its Mormon culture. Her work addresses issues ranging from ecology and wilderness preservation to women's health, to exploring our relationship to culture and nature. Among her many acclaimed books are *Refuge: An Unnatural History of Family and Place*; *Red: Patience and Passion in the Desert*; *The Open Space of Democracy*; and *Finding Beauty in a Broken World*. Among the many honors bestowed upon Williams are the Robert Marshall Award from The Wilderness Society, the Wallace Stegner Award given by the Center for the American West, and a John Simon Guggenheim Fellowship in creative nonfiction.

GEORGE WUERTHNER is the ecological projects director for the Foundation for Deep Ecology. He has visited and photographed hundreds of national park units in the United States, including all Alaskan park units, and even more wilderness areas, to gain first-hand knowledge of their ecology, and to see natural landscapes that operate with a minimum of human influence. He has published 36 books on a wide variety of topics including national parks, natural history, wilderness areas, and environmental issues.

NOTES

INTRODUCTION

1. E. Ellis, "Stop Trying to Save the Planet," *Wired*, May 2009. http://www.wired.com/wiredscience/2009/05/ftf-ellis-1/.

2. G. Snyder, pers. comm., 2013.

3. E. Abbey, *The Fool's Progress* (New York: Henry Holt & Co., 1988), p. 150.

4. C. A. Bowers, "Toward an Eco-Justice Pedagogy," 2003. http://www.bath.ac.uk/cree/resources/ecerbowers.pdf.

5. D. Ehrenfeld, *The Arrogance of Humanism* (Oxford, UK: Oxford University Press, 1979).

6. E. Ellis, "Neither Good nor Bad," *New York Times*, 23 May 2011. http://www.nytimes.com/roomfordebate/2011/05/19/the-age-of-anthropocene-should-we-worry/neither-good-nor-bad.

7. Lao-Tzu, *Tao Te Ching*, R. B. Blakney translation (New York: Penguin Putnam Inc., 1955), Signet Classic edition 2001, p. 29.

8. K. Sale, *After Eden: The Evolution of Human Domestication* (Durham, NC: Duke University Press, 2006), p. 120.

9. B. Kingsolver, *Small Wonder* (New York: Harper Collins Publishers, 2002), p. 40.

PAUL KINGSNORTH

1. http://www.eenews.net/greenwire/stories/1059962401

2. P. Kareiva, R. Lalasz, and M. Marvier, "Conservation in the Anthropocene: Beyond Solitude and Fragility," *Breakthrough Journal*, Fall 2011, p. 34.

3. Kareiva, Lalasz, and Marvier, "Conservation in the Anthropocene: Beyond Solitude and Fragility," *Breakthrough Journal*, p. 29.

4. http://www.emmamarris.com/rambunctious-garden/

5. E. Marris, *Rambunctious Garden: Saving Nature in a Post-Wild World* (New York: Bloomsbury, 2011).

6. Kareiva, Lalasz, and Marvier, "Conservation in the Anthropocene: Beyond Solitude and Fragility," *Breakthrough Journal*, p. 36.

DAVID W. KIDNER

1. P. Cushman, "Why the Self Is Empty: Toward a Historically Situated Psychology," *American Psychologist* 45, no. 5 (May 1990): 599–611.

2. G. Myers, *Children and Animals* (Boulder, CO: Westview Press, 1998).

3. D. Sobel, "Look, Don't Touch: The Problem with Environmental Education," *Orion Magazine* July/August 2012.

4. A. Franklin, *Nature and Social Theory* (London: Sage, 2001), 9.

5. Franklin, *Nature and Social Theory*, 86.

6. S. Vogel, "Environmental Philosophy after the End of Nature," *Environmental Ethics* 24, no. 1 (2002): 32.

7. Vogel, "Environmental Philosophy," 32.

8. C. Mann, "Three Trees: Inescapable Blendings of the Human and the Natural," *Harvard Design Magazine* Winter/Spring 2000, p. 32.

9. D. Kidner, *Nature and Experience in the Culture of Delusion* (Basingstoke: Palgrave Macmillan, 2012), 162.

10. W. Balée, "The Research Programme of Historical Ecology," *Annual Review of Anthropology* 35 (2006): 81.

11. W. Cronon, "The Trouble with Wilderness; Or, Getting Back to the Wrong Nature," in *Uncommon Ground: Rethinking the Human Place in Nature*, ed. W. Cronon (New York: W. W. Norton, 1995), 69.

12. S. Vogel, "The Nature of Artifacts," *Environmental Ethics* 25, no. 2 (Summer 2003): 149.

13. D. Botkin, *Discordant Harmonies: A New Ecology for the Twenty-First Century* (New York: Oxford University Press, 1992), 193.

14. P. Kareiva, S. Watts, R. McDonald, and T. Boucher, "Domesticated Nature: Shaping Landscapes and Ecosystems for Human Welfare," *Science* 316, no. 5833 (2007): 1869.

15. Ibid.

16. A. Gomez-Pompa and A. Kaus, "Taming the Wilderness Myth," *Bioscience* 42, no. 4 (April 1992): 274.

17. T. Strehlow, *Songs of Central Australia* (Sydney, Australia: Angus & Robertson, 1971).

18. G. Nabhan, *The Desert Smells Like Rain* (Tucson: University of Arizona Press, 1982); S. Atran, "Evolution and Devolution of Knowledge: A Tale of Two Biologies," *Journal of the Royal Anthropological Institute* 10 (2004): 395–420.

19. L. Maffi, ed., *On Biocultural Diversity* (Washington, D.C.: Smithsonian Institution, 2001).

20. T. Ingold, *The Perception of the Environment* (London: Routledge, 2002), 55.

21. P. Kareiva, "Part 2: Balancing the Needs of People and Nature," *Nature Conservancy Magazine,* Spring 2011. See http://www.nature.org/newsfeatures/magazine/part-two-balancing-the-needs-of-people-and-nature.xml.

22. Ibid.

23. G. Hardin, "The Tragedy of the Commons," *Science* 162 (1968): 1243–48.

EILEEN CRIST

1. On the idea of *oecumene* in the Hellenistic and Roman world, see F. Walbank, *Polybius, Rome and the Hellenistic World* (Cambridge: Cambridge University Press, 2002), 2, 8; D. Wilcox, *The Measure of Times Past: Pre-Newtonian Chronologies and the Rhetoric of Time* (Chicago: The University of Chicago Press, 1987), 85. For *oecumene* as a foreshadowing of globalization, see P. James, "Global Formation: From the *Oecumene* to Planet Exploitation," Globalism, Nationalism, Tribalism: Bringing Theory Back In (London: SAGE Publications, Ltd., 2006), 262–91.

2. Susan Bordo's (1977) expression. See S. Bordo, "Anorexia Nervosa: Psychopathology as the Crystallization of Culture," in *Food and Culture*, ed. C. Counihan and P. Van Esterik (New York: Routledge, 1997), 226–50.

3. I believe I owe the phrasing to animal rights writer and activist Tom Regan; see his *Defending Animal Rights* (Urbana: University of Illinois Press, 2001).

4. See Nicolaus Copernicus's famous "Letter to His Holiness Pope Paul III," published as the preface to the first edition of *On the Revolutions of the Heavenly Spheres* (1543): a remarkable document in endeavoring to placate the highest office of geocentric dogma, while also expressing great trepidation for "daring against the received opinion of mathematicians, and almost against common sense, to imagine some motion of the Earth." In A. M. Duncan, *Copernicus: On the Revolutions of the Heavenly Spheres* (New York: Barnes & Noble, 1976), 23–27.

5. Environmental "purists," opines columnist Margaret Wente in a recent stringing of labels, "have been terrible for environmentalism because they've alienated the public with their misanthropic, anti-growth, anti-technology, dogmatic, zealous, romantic, backward-looking message"; M. Wente, "Can Enviro-optimists Save the Movement from Itself?" *The Globe and Mail*, 20 April 2013. See George Monbiot's witty response to such name-calling in a recent *Guardian* publication; G. Monbiot, "I Love Nature. For This I am Called Bourgeois, Romantic—Even Fascist," *The Guardian* (8 July 2013).

6. "We've come through a period of finally understanding the nature and magnitude of humanity's transformation of the earth. Having realized it, can we become clever enough at a big enough scale to be able to maintain the rates of progress?" This quote from a Harvard biologist is a pithy, if bald-faced, representation of neo-green reasoning (cited in Andrew Revkin's *New York Times* report, aptly titled "Managing Planet Earth: Forget Nature. Even Eden is Engineered," *New York Times* 20 August 2002).

7. Key parameters, according to the planetary boundaries perspective, include anthropogenic nitrogen, greenhouse gases, and biodiversity loss. See J. Rockström et al., "A Safe Operating Space for Humanity," *Nature* 461, no. 24 (2009): 472–75; M. Lynas, *The God Species: How the Planet Can Survive the Age of Humans* (London: Fourth Estate, 2011). Identifying specific boundaries that should not be transgressed is the other side of the conceptual coin of "maximum sustainable yield." In both cases the logic goes as follows: How much can we take from the natural world, or up to what threshold can we pollute and degrade, without threatening boomeranging repercussions? The motive is to eat the planet

and have it too; or, to keep growing without collapsing. Exponent of planetary boundaries Mark Lynas is thus quick to differentiate "planetary boundaries" from the 1972 classic concept of "limits to growth": "The planetary boundaries concept does not necessarily imply any limit on human economic growth or productivity," he assures his readers (2011: 9).

8. This dream is taking the most immediately realizable form of aspirations to mine the Moon and nearby planets, given that no known life forms that could be exploited for human advantage exist within Earth's vicinity.

9. Ironically, the seemingly reasonable claim that human power is godlike is blind to its own entanglements with a monotheistic conception of a God, so improbably arrogant and callous, that the Gnostics unmasked him as an impostor of divinity. See H. Jonas, *The Gnostic Religion* (Boston: Beacon Press, 1958/1963). This is in agreement with professor John Gray's related point, "human uniqueness is a myth inherited from religion, which humanists have recycled into science." In J. Gray, *The Silence of Animals: On Progress and Other Modern Myths* (New York: Farrar, Straus and Giroux, 2013), 77.

10. S. Brand, *Whole Earth Discipline: An Ecopragmatist Manifesto* (London: Viking, 2009); M. Lynas, *The God Species: How the Planet Can Survive the Age of Humans* (London: Fourth Estate, 2011).

11. "In the Anthropocene we are the creators, engineers and *permanent global stewards* of a sustainable human nature" (emphasis added); E. Ellis, "Forget Mother Nature: This Is a World of Our Making," *New Scientist*, 14 June 2011. A similar idea is expressed by Marris: "We are already running the whole Earth, whether we admit it or not. To run it consciously and effectively, we must admit our role and even embrace it. We must temper our romantic notion of untrammeled wilderness and find room next to it for the more nuanced notion of a global, half-wild rambunctious garden, tended by us." E. Marris, "Ecology Without Wilderness: Tending the Global Garden We Call 'Nature'," *The Atlantic*, 15 September 2011.

12. E. Ellis, "Anthropogenic Transformation of the Terrestrial Biosphere," *Philosophical Transactions A* 369 (2011): 1029.

13. P. Kareiva, R. Lalasz, and M. Marvier, "Conservation in the Anthropocene: Beyond Solitude and Fragility," *Breakthrough Journal*, Fall 2011, pp. 29–37.

14. E. Ellis, "The Planet of No Return: Human Resilience on an Artificial Earth," *Breakthrough Journal*, (Winter 2012), http//thebreakthrough.org/index.php/journal/past.

15. Ibid.

16. See the entry about *The Matrix*: http://en.wikipedia.org/wiki/Red_pill_and_blue_pill

17. M. Lenzen et al., "International Trade Drives Biodiversity Threats in Developing Nations," *Nature* 486 (June 2012): 109–12.

18. J. Gray, *The Silence of Animals: On Progress and Other Modern Myths*, 156.

19. E. Marris, "Ecology: Ragamuffin Earth," *Nature* 460 (2009): 450–53.

20. F. Pearce, "True Nature: Revising Ideas on What Is Pristine and Wild," *Yale Environment 360* (13 May 2013). http://e360.yale.edu/feature/true_nature_

revising_ideas...is.../2649/. Understating, in passing, the importance of *the speed of change* that humans are effecting is an enormous obfuscation. Most changes in nature are not catastrophically rapid, which is why biodiversity tends to build over geological time, with the emergence of new species slightly outpacing background extinction. See E. O. Wilson, *The Diversity of Life* (Boston: Harvard University Press, 1999/2010). Mass extinctions, rare in Earth's history, are caused by catastrophic events—humanity's rapidly occurring and sustained impact being the current one.

21. See E. Crist, "Ecocide and the Extinction of Animal Minds," in *Ignoring Nature No More: The Case for Compassionate Conservation,* ed. M. Bekoff (Chicago: University of Chicago Press, 2013), 45–61.

22. Expressions such as "novel ecosystems" and neologisms such as *anthromes* may be viewed as Orwellian representations of the human reshaping of nature. Entitled human beings use what they want from ecosystems, while displacing or exterminating the parts that are in the way. For example, what European colonizers wanted to use from the North American prairie was its soil; everything else had to go, and ultimately of course so will the soil.

23. J. Derrida, "The Ends of Man," in *After Philosophy: End or Transformation?,* ed. K. Baynes et al. (Cambridge, MA: MIT Press, 1987), 131.

24. An observation made by many authors. For example: T. Adorno, *Minima Moralia: Reflections from Damaged Life* (London: NBL, 1978); J. Gould, *The Mismeasure of Man* (New York: W. W. Norton, 1981/1996), chapter 2; M. Calarco, "Identity, Difference, Indistinction," *The New Centennial Review* 11 (2012): 46.

25. P. Hawken, *Blessed Unrest* (London: Penguin Books, 2007), 190.

26. P. Kareiva, R. Lalasz, and M. Marvier, "Conservation in the Anthropocene: Beyond Solitude and Fragility," pp. 35, 36.

27. M. Shellenberger and T. Nordhaus, eds., *Love Your Monsters: Postenvironmentalism and the Anthropocene* (Oakland, CA: The Breakthrough Institute, 2011 PDF e-book).

28. See Global Witness cofounder Charmian Gooch's fascinating 2013 TED talk on corruption surrounding natural resource global deals. She argues persuasively that it is not just "greedy" people in positions of power who are implicated in corruption schemes, but a global network of banks, corporations, and governments who become complicit and also profit. While Gooch clearly sees the systemic, multidimensional character of how corruption works, especially when profits of millions or billions of dollars are at stake, she misses corruption's obvious, and hence invisible, foundation—the acted-upon assumption that Earth's places and beings are "natural resources." See C. Gooch, "Meet Global Corruption's Hidden Players," TEDGlobal, July 2013. This bedrock assumption, to borrow historian Leo Marx's words, is "so obvious that people do not know what they are assuming because no other way of putting things has ever occurred to them" (1996: 204–05); in L. Marx, "The Domination of Nature and the Redefinition of Progress," in *Progress: Fact or Illusion?,* ed. L. Marx and B. Mazlish (Ann Arbor: University of Michigan Press, 1996), 201–18.

29. See T. Kuhn, *The Structure of Scientific Revolutions* (Chicago: University of Chicago Press, 1970), 68–69.

DAVID JOHNS

1. B. Ewing, S. Goldfinger, A. Oursler, A. Reed, D. Moore, and M. Wackernagel, *The Ecological Footprint Atlas 2009* (Oakland, CA: Global Footprint Network, 2009); S. H. M. Butchart et al., "Global Biodiversity: Indicators of Recent Declines," *Science* 328 (28 May 2010): 1164–68; J. S. Brashares, "Filtering Wildlife," *Science* 329 (23 July 2010): 402–03.

2. G. Snyder, *The Practice of the Wild* (San Francisco: North Point Press, 1990).

3. R. Wright, *A Short History of Progress* (Toronto: Anansi, 2004).

4. B. Czech, *Supply Shock* (Gabriola, B.C.: New Society Publishers, 2013); R. L. Nadeau, *The Environmental Endgame* (New Brunswick, NJ: Rutgers University Press, 2006).

5. D. C. Burks, ed., *Place of the Wild* (Washington, D.C.: Island Press, 1994); J. B. Callicott and M. P. Nelson, eds., *The Great New Wilderness Debate* (Athens, GA: University of Georgia Press, 1998).

6. E. Hume, *Tabloids, Talk Radio, and the Future of News: Technology's Impact on Journalism* (The Annenberg Washington Program in Communications Policy Studies of Northwestern University, 1995).

7. R. A. Rappaport, "Adaptations and Maladaptations in Social Systems," in *The Ethical Basis of Economic Freedom*, ed. I. Hill (Chapel Hill, NC: American Viewpoint, 1976), 65.

8. C. Perrings et al., "Ecosystem Services for 2020," *Science* 330 (15 Oct. 2010): 323.

9. C. Perrings et al., "Response to Biodiversity Transcends Services," *Science* 330 (24 Dec. 2010): 1745.

10. P. Kareiva and M. Marvier, "Conservation for the People," *Scientific American* 297, no. 4 (October 2007): 50–57.

11. J. Grantham, "Be Persuasive. Be Brave. Be Arrested (If Necessary)," *Nature* 491, no. 303 (15 Nov. 2012).

12. R. J. Duffy, "Business, Elections and the Environment," in *Business and Environmental Policy*, ed. M. E. Kraft and S. Kamieniecki (Cambridge, MA: MIT Press, 2007), 61–90; S. Kamieniecki, *Corporate America and Environmental Policy* (Stanford, CA: Stanford University Press, 2006).

13. R. J. Duffy, ibid.; S. Kamieniecki, *Corporate America and Environmental Policy* (Stanford, CA: Stanford University Press, 2006); J. Layzer, "Deep Freeze: How Business Has Shaped the Global Warming Debate in Congress," in *Business and Environmental Policy*, ed. M. E. Kraft and S. Kamieniecki (Cambridge, MA: MIT Press, 2007), 93–125; R. T. Libby, *Eco-Wars: Political Campaigns and Social Movements* (New York: Columbia University Press, 1999).

14. G. A. Gonzalez, *Corporate Power and the Environment* (Lanham, MD: Rowman & Littlefield, 2001); W. F. Grover, *The President as Prisoner* (Albany, NY: State University Press of New York, 1989); S. Kamieniecki, ibid.; C. Lindblom, *Politics and Markets* (New York: Basic Books, 1977).

15. G. Cogkianese, "Business Interests and Information in Environmental Rulemaking," in *Business and Environmental Policy*, ed. M. E. Kraft and S. Kamieniecki (Cambridge, MA: MIT Press, 2007), 185–210.

16. G. W. Domhoff, *Who Rules America?*, 3rd ed. (Mountain View, CA: Mayfield Publishing, 1998). G. W. Domhoff, "Wealth, Income and Power," on G. W. Domhoff's official website http://whorulesamerica.net/power/wealth.html, accessed October 7, 2012; T. R. Dye, *Who's Running America?*, 8th ed. (Boulder, CO: Paradigm Publishers, 2014); S. R. Furlong, "Business and the Environment: Influencing Agency Policy Making," in *Business and Environmental Policy*, ed. M. E. Kraft and S. Kamieniecki (Cambridge, MA: MIT Press, 2006), 155–84; G. A. Gonzalez, *Corporate Power and the Environment.*

17. H. C. Kelman, "Reflections on Social and Psychological Processes of Legitimization and Delegitimization," in *The Psychology of Legitimacy*, ed. J. T. Jost and B. Major (Cambridge, UK: Cambridge University Press, 2001), 54–73; P. Stern, "Toward a Coherent Theory of Environmentally Significant Behavior," *Journal of Social Issues* 56, no. 3 (Fall 2000): 407–24.

18. F. Polletta, *It Was Like a Fever* (Chicago: University of Chicago Press, 2006).

19. S. Staggenborg, *Social Movements* (New York: Oxford University Press, 2011).

20. D. Johns, *New Conservation Politics* (Oxford, UK: Wiley-Blackwell, 2009); J. Rodman, "The Liberation of Nature?" *Inquiry* 20 (1977): 83–131.

21. A. Goudie, *The Human Impact on the Natural Environment*, 6th ed. (Oxford, UK: Blackwell, 2005); M. R. W. Rands et al., "Biodiversity Conservation: Challenges Beyond 2010," *Science* 329 (10 Sept. 2010): 1298–1303.

22. A. D. Barnosky, "Megafauna Biomass Tradeoff as a Driver of Quaternary and Future Extinction," *PNAS* 105 (12 August 2008): 11543–48; M. McGlone, "The Hunters Did It," *Science* 335 (23 March 2012): 1452–53; S. Rule et al., "The Aftermath of Megafaunal Extinction: Ecosystem Transformation in Pleistocene Australia," *Science* 335 (23 March 2012): 1483–86.

23. J. A. Alroy, "A Multispecies Overkill Simulation of the End-Pleistocene Megafaunal Mass Extinction," *Science* 292 (8 June 2001): 1893–96; J. McKee, "The Human Population Footprint on Global Biodiversity," in *Life on the Brink*, ed. P. Cafaro and E. Crist (Athens, GA: University of Georgia Press, 2012), 91–97.

24. C. Boehm, *Hierarchy in the Forest* (Cambridge, MA: Harvard University Press, 1999); A. W. Johnson and T. Earle, *The Evolution of Human Society*, 2nd ed. (Stanford: Stanford University Press, 2000).

25. A. Goudie, *The Human Impact on the Natural Environment*, 6th ed. (Oxford, UK: Blackwell, 2005); J. R. McNeill, *Something New Under the Sun* (New York: W. W. Norton, 2000); I. G. Simmons, *Global Environmental History* (Chicago: University of Chicago Press, 2007).

26. M. Williams, *The Deforestation of the World* (Chicago: University of Chicago Press, 2003).

27. P. G. Brewer and E. T. Peltzer, "Limits to Marine Life," *Science* 324 (17 April 2009): 347–48; B. Halperin et al., "An Index to Assess the Health and Benefits of the Global Ocean," *Nature* 488 (30 Aug. 2012): 615–20; E. A. Norse and L. Crowder, *Marine Conservation Biology* (Washington, D.C.: Island Press, 2005).

28. N. Jones, "Human Influence Comes of Age," *Nature* 473 (12 May 2011): 133.

29. D. Scott, " 'Untrammeled,' 'Wilderness Character,' and the Challenge of Wilderness Preservation," *Wild Earth* 11, nos. 3/4 (Fall/Winter 2001): 72–79.

30. J. H. C. Vest, "Will-of-the-Land," *Environmental Review* 9, no. 4: (Winter 1985): 321–29.

31. R. Noss, "Sustainability and Wilderness," *Conservation Biology* 5, no. 1 (March 1991): 120–22; M. Soulé and J. Terborgh, *Continental Conservation* (Washington, D.C.: Island Press, 1999).

32. B. Ewing, D. Moore, S. Goldfinger, A. Oursler, A. Reed, and M. Wackernagel, *The Ecological Footprint Atlas 2010* (Oakland, CA: Global Footprint Network, 2010).

33. J. Layzer, *The Environmental Case* (Washington, D.C.: CQ Press, 2011).

34. P. Kareiva, R. Lalasz, and M. Marvier, "Conservation in the Anthropocene: Beyond Solitude and Fragility," *Breakthrough Journal*, Fall 2011, pp. 29–37.

35. R. Noss, "The Wildlands Project Land Conservation Strategy," *Wild Earth* Special Issue 1 (1993): 10–25.

36. L. Gilbert-Norton, R. Wilson, J. R. Stevens, and K. H. Beard, "A Meta-Analytic Review of Corridor Effectiveness," *Conservation Biology* 24, no. 3: (June 2010): 660–68; R. Hilborn, P. Arcese, M. Borner, J. Hando, G. Hopcraft, M. Loibooki, S. Mduma, A. R. E. Sinclair, "Effective Enforcement in a Conservation Area," *Science* 314 (24 Nov. 2006): 1266; C. F. G. Jeffrey et al., "An Integrated Biogeographic Assessment of Reef Fish Populations and Fisheries in Dry Tortugas: Effects of No-Take Reserves," accessed 20 April 2013, NOAA Technical Memorandum NOS NCCOS 111 (Silver Spring, MD: NCCOS Center for Coastal Monitoring and Assessment Biogeography Branch, 2012). http://ccma.nos. noaa.gov/ecosystems/coralreef/TortugasAssessmentReport_final.pdf?utm; W. F. Laurence et al., "Averting Biodiversity Collapse in Tropical Forest Protected Areas," *Nature* 489 (13 Sept. 2012): 290; S. E. Lester et al., "Biological Effects Within No-Take Marine Reserves: A Global Synthesis," *Marine Ecology Progress Series* 384 (29 May 2009) 33–46; J. F. Oates, *Myth and Reality in the Rain Forest* (Berkeley, CA: University of California Press, 1999).

37. *Nature* magazine editors, "Think Big," *Nature* 469 (13 Jan. 2011), 131; *Nature* magazine editors, "Protect and Serve," *Nature* 487 (26 July 2012), 405–06.

38. R. Noss, "The Wildlands Project Land Conservation Strategy," *Wild Earth* Special Issue 1 (1993): 10–25; M. Soulé and J. Terborgh, *Continental Conservation* (Washington, D.C.: Island Press, 1999).

39. E. Marris, *Rambunctious Garden* (New York: Bloomsbury, 2011), 2.

40. W. M. Denevan, *The Native Population of the Americas in 1492*, 2nd ed. (Madison, WI: University of Wisconsin Press, 1992); J. Diamond, *The Third Chimpanzee* (New York: Harper Collins, 1992); R. Ellen, *Environment, Subsistence and System* (Cambridge, MA: Cambridge University Press, 1982); M. Harris and E. B. Ross, *Death, Sex and Fertility* (New York: Columbia University Press, 1987); R. Klein, *The Human Career* (Chicago: University of Chicago Press, 1989); J. R. McNeill, "Agriculture, Forests, and Ecological History: Brazil 1500–1983," *Environmental Review* 10 (Summer 1986): 122–33; I. G. Simmons, *Global Environmental History* (Chicago: University of Chicago Press, 2007).

41. C. H. McMichael et al., "Sparse Pre-Columbian Human Habitation in Western Amazonia," *Science* 336 (15 June 2012): 1429–31.

42. S. C. Chew, *World Ecological Degradation* (Walnut Creek, CA: Alta Mira Press, 2001); F. Essl, M. Winter, and P. Pyšek, "Trade Threat Could Be Even More Dire," *Nature* 487 (5 July 2011): 39; M. Harris, *Cannibals and Kings* (New York: Random House, 1977); A. W. Johnson and T. Earle, *The Evolution of Human Society,* 2nd ed.; M. Lenzen, D. Moran, K. Kanemoto, B. Foran, L. Lobefaro, and A. Geschke, "International Trade Drives Biodiversity Threats in Developing Nations," *Nature* 486 (7 June 2012), 109–12.

43. See, for example, A. Goudie, *The Human Impact on the Natural Environment*, 6th ed. (Oxford, UK: Blackwell, 2005); V. Smil, *Harvesting the Biosphere* (Cambridge, MA: MIT Press, 2013); R. Tucker, *Insatiable Appetite* (Berkeley and Los Angeles: University of California Press, 2000).

44. C. Chase-Dunn and E. N. Anderson, eds., *The Historical Evolution of World Systems* (New York: Palgrave Macmillan, 2005); C. Chase-Dunn and T. D. Hall, *Rise and Demise* (Boulder, CO: Westview Press, 1997).

45. P. Kareiva and M. Marvier, "Conservation for the People," *Scientific American* 297, no. 4 (Oct. 2007): 56.

46. J. Holdren, opening address to the 2007 Annual Meeting of the American Association for the Advancement of Science, quoted in R. Coontz, "Wedging Sustainability into Public Consciousness," *Science* 315 (23 Feb. 2007): 1068.

47. A. Leopold, *Round River* (New York: Oxford University Press, 1993).

48. D. Ehrenfeld, *The Arrogance of Humanism* (New York: Oxford University Press, 1979); J. Rodman, "The Liberation of Nature?"

49. S. Brand, *Whole Earth Catalog* (Fall 1968). Brand is quoting Edmund Leach in E. Leach, *A Runaway World?* (Oxford, UK: Oxford University Press, 1968).

50. E. Marris, *Rambunctious Garden* (New York: Bloomsbury, 2011).

51. R. Wright, *A Short History of Progress* (Toronto: Anansi, 2004).

52. D. Ehrenfeld, *The Arrogance of Humanism* (New York: Oxford University Press, 1979), 16–17.

53. In addition to D. Ehrenfeld, *The Arrogance of Humanism* (New York: Oxford University Press, 1979), see J. Peet, *Energy and the Ecological Economics of Sustainability* (Washington, D.C.: Island Press, 1992).

R. Dietz and D. O'Neill, *Enough Is Enough* (San Francisco: Berrett-Koehler, 2013) and B. Ewing, S. Goldfinger, A. Oursler, A. Reed, D. Moore, and M. Wackernagel, *The Ecological Footprint Atlas 2009.*

54. D. Ehrenfeld, *The Arrogance of Humanism,* 107.

55. M. Harris, *Cannibals and Kings* (New York: Random House, 1977); W. Jackson, *Alters of Unhewn Stone* (San Francisco: North Point Press, 1987); A. W. Johnson and T. Earle, *The Evolution of Human Society,* 2nd ed.

56. D. L. Guber and C. J. Bosso, "Framing ANWR," in *Business and Environmental Policy,* ed. M. E. Kraft and S. Kamieniecki (Cambridge, MA: MIT Press, 2007), 35–59; J. Layzer, "Deep Freeze: How Business Has Shaped the Global Warming Debate in Congress," in *Business and Environmental Policy*, ed. M. E. Kraft and S. Kamieniecki (Cambridge, MA: MIT Press, 2007), 93–125; C. Lindblom, *Politics and Markets.*

57. M. Klare, *Resource Wars* (New York: Metropolitan/Owl Books, 2002); P. W. Singer, *Corporate Warriors*, 2nd ed. (Ithaca, NY: Cornell University Press, 2007).

58. D. Dinnerstein, *The Mermaid and the Minotaur* (New York: Harper & Row, 1976), 254.

59. H. F. Searles, *The Nonhuman Environment in Normal Development and in Schizophrenia* (New York: International Universities Press, 1960), 78–101; P. Shepard, *Nature and Madness* (San Francisco: Sierra Club Books, 1982).

60. M. Berman, *Coming to Our Senses* (New York: Simon & Schuster, 1989); M. Harris, *Cannibals and Kings*; D. F. Lancy, *The Anthropology of Childhood* (Cambridge, UK: Cambridge University Press, 2008); H. F. Searles, *The Nonhuman Environment in Normal Development and in Schizophrenia*; P. Shepard, *Nature and Madness*.

61. C. Chase-Dunn and E. N. Anderson, eds., *The Historical Evolution of World Systems*; C. Chase-Dunn and T. D. Hall, *Rise and Demise*; A. Goudie, *The Human Impact on the Natural Environment*; J. Rodman, "The Liberation of Nature?"; V. Smil, *Harvesting the Biosphere*.

62. E. Fromm, *The Heart of Man* (New York: Harper & Row, 1964); D. Grossman, *On Killing*, 2nd ed. (New York: Little, Brown, 2009).

63. Ovid (Publius Ovidius Naso, ca. 16 BC), *The Love Poems* (Oxford, UK: Oxford University Press, 1990), 71.

64. Lao Tsu, *Tao te Ching* (New York: Knopf, 1972), ch. 29.

65. P. Shepard, *Nature and Madness*; F. Turner, *Beyond Geography* (New York: Viking, 1980

66. F. Fanon, *Wretched of the Earth* (New York: Grove Press, 1963); W. Jordan, *White over Black*, (Chapel Hill, NC: University of North Carolina Press, 1968).

67. A. W. Johnson and T. Earle, *The Evolution of Human Society*, 2nd ed.

68. M. N. Cohen and G. Crane-Kramer, eds., *Ancient Health* (Gainesville, FL: University of Florida Press, 2007).

69. P. Kareiva, R. Lalasz, and M. Marvier, "Conservation in the Anthropocene: Beyond Solitude and Fragility."

70. M. Klare, *Resource Wars*; F. Lawrence, "Britain's Water Habit Leaves Others Parched," *Guardian Weekly* (29 Aug. 2008): 15; G. Monbiot, "Trade Deals Are the New Gunboats," *Guardian Weekly* (9 May 2008), 24; R. Tucker, *Insatiable Appetite*.

71. Big Horn Association (editorial), *Cheyenne Daily Leader,* 3 March 1870.

72. I am indebted to John Rodman (1977) who to my knowledge first used the analogy of colonialism to describe the post-forager human relationship to the rest of Nature; see J. Rodman, "The Liberation of Nature?"

73. P. Kareiva, R. Lalasz, and M. Marvier, "Conservation in the Anthropocene: Beyond Solitude and Fragility"; E. Marris, *Rambunctious Garden* (New York: Bloomsbury, 2011).

74. S. Solomon, J. L. Greenberg, and T. A. Pyszczynski, "Lethal Consumption: Death-denying Materialism" in *Psychology and Consumer Culture,* ed. T. Kasser and A. D. Kanner (Washington, D.C.: American Psychological Association, 2004), 127–46.

75. P. Shepard, *The Sacred Game and the Tender Carnivore* (New York: Scribner's, 1973).

76. H. D. Thoreau, "Walden" (1854), in *The Portable Thoreau*, ed. C. Bode (New York: Viking, 1964), 335.

77. D. H. Lawrence, "A Propos of Lady Chatterley's Lover," in *Phoenix II* (London: Heinemann, 1968), 504.

CURT MEINE

1. J. B. Callicott, "The Wilderness Idea Revisited: The Sustainable Development Alternative," *The Environmental Professional* 13 (1991): 235–47; W. M. Denevan, "The Pristine Myth: The Landscape of the Americas in 1492," *Annals of the Association of American Geographers* 82 (1992): 369–85; W. Cronon, "The Trouble with Wilderness; or, Getting Back to the Wrong Nature," in W. Cronon, ed., *Uncommon Ground: Rethinking the Human Place in Nature* (New York: W. W. Norton & Co., 1995), 69–90. See also W. M. Denevan, "The Pristine Myth Revisited," *Geographical Review* 101 (2011): 576-91.

2. W. L. Thomas, ed., *Man's Role in Changing the Face of the Earth* (Chicago: University of Chicago Press, 1956), xxxvii.

3. L. Mumford, in *Man's Role in Changing the Face of the Earth*, 1146.

4. A. Leopold, *Game Management* (New York: Charles Scribner's Sons, 1933), 21.

5. L. Mumford, *The Brown Decades: A Study of Arts in America, 1865–1895*, rev. ed. (New York: Dover, 1955), 78; G. P. Marsh, *Man and Nature, or Physical Geography as Modified by Human Action* (New York: Charles Scribner, 1864), iii.

6. See R. S. Beeman and J. A. Pritchard, *A Green and Permanent Land: Ecology and Agriculture in the Twentieth Century* (Lawrence, KS: University Press of Kansas, 2001); and B. A. Minteer, *The Landscape of Reform: Civic Pragmatism and Environmental Thought in America* (Cambridge, MA: MIT Press, 2006).

7. See R. L. Knight and S. F. Bates, *A New Century for Natural Resources Management* (Washington, D.C.: Island Press, 1995); R. L. Knight and P. Landres, eds., *Stewardship Across Boundaries* (Washington, D.C.: Island Press, 1998); R. L. Knight and C. White, *Conservation for a New Generation: Redefining Natural Resources Management* (Washington, D.C.: Island Press, 2008).

8. See B. A. Minteer, *The Landscape of Reform*.

9. A. Leopold, "A Biotic View of Land," in *The River of the Mother of God and Other Essays by Aldo Leopold*, ed. S. L. Flader and J. B. Callicott (Madison, WI: University of Wisconsin Press, 1991), 267 (originally published in *Journal of Forestry* 37, no. 9 [1939]: 727–30). Leopold reiterated the point a number of times in his writings across his career, including in "The Land Ethic" in *A Sand County Almanac* (New York: Oxford University Press, 1949).

10. See D. Waller and T. Rooney, eds., *The Vanishing Present: Wisconsin's Changing Lands, Waters, and Wildlife* (Chicago: University of Chicago Press, 2008); K. D. Moore and M. P. Nelson, eds., *Moral Ground: Ethical Action for a Planet in Peril* (San Antonio, TX: Trinity University Press, 2010).

11. A. Leopold, "Conservation: In Whole or in Part?" in *The River of the Mother of God*, 318 (originally composed in 1944). See also: F. Berkes, N. C. Doubleday, and G. S. Cumming, "Aldo Leopold's Land Health from a Resilience Point of View: Self-renewal Capacity of Social–Ecological Systems," *EcoHealth* 9 (2012): 278–87; and P. Nadasdy, "Resilience and Truth: A Response to Berkes," *Maritime Studies* (MAST) 9 (2010): 41–45.

12. R. Marshall, *Arctic Village* (New York: The Literary Guild, 1933); R. Marshall, *Arctic Wilderness* (Berkeley, CA: University of California Press, 1956; republished as *Alaska Wilderness: Exploring the Central Brooks Range* (Berkeley, CA: University of California Press, 1970).

13. O. J. Murie, "Ethics in Wildlife Management," *Journal of Wildlife Management* 18, no. 3 (1954): 289–93.

14. M. E. Mulrennan, R. Mark, and C. H. Scott, "Revamping Community-based Conservation through Participatory Research," *The Canadian Geographer / Le Géographe Canadien* 56 (2012): 243–59. See http://wemindjiprotectedareapartnership.weebly.com.

15. H. McLeod, "Frog Bay Tribal National Park Now Open to the Public," *Ashland Daily Press*, 9 August 2012. Available online at http://www.ashlandwi.com/county_journal/article_f0b4deac-e22c-11e1-9535-001a4bcf887a.html.

16. P. Hawken, *Blessed Unrest: How the Largest Movement in the World Came into Being and Why No One Saw It Coming* (New York: Viking, 2007), 2.

17. A. Leopold, "The Ecological Conscience" in *The River of the Mother of God*, 345-46.

CLAUDIO CAMPAGNA AND DANIEL GUEVARA

1. Nature (with capital "N") indicates an idealization, not just what empirical science studies, for example. "Nature," as opposed to "nature," should suggest the object of ethical concern of a very high order. A controversial and, according to our own paper, fraught idea (perhaps in the end inexpressible in some sense, at least for now), it points to something we grasp only intuitively and darkly if we grasp it at all. It is what Thoreau and Muir and so forth are writing about. With a little "n," nature is not really controversial or essentially ethical at all. It is simply what empirical science studies.

2. P. Kareiva, R. Lalasz, and M. Marvier, "Conservation in the Anthropocene: Beyond Solitude and Fragility," *Breakthrough Journal*, Fall 2011, pp. 29–37.

3. Ibid.

4. Ibid.

5. M. Shellenberger and T. Nordhaus, *The Death of Environmentalism* (The Heartland Institute, 2004), http://heartland.org/policy-documents/death-environmentalism-0.

6. P. Kareiva, R. Lalasz, and M. Marvier, "Conservation in the Anthropocene: Beyond Solitude and Fragility."

7. Whether it is inconvenient or not depends on how you look at it (from the cabin or the corporate window, as it were), but it is not entirely new: John Muir encountered it in his battles with Gifford Pinchot (F. Turner, *John Muir: Rediscovering America* [Cambridge, MA: Da Capo Press, 2000]) and David Brower in his battles with Charles Park, among others (see chapter 1, J. McPhee, *Encounters with the Archdruid* [New York: Farrar, Straus and Giroux, 1971].).

8. M. Soulé, "The 'New' Conservation," *Conservation Biology* 27, no. 5 (2013): 895–97.

9. L. Wittgenstein, "Lecture on Ethics," *The Philosophical Review* 74, no. 1 (1965): 3–12.

10. M. Heidegger, *The Fundamental Concepts of Metaphysics: World, Finitude, Solitude* (Bloomington, IN: Indiana University Press, 2001).

11. M. C. Nussbaum, *Frontiers of Justice: Disability, Nationality, Species Membership* (Cambridge, MA: Belknap Press of Harvard University, 2007), 374.

12. L. Wittgenstein, "Lecture on Ethics."

13. It is inconsistent with how we and many others experience the beauty and sublimity of Nature, for one thing. See Elaine Scarry's book, for a wonderful exploration in right direction (E. Scarry, *On Beauty and Being Just* [Princeton, NJ: Princeton University Press, 2001].).

14. An obvious contemporary place for a philosopher to mine, in this regard, is in the work of Gary Snyder, unsurpassed in its poetic and broadly informed sensitivity to language, including of course language entirely outside of the influence of Western philosophical sources. But we emphasize that it *must be mined*; everything is virgin territory philosophically in this area of thought.

15. C. Campagna, *Bailando en Tierra de Nadie: Hacia un nuevo discurso del ambientalismo* (Buenos Aires, Argentina: Editorial Del Nuevo Extremo, 2013).

MICHAEL SOULÉ

1. D. Foreman, *Man Swarm and the Killing of Wildlife* (Durango, CO: Raven's Eye Press, 2011).

2. See, for example, www.culturalsurvival.org/.

3. B. McKibben, "Global Warming's Terrifying New Math," *Rolling Stone*, 19 July 2012.

4. The animal welfare movement will not be discussed further, here, because domesticated, kept animals were bred by people for utilitarian purposes; thus animal welfare is logically a section of humanitarianism.

5. www.nps.gov/partnerships/fundraising_individuals_statistics.htm

6. M. S. Gazzaniga, *Human: The Science Behind What Makes Your Brain Unique* (New York: HarperCollins, 2008).

7. J. Haidt, *The Righteous Mind* (New York:. Pantheon Books, 2012).

8. D. Pfaff, *The Neuroscience of Fair Play: Why We (Usually) Follow the Golden Rule* (Washington, D.C.: Dana Press, 2007).

9. E. Abbey, "Down the River," in *The Best of Edward Abbey* (San Franscisco: Sierra Club Books, 1984), 272–307.

10. B. Devall and G. Sessions, *Deep Ecology: Living as if Nature Mattered* (Layton, UT: Gibbs Smith, 2001). http://en.wikipedia.org/wiki/Deep_ecology.

11. D. Foreman, *Take Back Conservation* (Durango, CO: Raven's Eye Press, 2012).

12. Critics of conservation including the Breakthrough Institute, its funders, and Santa Clara University faculty Peter Kareiva and Michelle Marvier claim that traditional wilderness/biodiversity conservation is an impossible and illogical enterprise because there is no pristine nature; therefore the goal of nature protection is futile and oxymoronic. This black-and-white portrayal of conservation is like believing that because no book is absolutely true, we must burn all libraries. In fact, educated conservationists have not believed in the existence of pristine places or systems since at least the 1970s, when DDT was found in animal tissues everywhere, including in the milk of human mothers.

13. The current rate is estimated to be about one thousand times higher than it was prior to the agricultural revolution and the human occupation of Oceania and the Americas. Several scientists estimate that about half of existing species will have disappeared by the middle of this century.

14. See M. Shellenberger and T. Nordhaus, eds., *Love Your Monsters: Postenvironmentalism and the Anthropocene* (Oakland, CA: The Breakthrough Insititute, 2011), PDF e-book.

15. P. Kareiva, R. Lalasz, and M. Marvier, "Conservation in the Anthropocene: Beyond Solitude and Fragility," *Breakthrough Journal*, Fall 2011, p. 36. The humanitarian program of Kareiva and his colleagues is also presented in many interviews, blogs, and articles. Among the most useful, I believe, are articles about Kareiva by Paul Voosen in Greenwire, entitled "Conservation: Myth-busting Scientist Pushes Greens Past Reliance on 'Horror Stories.'" http://www. eenews.net/public/Greenwire/2012/04/03/1. Also informative is a YouTube video of a talk by Kareiva: http://dotearth.blogs.nytimes.com/2012/04/03/peter-kareiva-an-inconvenient-environmentalist/.

16. D. Foreman, *Take Back Conservation* (Durango, CO: Raven's Eye Press, 2012).

17. See "Letters" in *BioScience* 63, no. 4 (April 2012): 242–43.

18. http://www.nationalparksstraveler.com/2012/08/polls-shows-vast-majority-voters-believe-federal-government-has-responsibility-safeguard-nati10342.

19. M. E. Soulé, "The Social Siege of Nature" in *Reinventing Nature?: Responses to Postmodern Deconstruction*, ed. M. E. Soulé and G. Lease (Washington, D.C.: Island Press, 1995), 137–70. See also, J. F. Oates, *Myth and Reality in the Rainforest: How Conservation Strategies Are Failing in West Africa* (Berkeley, CA: University of California Press: 1999). No such ethical awakening has occurred among the wealthy in the United States.

20. E. Marris, *Rambunctious Garden* (New York: Bloomsbury, 2011).

21. J. A. Estes et al., "Trophic Downgrading of Planet Earth," *Science* 333, no. 6040 (15 July 2011): 301–306.

22. D. Tilman, "Biodiversity and Environmental Sustainability amid Human Domination of Global Ecosystems," *Daedalus*, Summer 2012, pp. 102–20.

23. The new environmentalists also neglect to mention the growing support by ecologists for the view that a major driver of extinction is the global disappearance of keystone species, particularly large carnivores; see J. E. Estes, J. Terborgh, J. Berger et al., "Trophic Downgrading of Planet Earth," *Science* 333, no. 6040 (15 July 2011): 301–306.

24. S. Pinker, *The Better Angels of Our Nature: Why Violence Has Declined* (New York: Viking, 2011).

25. Incidentally, the Endangered Species Act has been highly successful in rescuing species from the brink; see D. Goble, J. M. Scott, and F. Davis, *The Endangered Species Act at Thirty*, Vols. 1 & 2 (Washington, D.C.: Island Press, 2006).

26. W. F. Laurance et al., "Averting Biodiversity Collapse in Tropical Forest Protected Areas," *Nature* 489 (13 September 2012): 290–94. doi:10.1038/nature11318.

27. The phrase "tenacity of benevolence" is from Jean Giono's *The Man Who Planted Trees*.

DAVID EHRENFELD

1. F. Pearce, "New Green Vision: Technology as Our Planet's Last Best Hope," *Yale Environment* 360 (15 July 2013).

2. L. Brown, "Can We Raise Grain Yields Fast Enough?," *World-Watch*, Worldwatch Institute (July–August 1997): 8–17; see also F. Magdoff and B. Tokar, "Agriculture and Food in Crisis: An Overview," in *Agriculture and Food in Crisis: Conflict, Resistance, and Renewal*, ed. F. Magdoff and B. Tokar (New York: Monthly Review Press, 2010), pp. 10–17; D. Ehrenfeld, "Agriculture in Transition," in *Beginning Again: People and Nature in the New Millennium* (New York: Oxford University Press, 1993/1995), 164–74.

3. B. Halweil, "Grain Harvests Flat," in *Vital Signs 2006–2007: The Trends That Are Shaping Our Future* (New York: Norton, 2006), 22–24.

4. M. A. Altieri, *Genetic Engineering in Agriculture: The Myths, Environmental Risks, and Alternatives*, 2nd ed. (Oakland, CA: Food First Books, 2004); D. Ehrenfeld, *Becoming Good Ancestors: How We Balance Nature, Community, and Technology* (New York: Oxford University Press, 2009), 4–13; C. M. Benbrook, "Who Controls and Who Will Benefit from Plant Genomics?" Presented at the 2000 Genomic Seminar *Genomic Revolution in the Fields: Facing the Needs of the New Millennium* (Washington, D.C.: American Association for the Advancement of Science Annual Meeting, 19 Feb. 2000). http://www.biotech-info.net/AAASgen.html.

5. APHIS (Animal and Plant Health Inspection Services), U.S. Department of Agriculture, "Monsanto Company Petition (07-CR-191U) for Determination of Non-regulated Status of Event MON 87460, OECD Unique Identifier: MON 87460-4, Final Environmental Assessment" (Washington, D.C.: U.S.D.A/APHIS, Nov. 2011).

6. J. Qiu, "GM Crop Use Makes Minor Pests Major Problems," *Nature* (13 May 2010). doi:10.1038/news.2010.242.

7. H. Sudarshan, "Foreword" in V. Ramprasad, *Hidden Harvests: Community Based Biodiversity Conservation* (Bangalore, India: Green Foundation, 2002), 4–6.

8. J. Qiu, "Genetically Modified Crops Pass Benefits to Weeds," *Nature* (16 Aug. 2013). doi:10.1038/nature.2013.13517; H. Thompson, "War on Weeds Loses Ground: The Rise of Herbicide-resistant Varieties Drives a Search for Fresh Methods of Control," *Nature* 485 (24 May 2012): 430.

9. V. Shiva, "Globalization and the War Against Farmers and the Land," in *The Essential Agrarian Reader*, ed. N. Wirzba (Lexington, KY: University Press of Kentucky, 2003), 121–39.

10. A. A. Bartlett, "Forgotten Fundamentals of the Energy Crisis," *Am J. of Physics* 46 (1978): 876–88.

11. V. Smil, "Global Energy: The Latest Infatuations," *American Scientist* 99, no. 3 (2011): 212–19.

12. M. Bittman, "The New Nuclear Craze," *The New York Times*, 24 Aug. 2013, p. A21.

13. For the cost of the *Deepwater Horizon* drilling platform, see J. Tainter and T. Patzek, *Drilling Down: The Gulf Oil Debacle and Our Energy Dilemma* (New York: Springer, 2012), 5.

14. Smil, "Global Energy: The Latest Infatuations," *American Scientist* 99, no. 3 (2011): 212–19.

15. O. Zehner, "Solar Cells and Other Fairy Tales" in *Green Illusions: The Dirty Secrets of Clean Energy and the Future of Environmentalism* (Lincoln, NE: University of Nebraska Press, 2012), 3–30.

16. Ibid.

17. D. Cardwell, "Grappling with the Grid: Intermittent Nature of Green Power Is Challenge for Utilities," *The New York Times*, 15 Aug. 2013, pp. B1, B6; see also O. Zehner, "Wind Power's Flurry of Limitations," in *Green Illusions*, 31–60.

18. Cardwell, "Grappling with the Grid: Intermittent Nature of Green Power Is Challenge for Utilities," *The New York Times*, 15 Aug. 2013, pp. B1, B6.

19. K. French, "'Never Stops, Never Stops. Headache. Help.': Some People Living in the Shadows of Wind Turbines Say They're Making Them Sick. Almost As Upsetting: Their Neighbors Don't Feel a Thing," *New York Magazine*, 23 Sept. 2013, p. 28.

20. T. Beardsley, "Biofuels Reassessed," *BioScience* 62 (2012): 855; see also S. Raghu et al., "Adding Biofuels to the Invasive Species Fire," *Science* 313 (2006): 293.

21. Beardsley, "Biofuels Reassessed," *BioScience* 62 (2012).

22. Smil, "Global Energy: The Latest Infatuations," *American Scientist* 99, no. 3 (2011): 212–19.

23. J. Major, "1981 Climate Change Predictions Were Eerily Accurate," io9 (16 Aug. 2012). http://io9.com/5899907/1981-climate-change-predictions-were-eerily-accurate.

24. J. Hansen, "Game Over for the Climate," *The New York Times*, 9 May 2012.

25. See S. Battersby, "Cool It: From Sunshades to Making the Seas Bloom, There Are Plenty of Ideas About How to Stop the Planet Warming. But Will Any of Them Work?" *New Scientist* 215, no. 2883 (22 Sept. 2012): 31–35; J. Winston, "Geoengineering Could Backfire, Make Climate Change Worse," *Wired UK*, 16 July 2012, http://www.wired.com/wiredscience/2012/07/geoengineering-climate-change/; C. Hamilton, "Geoengineeering: Our Last Hope, Or a False Promise?" *The New York Times*, 27 May 2013.

26. V. Havel, "Our Moral Footprint: The Earth Will Survive—But Will We?" *The New York Times*, 27 September 2007, p. A33.

27. O. H. Pilkey and L. Pilkey-Jarvis, *Useless Arithmetic: Why Environmental Scientists Can't Predict the Future* (New York: Columbia University Press, 2007).

28. Pilkey and Pilkey-Jarvis, *Useless Arithmetic: Why Environmental Scientists Can't Predict the Future*, 101.

29. Pilkey and Pilkey-Jarvis, *Useless Arithmetic: Why Environmental Scientists Can't Predict the Future*, 107.

30. C. Perrow, *Normal Accidents: Living With High-Risk Technologies* (Princeton, NJ: Princeton University Press, 1999); see also D. Ehrenfeld, "When Risk Assessment Is Risky: Predicting the Effects of Technology" in *The Energy Reader: Overdevelopment and the Delusion of Endless Growth*, ed. T. Butler, D. Lerch, and G. Wuerthner (Sausalito, CA: Foundation for Deep Ecology in collaboration with Watershed Media and Post Carbon Insititute, 2012), 77–83.

31. C. Perrow, *Normal Accidents: Living With High-Risk Technologies* (Princeton, NJ: Princeton University Press, 1999), p. 28.

32. J. Tainter and T. Patzek, *Drilling Down: The Gulf Oil Debacle and Our Energy Dilemma* (New York: Springer, 2012), pp. 7–8.

33. Tainter and Patzek, *Drilling Down: The Gulf Oil Debacle and Our Energy Dilemma*.

34. C. Sullivan and ClimateWire, "Human Population Growth Creeps Back Up," *Scientific American* (June 14, 2013). http://www.scientificamerican.com/article.cfm?id=human-population-growth-creeps-back-up&print=true.

35. Convention on International Trade in Endangered Species of Wild Fauna and Flora, http://www.cites.org/eng/disc/what.php (accessed Sept. 12, 2013).

36. E. M. Forster, "The Machine Stops" (1909) in *The Collected Tales of E. M. Forster* (New York: Modern Library, 1968), 144–97.

37. W. Berry, *The Unsettling of America* (San Francisco: Sierra Club Books, 1977), 56.

38. D. Ehrenfeld, *The Arrogance of Humanism* (New York: Oxford University Press, 1981): 211, 228–29.

TIM CARO ET AL.

1. A. D. Barnosky, P. L. Koch, R. S. Feranec, S. L. Wing, and A. B. Shabel, "Assessing the Causes of Late Pleistocene Extinctions on the Continents," *Science* 306 (2004): 70–75.

2. J. B. C. Jackson et al., "Historical Overfishing and the Recent Collapse of Coastal Ecosystems," *Science* 293 (2001): 629–38.

3. S. Lavergne, N. Mouquet, W. Thuiller, and O. Ronce, "Biodiversity and Climate change: Integrating Evolutionary and Ecological Responses of Species and Communities," *Annual Review of Ecology, Evolution, and Systematics* 41 (2010): 321–50.

4. N. W. Van den Brink, M. J. Riddle, M. Van den Huevel-Greve, and J. A. Van Franeker, "Contrasting Time Trends of Organic Contaminants in Antarctic Pelagic and Benthic Food Webs," *Marine Pollution Bulletin* 62 (2011): 128–32.

5. C. Collins and R. Kays, "Causes of Mortality in North American Populations of Large and Medium-sized Mammals," *Animal Conservation* (2011). doi:10.1111/ j.1469-1795.2011.00458.x; and C. T. Darimont, S. M. Carlson, M. T. Kinnison, P. C. Paquet, T. E. Reimchen, and C. C. Wilmers, "Human Predators Outpace Other Agents of Trait Change in the Wild," *Proceedings of the National Academy of Sciences* 106 (2009): 952–54.

6. W. Sanderson, M. Jaiteh, M. A. Levy, K. H. Redford, A. V. Wannebo, and G. Woolmer, "The Human Footprint and the Last of the Wild," *BioScience* 52 (2002): 891–904.

7. P. J. Crutzen and E. F. Stoermer, "The 'Anthropocene,'" *Global Change Newsletter* 41 (2000): 17–18.

8. W. F. Ruddiman, "The Anthropogenic Greenhouse Era Began Thousands of Years Ago," *Climatic Change* 61 (2003): 261–93; J. Zalasiewicz et al., "Stratigraphy of the Anthropocene," *Philosophical Transactions of the Royal Society A* 369 (2011): 1036–55.

9. P. Kareiva, S. Watts, R. McDonald, and T. Boucher, "Domesticated Nature: Shaping Landscapes and Ecosystems for Human Welfare," *Science* 316 (2007): 1866–69.

10. R. A. Mittermeier, C. G. Mittermeier, T. M. Brooks, J. D. Pilgrim, W. R. Konstant, G. A. B. da Fonseca, and C. Kormos, "Wilderness and Biodiversity Conservation," *Proceedings of the National Academy of Sciences* 100 (2003): 10309–313.

11. A. Brandt et al., "First Insights into the Biodiversity and Biogeography of the Southern Ocean Deep Sea," *Nature* 447 (2007): 307–11; J. Laybourn-Parry and D. A. Pearce, "The Biodiversity and Ecology of Antarctic Lakes: Models for Evolution," *Philosophical Transactions of the Royal Society B* 362 (2007): 2273–89.

12. R. A. Mittermeier et al., "Wilderness and Biodiversity Conservation."

13. J. C. Brito, A. L. Acosta, F. Álvares, and F. Cuzin, "Biogeography and Conservation of Taxa from Remote Regions: An Application of Ecological-niche Based Models and GIS to North-African Canids," *Biological Conservation* 142 (2009): 3020–29; H. D. Thing, D. R. Klein, K. Jingfors, and S. Holt, "Ecology of Muskoxen in Jameson Land, Northeast Greenland," *Holarctic Ecology* 10 (1987): 95–103; P. Wilson, "Ecology and Habitat Utilization of Blue Sheep (*Pseudois nayaur*) in Nepal," *Biological Conservation* 21 (1981): 55–74.

14. S. A. Sandin et al., "Baselines and Degradation of Coral Reefs in the Northern Line Islands," *PLoS ONE* 3, no. 2 (2008): e1548. doi:10.1371/journal. pone.0001548; E. J. Stokes et al., "Monitoring Great Ape and Elephant Abundance at Large Spatial Scales: Measuring Effectiveness of a Conservation Landscape," *PLoS ONE* 5, no. 4 (2010): e10294. doi:10.1371/journal.pone.0010294; M. Van Heist, D. Sheil, I. Rachmann, P. Gusbager, C. O. Raweyai, and H. S. M. Yoteni, "The Forests and Related Vegetation of Kwerba, on the Foja Foothills, Mamberamo, Papua (Indonesia New Guinea)," *Blumea* 55 (2010): 153–61.

15. J. E. Garcia and J. Mba, "Distribution, Status and Conservation of Primates in Monte Alen National Park, Equatorial Guinea," *Oryx* 31 (1997): 67–76; H. W. Herrmann, W. Bohme, O. Euskirchen, P. A. Herrmann, and A. Schmitz, "African Biodiversity Hotspots: The Reptiles of Mt Nlonako, Cameroon," *Revue Suisse de Zoologie* 112 (2005): 1045–69; N. Myers, R. A. Mittermeier, C. G. Mittermeier, G. A. B. da Fonseca, and J. Kent, "Biodiversity Hotspots for Conservation Priorities," *Nature* 403 (2000): 853–58.

16. W. Sanderson et al., "The Human Footprint and the Last of the Wild."

17. L. J. Hannah, *Climate Change Biology*, (Burlington, MA: Elsevier, 2010).

18. R. A. Mittermeier et al., "Wilderness and Biodiversity Conservation."

19. C. D. Thomas, "Translocation of Species, Climate Change, and the End of Trying to Recreate Past Ecological Communities," *Trends in Ecology & Evolution* 26 (2011): 216–21.

20. C. J. Donlan et al., "Pleistocene Rewilding: An Optimistic Agenda for Twenty-first Century Conservation," *The American Naturalist* 168 (2006): 660–81.

21. T. Caro, "The Pleistocene Re-wilding Gambit," *Trends in Ecology & Evolution* 22 (2007): 281–83; A. Ricciardi, and D. Simberloff, "Assisted Colonization Is Not a Viable Conservation Strategy," *Trends in Ecology & Evolution* 24 (2009): 248–53.

22. J. R. Karr and D. R. Dudley, "Ecological Perspectives on Water Quality Goals," *Environmental Management* 5 (1981): 55–68.

23. L. McClenachan, "Documenting Loss of Large Trophy Fish from the Florida Keys with Historical Photographs," *Conservation Biology* 23 (2009): 636–43; Sáenz-Arroyo, C. M. Roberts, J. Torre, M. Carino-Olvera, and R. R. Enríquez-Andrade, "Rapidly Shifting Environmental Baselines Among Fishers of the Gulf of California," *Proceedings of the Royal Society B* 272 (2005): 1957–62.

24. S. A. Sandin et al., "Baselines and Degradation of Coral Reefs in the Northern Line Islands."

DAVE FOREMAN

1. W. M. Denevan, "The Pristine Myth: The Landscape of the Americas in 1492," *Annals of the Association of American Geographers* (1992): 369–85.

2. A. Gomez-Pompa and A. Kaus, "Taming the Wilderness Myth," *BioScience* 42, no. 4 (April 1992): 271–79.

3. J. Baird Callicott, "The Wilderness Idea Revisited: The Sustainable Development Alternative," *The Environmental Professional* 13 (1991): 240.

4. C. Whitlock and M. A. Knox, "Prehistoric Burning in the Pacific Northwest: Human Versus Climatic Influences," in *Fire, Native Peoples, and the Natural Landscape*, ed. T. R. Vale (Washington, D.C.: Island Press, 2002), 222–23.

5. D. Dagget, *Gardeners of Eden: Rediscovering Our Importance to Nature* (Reno, NV: University of Nevada Press, 2005). How they did this without the godlike cattle, which Dagget and his rancher friends hold sacred, I do not know.

6. M. E. Soulé, "The Social Siege of Nature," in Reinventing Nature?: Responses to Postmodern Deconstruction, ed. M. E. Soulé and G. Lease (Washington, D.C.: Island Press, 1995), 155–56.

7. Denevan, "The Pristine Myth," 370.

8. D. H. Ubelaker "North American Indian Population Size, A.D. 1500 to 1985," *American Journal of Physical Anthropology* 77 (1988): 291.

9. W. M. Denevan, ed., Introduction to *The Native Population of the Americas in 1492*, 2nd ed. (Madison, WI: The University of Wisconsin Press, 1992), p. xx.

10. T. R. Vale, "The Pre-European Landscape of the United States: Pristine or Humanized?" in *Fire, Native Peoples, and the Natural Landscape* (Washington, D.C.: Island Press, 2002), 10–31.

11. W. R. Baker, "Indians and Fire in the Rocky Mountains: The Wilderness Hypothesis Renewed," in *Fire, Native Peoples, and the Natural Landscape*, ed. T. R. Vale (Washington, D.C.: Island Press, 2002), 50.

12. D. Foreman, *Rewilding North America: A Vision for Conservation in the 21st Century* (Washington, D.C.: Island Press, 2004), 25–44.

13. W. Cronon, *Changes in the Land: Indians, Colonists, and the Ecology of New England* (New York: Hill & Wang, 1983), 56.

14. T. R. Vale, "The Myth of the Humanized Landscape: An Example from Yosemite National Park," *Natural Areas Journal* 18, no. 3 (1998): 231–36; this article later published under the same title, in *Wild Earth*, Fall 1999, pp. 34–40.

15. J. Donlan, H. W. Greene, J. Berger, C. E. Bock, J. H. Bock, D. A. Burney, J. A. Estes, D. Foreman, Paul S. Martin, Gary W. Roemer, Felisa A. Smith, and Michael E. Soulé, "Re-wilding North America," *Nature* 436 (18 August 2005): 913–14 (The original title of this piece was "Pleistocene Rewilding," but the editors at *Nature* unfortunately changed the title; see also C. J. Donlon et al., "Pleistocene Rewilding: An Optimistic Agenda for Twenty-first Century Conservation," *The American Naturalist* 168 [2006]: 660–81); C. Barlow, *The Ghosts of Evolution: Nonsensical Fruit, Missing Partners, and Other Ecological Anachronisms* (New York: Basic Books, 2000); P. S. Martin and D. A. Burney, "Bring Back the Elephants!" *Wild Earth*, Spring 1999, pp. 57–64; P. Martin, *Twilight of the Mammoths: Ice Age Extinctions and the Rewilding of America* (Berkeley, CA: University of California Press, 2005).

16. D. Worster, "The Wilderness of History," *Wild Earth*, Fall 1997, p. 10; Worster writes, "I am using the cautious but authoritative estimate of Douglas H. Ubelaker of the Smithsonian Institution, in his article 'North American Indian Population Size, A.D. 1500 to 1985,' *American Journal of Physical Anthropology* 77 (1988): 291."

17. R. Noss, "Wilderness: Now More than Ever," *Wild Earth,* Winter 1994/95, pp. 60–63.

18. C. D. Allen, "Where Have All the Grasslands Gone? Fires and Vegetation Change in Northern New Mexico," *The Quivira Coalition Newsletter,* May 1998.

19. D. R. Foster, "New England's Forest Primeval," *Wild Earth,* Spring 2001, pp. 42–43.

20. D. Foster, "*Wild Earth* Interview" by Jamie Sayen, *Wild Earth,* Spring 2001, p. 35.

21. Vale, "The Myth of the Humanized Landscape," 231.

22. Vale, "The Myth of the Humanized Landscape," 232.

23. M. E. Soulé, "Social Siege of Nature," in *Reinventing Nature?: Responses to Postmodern Deconstruction,* ed. M. E. Soulé and G. Lease (Washington, D.C.: Island Press, 1995), 157. In an e-mail to me, Soulé writes that his "statement applies to all kinds of species, except those that have been mostly eliminated by human enterprise or transport (including large mammals and other exploited species, and many exotic species). But numerically, the species whose geographic ranges are not determined by biogeography or ecology are a minority."

24. Vale, "The Myth of the Humanized Landscape," 232.

25. Vale, "The Myth of the Humanized Landscape," 233.

26. A. J. Parker, "Fire in Sierra Nevada Forests: Evaluating the Ecological Impact of Burning by Native Americans," in *Fire, Native Peoples,* 255–56.

27. T. Vale, "The Myth of the Humanized Landscape," 234. The reference is to D. Flores, "The West that Was, and the West that Can Be," *High Country News* 29, no. 15 (1997): 1, 67.

28. C. D. Allen, "Lots of Lightning and Plenty of People: An Ecological History of Fire in the Upland Southwest," in *Fire, Native Peoples, and the Natural Landscape,* 162.

29. Allen, "Lots of Lightning," 162–63.

30. Allen, "Lots of Lightning," 145.

31. Allen, "Lots of Lightning," 146.

32. Parker, "Fire in Sierra Nevada Forests," 254.

33. Allen, "Lots of Lightning," 170–71.

34. Allen, "Lots of Lightning," 180.

35. Allen, "Lots of Lightning," 180.

36. Parker, "Fire in Sierra Nevada Forests," 258–59.

37. Parker, "Fire in Sierra Nevada Forests," 259.

38. Gomez-Pompa and Kaus, "Taming the Wilderness Myth," 274.

39. J. Diamond, *Collapse: How Societies Choose to Fail or Succeed* (New York: Viking, 2005); S. A. LeBlanc with K. Register, *Constant Battles: The Myth of the Peaceful, Noble Savage* (New York: St. Martin's Press, 2003); and R. Wright, *A Short History of Progress* (New York: Carroll & Graf Publishers, 2005).

40. Diamond, *Collapse,* 175.

41. Soulé, "The Social Siege of Nature," 155–56.

42. R. T. Simmons, "Nature Undisturbed: The Myth behind the Endangered Species Act," *PERC Reports,* March 2005, 2–5.

43. Denevan, "The Pristine Myth," 369.

44. A. Leopold, "The Last Stand of the Wilderness," *American Forests and Forest Life* 31, no. 382 (October 1925): 603.

45. The Spring 2001 issue of *Wild Earth*, with a theme of the "Wild, Wild East," should lay to rest misunderstandings about pristine areas. Particularly noteworthy are: J. M. Turner, "Wilderness East: Reclaiming History," pp. 19–26; D. W. Scott, "Eastern Wilderness Areas Act: What's in a Name?" p. 24; and D. W. Scott, "Congress's Practical Criteria for Designating Wilderness," 28–32. See also Scott's technical memo to Sally Miller, "What Lands Qualify for Wilderness Designation: A Review of the Wilderness Act and Congressional Precedents," 23 July 2001, available from the Campaign for America's Wilderness. This memo crushes the Pristine Myth of wilderness areas. Scott's recent book also very effectively covers the issue: see D. Scott, *The Enduring Wilderness: Protecting Our Natural Heritage through the Wilderness Act* (Golden, CO: Fulcrum Publishing, 2004).

46. A. Leopold, *A Sand County Almanac* (New York: Oxford University Press, 1949), 189.

47. F. Church, "The Wilderness Act Applies to the East," *Congressional Record— Senate*, 16 January 1973, 737.

48. W. Cronon, "Landscape and Home: Environmental Traditions in Wisconsin," bound reprint, originally published in *Wisconsin Magazine of History* 74 (Winter 1990–91).

49. T. R. Vale, "Reflections," in *Fire, Native Peoples*, 300.

BRENDAN MACKEY

1. Official website of Dorothea Mackellar; http://www.dorotheamackellar.com.au/archive/mycountry.html.

2. M. A. Gray, "The International Crime of Ecocide," *California Western International Law Journal* 26 (1996): 215–71.

3. Camel infestations are perhaps a novel Australian environmental threat; http://www.abc.net.au/news/2009-11-26/town-under-siege-6000-camels-to-be-shot/1157190.

4. State of the Environment 2011 Committee, *Australia State of the Environment 2011*, independent report to the Australian Government Minister for Sustainability, Environment, Water, Population and Communities (Canberra: DSEWPaC, 2011).

5. Here I am referring to the systemic relationships between social justice and environmental degradation; see L. Boff, *Cry of the Earth, Cry of the Poor* (Maryknoll, NY: Orbis Books , 2000).

6. O. Noonuccal, *We Are Going: Poems* (Brisbane: Jacaranda Press, 1964).

7. B. Mackey, J. E. M. Watson, and G. Hope, "Climate Change, Biodiversity Conservation, and the Role of Protected Areas: An Australian Perspective," *Biodiversity* 9 (2008): 11–18.

8. This is because the lifetime of the airborne fraction of a pulse of CO_2 is tens of thousands of years and therefore current emissions will continue to disrupt Earth's climate systems effectively "forever" from a human perspective; see D. Archer and V. Brovkin, "The Millennial Atmospheric Lifetime of Anthropogenic CO_2," *Climatic Change* 90 (2008): 283–97.

9. S. Berry, B. Mackey, and T. Brown, "Potential Applications of Remotely Sensed Vegetation Greenness to Habitat Analysis and the Conservation of Dispersive Fauna," *Pacific Conservation Biology* 13, no. 2 (2007): 120–27.

10. "Coal Seam Gas-produced Water and Site Management," CSIRO Fact Sheets, 2012. http://www.csiro.au/news/coal-seam-gas#FactSheets.

11. A. D. Barnofsky et al., "Has the Earth's Sixth Mass Extinction Already Arrived?" *Nature* 471 (2011): 51–57.

12. P. Kareiva, S. Watts, R. McDonald, and T. Boucher, "Domesticated Nature: Shaping Landscapes and Ecosystems for Human Welfare," *Science* 316 (2012): 1866–69.

13. P. J. Crutzen and E. F. Stoermer, "The 'Anthropocene,'" *Global Change Newsletter* 41 (2000): 17–18.

14. J. Rockstrom et al., "A Safe Operating Space for Humanity," *Nature* 461, no. 7263 (2009): 472–75.

15. J. L. Grenfell et al., "Co-evolution of Atmospheres, Life, and Climate," *Astrobiology* 10 (2010): 77–88. doi:10.1089/ast.2009.0375.

16. D. Meadows, *Thinking in Systems—A Primer* (Earthscan, 2008). ISBN 978-1-84407-726-7.

17. M. E. Soulé, J. A. Estes, R. B. Miller, and D. L. Honnold, "Strongly Interacting Species: Conservation Policy, Management, and Ethics," *BioScience* 55 (2005): 168–76. http://dx.doi.org/10.1641/0006-3568(2005)055[0168:SISCPM]2.0.CO;2.

18. I. Thompson, B. Mackey, S. McNulty, and A. Mosseler, *Forest Resilience, Biodiversity, and Climate Change: A Synthesis of the Biodiversity/ Resilience/ Stability Relationship in Forest Ecosystems* (Montreal: Secretariat of the Convention on Biological Diversity, Technical Series, no. 43, 2009, 67 pages).

19. R. Bliege Bird et al., "The 'Fire Stick Farming' Hypothesis: Australian Aboriginal Foraging Strategies, Biodiversity and Anthropogenic Fire Mosaics," *Proceedings of the National Academy of Sciences* 105 (2008): 14796–801.

20. B. Mackey, J. E. M. Watson, and G. Hope, "Climate Change, Biodiversity Conservation, and the Role of Protected Areas: An Australian Perspective," *Biodiversity* 9 (2008): 11–18.

21. W. R. Barker and P. J. M. Greenslade, *Evolution of the Flora and Fauna of Arid Australia* (Adelaide, S.A., Australia: Peacock Publications, 1982); M. E. White, *The Greening of Gondwana* (Frenchs Forest, N.S.W., Australia: Reed, 1986).

22. B. A. Barlow, *Flora and Fauna of Alpine Australia: Ages and Origins* (Melbourne: CSIRO, 1986); R. Hill, *History of Australian Vegetation: Cretaceous to Recent* (Cambridge, MA: Cambridge University Press, 1994); G. S. Hope, "Quaternary Vegetation" in *History of Australian Vegetation: Cretaceous to Recent*, ed. R. Hill (Cambridge, MA: Cambridge University Press, 1994), 368–89.

23. J. A. Norman, F. E. Rheindt, D. E. Rowe, and L. Christidis, "Speciation Dynamics in the Australo-Papuan *Meliphaga* Honeyeaters," *Molecular Phylogenetics and Evolution* 42 (2007): 80–91.

24. M. Archer and S. J. Hand, "The Australian Marsupial Radiation" in *Evolution and Biogeography of Australasian Vertebrates*, ed J. Merrick, M., Archer, G. M., Hickey, and M. S. Y. Lee (Sydney: Auscipub Pty Ltd, 2006), 575–646; M. J. Osborne and L. Christidis, "Molecular Relationships of the Cuscuses, Brushtail and Scaly-tailed Possums," *Australian Journal of Zoology* 50 (2002): 135–49.

25. L. K. Corbett, *The Dingo in Australia and Asia* (Sydney: UNSW Press, 1995).

26. R. A. Bradstock, "A Biogeographic Model of Fire Regimes in Australia: Current and Future Implications," *Global Ecology and Biogeography* 19 (2010): 145–58.

27. B. G. Mackey, D. B. Lindenmayer, A. M. Gill, A. M. McCarthy, and J. A. Lindesay, *Wildlife, Fire and Future Climate: A Forest Ecosystem Analysis* (Melbourne: CSIRO Publishing, 2002).

28. For example, most tree species in the *Eucalyptus* genus are not killed by fires and quickly re-sprout foliage from epicormic growth; A. M. Gill, "Adaptive Responses of Australian Vascular Plant Species to Fires," in *Fire and the Australian Biota*, ed. A. M. Gill, R. H. Groves, and I. R. Noble (Canberra: Australian Academy of Science, 1981a).

29. R. Kennett, M. Jackson, J. Morrison, and J. Kitchens, "Indigenous Rights and Obligations to Manage Traditional Land and Sea Estates in North Australia: The Role of Indigenous Rangers and the I-Tracker Project Collection and Management Program Across North Australia," *Policy Matters* 17 (2010): 135–42.

30. J. C. Z. Woinarski, B. G. Mackey, H. Nix, and B. Trail, *The Nature of Northern Australia: Its Natural Values, Ecology, and Future Prospects* (Canberra: ANU E Press, 2007). http://epress.anu.edu.au/nature_na_citation.html.

31. M. Ziembicki, J. C. Z. Woinarski, and B. Mackay, "The Changing Status of the Native Mammal Fauna of Northern Australia: Indigenous Perspectives," *Conservation Biology* 157 (2013): 78–92.

32. Between 2011 and 2050, the world population is expected to increase by 2.3 billion, passing from 7.0 billion to 9.3 billion (United Nations, 2011). At the same time, the population living in urban areas is projected to gain 2.6 billion, passing from 3.6 billion in 2011 to 6.3 billion 205; *World Urbanization Prospects, The 2011 Revision—Highlights*, United Nations, Department of Economic and Social Affairs Population Division, 2012. http://esa.un.org/unup/pdf/WUP2011_Highlights.pdf.

33. J. Rockström et al., "A Safe Operating Space for Humanity," *Nature* 461 (2009): 472–75.

34. The Convention on Biological Diversity defines biological diversity as the variability among living organisms from all sources including, among other things, terrestrial, marine, and other aquatic ecosystems and the ecological complexes of which they are part; this includes diversity within species, between species, and of ecosystems; Article 2, Use of Terms, Secretariat for The Convention on Biological Diversity; http://www.cbd.int/convention/articles/default.shtml?a=cbd-02.

35. D. VanDeVeer and C. Pierce, eds., *The Environmental Ethics and Policy Book: Philosophy, Ecology, Economics* (Belmont, CA: Dadsworth, 1994), 57.

36. V. Plumwood, "Androcentrism and Anthropocentricism: Parallels and Politics," in *Ecofeminism: Women, Culture, Nature*, ed. K. J. Warren (Bloomington: Indiana University Press, 1997), 327–55.

37. J. R. Des Jardins, *Environmental Ethics: An Introduction to Environmental Philosophy* (Belmont, CA: Wordsworth, 1993).

38. J. Baird Callicott, "Animal Liveration: A Triangular Affair," in *The Animal Rights/ Environmental Ethics Debate: The Environmental Perspective* (New York, NY: University of New York Press, 1992), 36–69.

39. A. Leopold, *A Sand County Almanac* (New York: Oxford University Press, 1949).

40. Secretariat for the CBD, "Preamble," *The Convention on Biological Diversity.* http://www.cbd.int/convention/articles/default.shtml?a=cbd-00.

41. For the full text of the Earth Charter, and documentation of its history and the associated initiative, see www.earthcharter.org.

42. R. Peakall, L. Jones, C. C. Bower, and B. G. Mackey, "Bioclimatic Assessment of the Geographic and Climatic Limits to Hybridisation in a Sexually Deceptive Orchid System," *Australian Journal of Botany* 50 (2002): 21–30.

43. M. K. Fujita, J. A. McGuire, S. C. Donnellan, and C. Moritz, "Diversification & Persistence at the Arid-monsoonal Interface: Australia-wide Biogeography of the Bynoe's Gecko (Heteronotia binoei; Gekkonidae)," *Evolution* 64 (2010): 2293–314.

44. B. Brown, "Environmental Flows: How the Franklin Was Saved," *The Monthly*, no. 85 (Dec. 2012–Jan. 2013). http://www.themonthly.com.au/how-franklin-was-saved-environmental-flows-bob-brown-7135.

45. M. E. Soulé et al., "Continental Connectivity: Its Role in Australian Conservation," *Pacific Conservation Biology* 10 (2004): 266–79; K. R. Crooks and M. Sanjayan, ed.s, *Conservation Biology, Book 14, Conservation Connectivity* (Cambridge, MA: Cambridge University Press, 2006).

46. See National Wildlife Corridors Plan (http://www.environment.gov.au/ biodiversity/wildlife-corridors/index.html); Gondwana link (http://www. gondwanalink.org/); The Great Eastern Ranges Initiative (http://www. greateasternranges.org.au/).

47. This theme is robustly investigated in Reinhold Niebuhr's *The Children of Light and the Children of Darkness: A Vindication of Democracy and a Critique of Its Traditional Defense* (Chicago, IL: University of Chicago Press, 2011), first published 1944.

48. M. O'Connor, *The Olive Tree: Collected Poems 1972–2000*, ISBN: 868066974. http://www.poetrylibrary.edu.au/poems-book/the-olive-tree-0161000.

PHILIP CAFARO

1. A. Revkin, video interview, "Emma Marris Explores Earth's 'Rambunctious Garden,'" embedded in A. Revkin, "Emma Marris: In Defense of Everglades Pythons," *New York Times* Dot.earth blog, 17 August 2012.

2. P. Kareiva and M. Marvier, "What Is Conservation Science?," *BioScience* 62, no. 9 (2012): 962–69.

3. A. Revkin, "Emma Marris Explores Earth's 'Rambunctious Garden.'"

4. Examples include W. Steffen et al., "The Anthropocene: From Global Change to Planetary Stewardship," *AMBIO* 40 (2011): 739–61; and R. Bradbury, "A World Without Coral Reefs," *New York Times*, 13 July 2012.

5. Intergovernmental Panel on Climate Change (IPCC), *Climate Change 2007: Synthesis Report*, pp. 51–52, accessed at www.ipcc.ch.

6. P. Kareiva, R. Lalasz, and M. Marvier, "Conservation in the Anthropocene: Beyond Solitude and Fragility," *Breakthrough Journal*, Fall 2011, p. 33.

7. Ibid., pp. 34–35.

8. Ibid., p. 29.

9. For a more fully developed argument that other species have a right to continued existence free from anthropogenic extinction, see W. Staples III and P. Cafaro, "For a Species Right to Exist" in *Life on the Brink: Environmentalists Confront Overpopulation*, ed. P. Cafaro and E. Crist (Athens, GA: University of Georgia Press, 2012), pp. 283–300.

10. See P. Cafaro and E. Crist, *Life on the Brink: Environmentalists Confront Overpopulation*, for a comprehensive discussion of the issues raised in this paragraph.

11. Valuable contributions to specifying the parameters of a sustainable economy include H. Daly and J. Cobb, *For the Common Good: Redirecting the Economy toward Community, the Environment, and a Sustainable Future* (Boston: Beacon Press, 1989); S. Alexander, ed. *Voluntary Simplicity: The Poetic Alternative to Consumer Culture* (Whanganui, New Zealand: Stead & Daughters, 2009); and T. Jackson, *Prosperity without Growth? The Transition to a Sustainable Economy* (European Union Sustainable Development Commission: 2009).

12. For an overview of observed and anticipated impacts of climate change in U.S. national parks, see the website for the National Park Service's Climate Change Response Program (www.nps.gov/orgs/ccrp/index.htm).

HARVEY LOCKE

1. R. J. Bidinotto, "Environmentalism: Freedom's Foe for the '90s," *The Freeman* 40 (November 1990): 409–20.

2. P. Kareiva, R. Lalasz, and M. Marvier, "Conservation in the Anthropocene: Beyond Solitude and Fragility," *Breakthrough Journal,* Fall 2011, pp. 29–37.

3. M. Wente, "Can Enviro-optimists Save the Movement from Itself?" Toronto *Globe and Mail*, 20 April 2013.

4. G. Ward, *Teach Yourself: Postmodernism* (Blacklick, OH: McGraw-Hill, 2003), 176–77; R. Appignanesi, C. Garratt, Z. Sardar, and P. Curry, *Introducing Postmodernism* (Thriplow, Royston, UK: Icon Books, 2004).

5. Ward, *Teach Yourself: Postmodernism*.

6. D. Mitchell, *Cloud Atlas* (New York: Random House, 2004), 403.

7. J. F. Lyotard, *The Post Modern Condition: A Report on Knowledge* (Manchester, UK: Manchester University Press, 1992).

8. Ward, *Teach Yourself: Postmodernism.*

9. T. Judt, *Postwar: A History of Europe Since 1945* (New York: Penguin Press, 2005).

10. A. Phillips, "Landscape Approaches to National Parks and Protected Areas," in *National Parks and Protected Areas,* ed J. G Nelson and A. Serrafin (Berlin and Heidelberg: Springer Verlag, 1999), 31–37; see also A. Phillips, "Turning Ideas on Their Heads: A New Paradigm for Protected Areas," *George Wright Forum* 20 (2003): 8–32.

11. R. Barbault, *Protected Areas: Combining Biodiversity Conservation and Sustainable Development: Foundations and Recommendations for a Development Cooperation Strategy on Protected Area Management,* (Paris, FR: Institut Français de la Biodiveristé, 2003).

12. H. Locke and P. Dearden, "Rethinking Protected Area Categories and the New Paradigm," *Environmental Conservation* 32, no. 1 (Cambridge University Press, UK: Foundation for Environmental Conservation, 2005).

13. J. M. Mallarach, J. Morrison, A. Kothari, F. Sarmiento, J.-A. Atauri, and B. Wishitemi, "In Defence of Protected Landscapes: A Reply to Some Criticisms of Catgeory V Protected Areas and Suggestions for Improvement," (2007) in *Defining Protected Areas: An International Conference in Almeria, Spain*, ed. N. Dudley and S. Stolton (Gland, Switzerland: IUCN, 2008), 30–36.

14. Mallarach et al., "In Defence of Protected Landscapes: A Reply to Some Criticisms of Catgeory V Protected Areas and Suggestions for Improvement," 33.

15. N. Dudley and S. Stolton, Defining Protected Areas: An International Conference in Almeria, Spain, May 2007 (Gland, Switzerland: IUCN, 2008), 189; N. Dudley, ed., "IUCN Guidelines for Applying Protected Area Management Categories," 2008. www.iucn.org/about/union/commissions/wcpa/wcpa_puball/wcpa_pubsubject/wcpa_categoriespub/index.cfm?uNewsID=1662; N. Dudley, *Authenticity in Nature: Making Choices about the Naturalness of Ecosystems* (London, UK: Earthscan, 2011).

16. R. Crofts and A. Phillips, "Putting Nature on the Map: Applying the IUCN Protected Areas Management Categories in the UK," *Parks* 19, no. 1, (March 2013): 81–90.

17. Crofts and Phillips, "Putting Nature on the Map: Applying the IUCN Protected Areas Management Categories in the UK," 82.

18. W. Cronon, "The Trouble with Wilderness" in *Uncommon Ground: Rethinking the Human Place in Nature,* ed. W. Cronon (New York: W. W. Norton, 1995), 69–90. http://www.williamcronon.net/writing/Trouble_with_Wilderness_Main.html.

19. J. Baird Callicott and M. P. Nelson, *The Great New Wilderness Debate (Athens, GA: University of Georgia Press, 1999).*

20. M. Chapin, "A Challenge to Conservationists," *Worldwatch Magazine (November/December 2004).*

21. M. Wente, "Can Enviro optimists Save the Movement from Itself?" Toronto *Globe and Mail,* 20 April 2013.

22. Kareiva et al., "Conservation in the Anthropocene," p. 36.

23. G. Monbiot, "The Culture of Nature" (July 8, 2013), on Monbiot's website www. monbiot.com. http://www.monbiot.com/2013/07/08/the-culture-of-nature/.

24. Kareiva et al., "Conservation in the Anthropocene," p. 36.

25. Kareiva et al., "Conservation in the Anthropocene"; for quotes in this paragraph, see pages 30–33.

26. Kareiva et al., "Conservation in the Anthropocene," p. 31.

27. Kareiva et al., "Conservation in the Anthropocene," p. 31.

28. Kareiva et al., "Conservation in the Anthropocene," p. 32.

29. Kareiva et al., "Conservation in the Anthropocene," p. 37.

30. I. McEwen, *Solar* (London: Vintage Books, 2011), 182.

31. A. Sokal, "Transgressing Boundaries: Toward a Transformative Hermeneutics of Quantum Gravity," *Social Text* (Summer/Spring 1996), pp. 217–52.

32. M. Kingwell, "Taking on Scientism's Big Bullies: Hitchens, Dawkins and Pinker," Review of Curtis White's *The Science Delusion. The Globe and Mail*, 14 June 2013.

33. P. Neubauer, O. P. Jensen, J. A. Hutchings, and J. K. Baum, "Resilience and Recovery of Overexploited Marine Populations," *Science* 340 (2013): 347–49.

34. For further information, see the IUCN Red List; www.iucnredlist.org/details/39994/0.

35. P. Neubauer et al., "Resilience and Recovery of Overexploited Marine Populations."

36. P. Neubauer, O. P. Jensen, J. A. Hutchings, and J. K. Baum, "Resilience and Recovery of Overexploited Marine Populations," *Science* 340, no. 6130 (2013): 347–49.

37. CBC, "Cod Stocks May Never Recover, Study Finds: Report Says Human Error, Industry Pressure to Blame," 21 April 2013. http://www.cbc.ca/news/canada/newfoundland-labrador/story/2013/04/21/nl-cod-stocks-hutchings-study-421.html.

38. D. Pauley, V. Christensen, J. Dalsgaard, R. Froese, and F. Torres, "Fishing Down Marine Food Webs," Science 279 (1998): 860–63; B. Worm et al., "Impacts of Biodiversity Loss on Ocean Ecosystem Services," *Science* 314, no. 5800 (2006): 787–90.

39. Ministry of Environment and Forests 2010; baraza.wildlifedirect.org/tag/mountain-gorilla; http://www.iucnredlist.org/details/39994/0.

40. G. Himmelfarb, "Postmodernist History," pages 71–93 in *Reconstructing History: The Emergence of a New Historical Society,* ed. E. Fox-Genovese and E. Lasch-Quinn (London: Routledge, 1999), 74.

41. P. Nabokov and L. Loendorf, *Restoring a Presence: American Indians and Yellowstone National Park* (Norman, OK: University of Oklahoma Press, 2002).

42. P. Nabokov and L. Loendorf, quoting Hayden, in *Restoring a Presence: American Indians and Yellowstone National Park.*

43. D. Brown, *Bury My Heart at Wounded Knee* (New York: Holt Reinhart Winston, 1970).

44. Kareiva et al., "Conservation in the Anthropocene," p. 35.

45. E. C. Ellis, J. O. Kaplan, D. Q. Fuller, S. Vavrus, K. K. Goldewijk, and P. H. Verburg, "Used Planet: A Global History," *PNAS* Early Edition, 2013. http://www.pnas.org/content/early/2013/04/25/1217241110.full.pdf+html, p. 3 of 8.

46. E. W. Sanderson, M. Jaiteh, M. A. Levy, and K. H. Redford, "The Human Footprint and the Last of the Wild," Bioscience 52, no. 10 (2002): 891; C. Kormos and H. Locke, "Introducing the Wilderness Concept," in *A Handbook on International Wilderness Law and Policy,* ed. C. Kormos (Golden, CO: Fulcrum Publishing, 2008).

47. H. Locke, "Wilderness and Spirituality," *Wild Earth* 9, no. 1 (Spring 1999); H. Locke, "The Spiritual Dimension of Moving to the Mountains," in *The Amenity Migrants: Seeking and Sustaining Mountains and Their Cultures,* ed. L. A. G. Moss (Cambridge, MA: CABI, 2008).

48. H. Locke and P. Dearden, "Rethinking Protected Area Categories and the New Paradigm," *Environmental Conservation* 32, no. 1 (Cambridge University Press, UK: Foundation for Environmental Conservation, 2005).

49. C. Kormos and H. Locke, "Introducing the Wilderness Concept," in *A Handbook on International Wilderness Law and Policy,* ed. C. Kormos (Golden, CO: Fulcrum Publishing, 2008); H. Locke, "Civil Society and Protected Areas: Lessons from Canada," *George Wright Forum* 26, no. 2 (2009).

50. J. Cajune, V. G. Martin, and T. Tanner, eds., *Protecting Wild Nature on Native Lands: Case Studies by Native Peoples from Around the World (Golden, CO: Fulcrum Publishing, 2008).*

51. N. Dudley, *Authenticity in Nature: Making Choices about the Naturalness of Ecosystems.*

52. Kareiva et al., "Conservation in the Anthropocene," p. 36.

53. Kareiva et al., "Conservation in the Anthropocene," p. 37.

54. J. A. Stanford, M. S. Lorang, and F. R. Hauer, "The Shifting Habitat Mosaic of River Ecosystems," *Verh. Internat. Verein. Limnol.* 29, no. 1 (2005): 123–36.

55. European Commission, "LIFE and Human Co-existence with Large Carnivores," Environment Directorate (Luxembourg: European Union, 2013).

56. J. Timblin Maupin, Facebook posting (by Jennifer Timblin Maupin) on March 3, 2013; mju1hhwm@facebookmail.com.

57. J. Zalasiewicz, M. Williams, A. Haywood, and M. Ellis, "The Anthropocene: A New Epoch of Geological Time?" *Phil. Trans. R. Soc. A* (2011): 369.

58. J. A. Hodgson, C. D. Thomas, B. A. Wintle, and A. Moilanen, "Climate Change, Connectivity and Conservation Decision Making: Back to Basics," *Journal of Applied Ecology* 46, no. 5 (2009): 964–69.

59. *Nature* editorial, "Think Big," *Nature* 469, no. 131 (January 13, 2011). doi:10.1038/469131a; H. Locke, "Transboundary Cooperation to Achieve Wilderness Protection and Large Landscape Conservation," *Park Science* 28, no. 3 (Winter 2011–2012) (Washington, D.C.: Department of the Interior).

60. R. F. Noss et al., "Bolder Thinking for Conservation," *Conservation Biology* 26, no. 1 (Feb. 2012): 1–4; H. Locke, "Why Nature Needs Half: A Necessary and Hopeful New Agenda for Parks and Protected Areas," *PARKS: The International Journal of Protected Areas and Conservation* 19, no. 2 (26 September 2013) (Gland, Switzerland: IUCN); see also www.natureneedshalf.org.

GEORGE WUERTHNER

1. C. White, "The Working Wilderness: A Call for a Land Health Movement." http://www.awestthatworks.com/2Essays/Working_Wilderness/The_Working_Wilderness.pdf.

2. "Keeping Maine Forests." http://www.keepingmainesforests.org/Maine%20Woods%20brochure.pdf.

3. Institute for Agriculture and Trade Policy, "Working Landscapes." http://www.iatp.org/issue/rural-development/environment/agriculture/working-landscapes.

4. N. F. Sayre, "Working Wilderness: The Malpai Borderlands Group and the Future of the Western Range," Terrain.org. http://www.terrain.org/essays/18/sayre.htm.

5. Exploring Vermont's Working Landscape at Groton State Forest, *Vermont Business Magazine* (Aug. 27, 2013). http://www.vermontbiz.com/event/august/exploring-vt%E2%80%99s-working-landscape-groton-state-forest-0.

6. P. Kareiva, M. Marvier, and R. Lalasz, "Conservation in the Anthropocene: Beyond Solitude and Fragility," *Breakthrough Journal* (Winter 2012). http://thebreakthrough.org/index.php/journal/past-issues/issue-2/conservation-in-the-anthropocene/.

7. Interview with Peter Kareiva, "The End of the Wild," The Nature Conservancy. http://www.nature.org/science-in-action/our-scientists/the-end-of-the-wild.xml.

8. A Working Forest: Its Future With Fire, People and Wildlife. http://aworkingforest.com/a-working-forest/

9. Idaho Forest Products Commission. http://www.idahoforests.org/iwfdvd.htm.

10. G. Hoch, "Where Cattle Roam and Wild Grasses Grow," *Minnesota Conservation Volunteer Magazine* (July/August 2013). http://www.dnr.state.mn.us/volunteer/julaug13/grazing.html.

11. Iowa Public Television, "Explore More: Working Landscapes." http://www.youtube.com/watch?v=0MorL44Ef-c&list=PL6E20820D75851E7A&index=1

12. Department of Environmental Science, Policy, and Management at UC Berkeley, "Working Landscapes," Our Environment at Berkeley. http://ourenvironment.berkeley.edu/research/research-themes/working-landscapes/

13. Many slave owners argued that slaves were better off enslaved than free because, if freed, the slaves would not be able to take care of themselves. Slave owners saw themselves as being parental and providing the slaves with housing, etc. Here's one link that discusses this further: http://answers.yahoo.com/question/index?qid=20100708220047AA4E7yt.

14. L. Huntsinger and N. Sayre, "Introduction: The Working Landscapes Special Issue," *Rangelands* 29, no. 3 (June 2007).

15. C. Morse et al. (2010) "Strategies for Promoting Working Landscapes in North America and Europe.," http://vtworkinglands.org/sites/default/files/library/files/working%20landscape/UVM_StrategiesforPromotingWorkingLandscapes.pdf

16. Idaho Forest Products Commission. http://www.idahoforests.org/iwfdvd.htm.

17. T. Tscharntke et al., "Landscape Perspective on Agricultural Intensification and Biodiversity—Ecosystem Service Management," *Ecology Letters* 8, no. 8 (2005): 857–87.

18. Fridolin Krausmanna,1, Karl-Heinz Erba, Simone Gingricha, Helmut Haberla, Alberte Bondeaub,c, Veronika Gaubea, Christian Lauka, Christoph Plutzara, and Timothy D. Searchingerd 2013. Global human appropriation of net primary production doubled in the 20th century. Published online before print June 3, 2013, doi: 10.1073/pnas.1211349110 PNAS June 3, 2013

19. EuropaBio: How does Agriculture Affect Biodiversity? http://www.europabio. org/how-does-agriculture-affect-biodiversity

20. G. P. Buchert et al.,"Effects of Harvesting on Genetic Diversity in Old-Growth Eastern White Pine in Ontario, Canada," *Biology* 11, .3(June 1997): 747–58.

21. G. Wuerthner, *Wildfire: A Century of Failed Forest Policy* (Covelo, CA: Island Press, 2006).

22. R. L. Beschta and W. J. Ripple "Large Predators and Trophic Cascades in Terrestrial Ecosystems of the Western United States," *Biological Conservation* 142 (2009): 2401–14.

23. The World Bank. http://data.worldbank.org/indicator/AG.LND.AGRI.ZS/ countries/1W?display=graph.

24. G. P. Asner et al., "Grazing Systems, Ecosystem Responses, and Global Change," *Annual Review of Environment and Resources* 29 (2004): 261–99. doi:10.1146/ annurev.energy.29.062403.102142.

25. R. Alkemade et al., "Assessing the Impacts of Livestock Production on Biodiversity in Rangelands Ecosystems," *PNAS* 110, no. 52 (December 2013). www.pnas.org/cgi/doi/10.1073/pnas.1011013108.

26. G. Wuerthner and M. Matteson, *Welfare Ranching: The Subsidized Destruction of the American West* (Covelo, CA: Island Press, 2002).

27. T. Howard, "Disease Transmission from Domestic Sheep to Bighorn Sheep." http://www.bighorndiseaseinfo.org/.

28. J. A. Estes and J. Terborgh, *Trophic Cascades: Predators, Prey, and the Changing Dynamics of Nature* (Washington, D.C.: Island Press, 2010).

29. S. Trombulak and C. Frissell, "Review of the Ecological Effects of Roads on Terrestrial and Aquatic Ecosystems," *Conservation Biology* 14, no. 1 (February 2000): 18–30.

30. J. Strittholt et al., "Status of Mature and Old-Growth Forests in the Pacific Northwest," *Conservation Biology* 20, no. 2 (April 2006): 36374.

31. World Bank Data base. http://data.worldbank.org/topic/agriculture-and-rural-development.

32. J. Owen, "Farming Claims Almost Half Earth's Land, New Maps Show," *National Geographic News* (December 9, 2005). http://news.nationalgeographic.com/ news/2005/12/1209_051209_crops_map.html.

33. E. Maris, P. Kareiva, J. Mascaro, and E. Ellis, "Hope in the Age of Man," *New York Times* (7 December 2011). http://www.nytimes.com/2011/12/08/opinion/the-age-of-man-is-not-a-disaster.html?ref=opinion.

34. W. D. Newmark, "Extinction of Mammal Populations in Western North American National Parks," *Conservation Biology* 9, no. 3 (2002): 512–26.

35. H. Nagendra, "Do Parks Work? Impacts of Protected Areas on Land Clearing," *AMBIO: A Journal of the Human Environment* 37, no. 5 (2008): 330–37.

36. B. Halpern, "The Impact of Marine Reserves: Do Reserves Work and Does Size Matter?" Supplement to *Ecological Applications* 13, no. 1 (2003): S117–S137.

37. M. Soulé and J. Terborgh, *Continental Conservation: Scientific Foundations of Regional Reserve Networks* (Washington, D.C.: Island Press, 1999).

38. L. N. Joppa, P. Visconti, C. J. Jenkins, and S. L. Pimm, "Achieving the Convention on Biological Diversity's Goals for Plant Conservation," *Science* 341, no. 6150 (6 September 2013): 1100–103. doi:10.1126/science.1241706.

39. R. F. Noss, C. Carroll, K. Vance-Borland, and G. Wuerthner, "A Multicriteria Assessment of the Irreplaceability and Vulnerability of Sites in the Greater Yellowstone Ecosystem," *Conservation Biology* 16 (2002): 895–908.

40. L. N. Joppa, S. R. Loarie, and S. L. Pimm, "On the Protection of 'Protected Areas'," PNAS 105, no. 18 (May 2008). www.pnas.org_cgi_doi_10.1073_pnas.0802471105 PNAS _ May 6, 2008 _ vol. 105 _ no. 18.

41. Interview with Emma Marris, American Society of Landscape Architects. http://www.asla.org/ContentDetail.aspx?id=34133.

42. D. W. Tallamy, *Bringing Nature Home: How Native Plants Sustain Wildlife in Our Gardens* (Portland, Oregon: Timber Press, 2007). http://bringingnaturehome.net.

43. E. Ellis, "Overpopulation Is Not a Problem," *New York Times*, 13 September 2013.

NED HETTINGER

1. P. Crutzen, "Geology of Mankind: The Anthropocene," *Nature* 415 (2002): 23.

2. P. Vitousek, H. Mooney, J. Lubchenco, and J. Melillo, "Human Domination of Earth's Ecosystems," *Science* 277, no. 5325 (1997): 494–99.

3. R. Monastersky, "Earthmovers: Humans Take Their Place Alongside Wind, Water, and Ice," *Science News* 146 (1994): 432–33.

4. J. Zalasiewicz, M. Williams, W. Steffen, and P. Crutzen, "The New World of the Anthropocene," *Environmental Science & Technology* 44, no. 7(2010): 2228–31.

5. Ibid.

6. P. Kareiva, S. Watts, R. McDonald, and T. Boucher, "Domesticated Nature; Shaping Landscapes and Ecosystems for Human Welfare," *Science* 316, no. 5833 (2007): 1866–69. http://www.sciencemag.org/content/316/5833/1866.full.

7. E. Marris, P. Kareiva, J. Mascaro, and E. Ellis, "Hope in Age of Man," op-ed, *New York Times* 7 December 2011. http://www.nytimes.com/2011/12/08/opinion/the-age-of-man-is-not-a-disaster.html.

8. A. Thompson, "Responsibility for the End of Nature: Or, How I Learned to Stop Worrying and Love Global Warming," *Ethics and the Environment* 79, no. 1 (2009): 79–99.

9. A. Thompson, "Responsibility for the End of Nature: Or, How I Learned to Stop Worrying and Love Global Warming," p. 97.

10. A. Thompson, "Radical Hope for Living Well in a Warmer World," *Journal of Agricultural and Environmental Ethics* 23, no. 1(2010): 43–55.

11. A. Thompson, "Responsibility for the End of Nature: Or, How I Learned to Stop Worrying and Love Global Warming," p. 96.

12. A. Thompson, "Responsibility for the End of Nature: Or, How I Learned to Stop Worrying and Love Global Warming," p. 97.

13. Ibid.

14. Ibid.

15. H. Rolston III, *A New Environmental Ethics: The Next Millennium for Life on Earth* (New York: Routledge, 2012), 46.

16. A. Thompson, "Responsibility for the End of Nature: Or, How I Learned to Stop Worrying and Love Global Warming," p. 97.

17. A. Thompson, "Radical Hope for Living Well in a Warmer World," p. 54.

18. B. McKibben , *The End of Nature* (New York: Doubleday, 1989).

19. E. Ellis, (Video, interview), "Erle Ellis on the Anthropocene," *The Economist*, Multimedia Library accessed February 2012.

20. P. Kareiva, S. Watts, R. McDonald, and T. Boucher, "Domesticated Nature; Shaping Landscapes and Ecosystems for Human Welfare," *Science* 316, no. 5833 (2007): 1866–69. http://www.sciencemag.org/content/316/5833/1866.full.

21. B. McKibben, *The End of Nature* (New York: Doubleday, 1989), 85.

22. N. Hettinger and B. Throop, "Refocusing Ecocentrism: De-emphasizing Stability and Defending Wildness," *Environmental Ethics* 21, no. 1 (Spring 1999): 3–21.

23. T. Caro, J. Darwin, T. Forrester, C. Ledeoux-Bloom, and C. Wells, "Conservation in the Anthropocene," *Conservation Biology* 26, no. 1 (2011): 185–88.

SANDRA LUBARSKY

1. A. Leopold, *Sand County Almanac: With Essays on Conservation from Round River* (New York: Ballantine Books, 1970), 229.

2. Ibid., 230.

3. Ibid., 282.

4. Ibid, 230.

5. J. J. Yates, "A Conversation with Wendell Berry and Wes Jackson," *The Hedgehog Review* 14, no. 2 (Summer 2012), accessed Sept. 12, 2013, http://www.iasc-culture.org/THR/THR_article_2012_Summer_Interview_Berry_Jackson.php.

6. A. N. Whitehead, *Science and the Modern World* (New York: Free Press, 1967), vii.

7. A. N. Whitehead, *Modes of Thought* (New York: Free Press, 1968), 135.

8. W. Berry, *A Continuous Harmony: Essays Cultural and Agricultural* (San Diego, CA: Harcourt Brace Jovanovich, 1970), 12.

LISI KRALL

1. A. Leopold, *A Sand County Almanac: With Essays on Conservation from Round River* (New York: Oxford University Press, 1966), 262.

INDEX

ABOUT ISLAND PRESS

Since 1984, the nonprofit organization Island Press has been stimulating, shaping, and communicating ideas that are essential for solving environmental problems worldwide. With more than 800 titles in print and some 40 new releases each year, we are the nation's leading publisher on environmental issues. We identify innovative thinkers and emerging trends in the environmental field. We work with world-renowned experts and authors to develop cross-disciplinary solutions to environmental challenges.

Island Press designs and executes educational campaigns in conjunction with our authors to communicate their critical messages in print, in person, and online using the latest technologies, innovative programs, and the media. Our goal is to reach targeted audiences—scientists, policymakers, environmental advocates, urban planners, the media, and concerned citizens—with information that can be used to create the framework for long-term ecological health and human well-being.

Island Press gratefully acknowledges major support of our work by The Agua Fund, The Andrew W. Mellon Foundation, Betsy & Jesse Fink Foundation, The Bobolink Foundation, The Curtis and Edith Munson Foundation, Forrest C. and Frances H. Lattner Foundation, G.O. Forward Fund of the Saint Paul Foundation, Gordon and Betty Moore Foundation, The Kresge Foundation, The Margaret A. Cargill Foundation, New Mexico Water Initiative, a project of Hanuman Foundation, The Overbrook Foundation, The S.D. Bechtel, Jr. Foundation, The Summit Charitable Foundation, Inc., V. Kann Rasmussen Foundation, The Wallace Alexander Gerbode Foundation, and other generous supporters.

The opinions expressed in this book are those of the author(s) and do not necessarily reflect the views of our supporters.